KinderUnits

Revised

By Esther Moore Howard and Dianne Faulk
Revisions by Rebecca Shimek Hanel

A Preplanned Calendar of Thematic Kindergarten Activities September-May

Fearon Teacher Aids
A Division of Frank Schaffer Publications, Inc.

Acknowledgments

We would like to thank Dr. Gloria Correro and Dr. Jim Turner for making
the Cooperative Demonstration Kindergarten a reality.
Without them, the program would not have become a model kindergarten.
Also, we extend our gratitude to Vicki Potter, Sheila Reeves,
Sherley Gillespie, and Denise Parrish for using their expert typing skills
in preparing these activities for publication.
Most important, we want to thank our husbands for their patience
and understanding during our pursuit in developing a quality
education program for five- and six-year-old children.

This Fearon Teacher Aids product was formerly manufactured and
distributed by American Teaching Aids, Inc., a subsidiary of Silver Burdett
Ginn, and is now manufactured and distributed by Frank Schaffer
Publications, Inc. FEARON, FEARON TEACHER AIDS and the FEARON
balloon logo are marks used under license from Simon & Schuster, Inc.

Editorial Director: Virginia L. Murphy
Revision Editor: Rebecca Shimek Hanel
Copyeditor: Kristin Eclov
Original Illustration: Marilynn Barr
Cover and Spot Illustration: Janet Skiles
Inside Design: Teena Remer
Cover Design: Lucyna Green

Entire contents copyright © 1994 by
Fearon Teacher Aids, a Division of
Frank Schaffer Publications, Inc.

ISBN 0-86653-910-7
Printed in the United States of America
1.9 8 7

Dedication

We dedicate this resource book to the children who attended the Cooperative Demonstration Kindergarten. We hope that the curriculum we provided made them want to learn more about their world.

We also dedicate this book to our children, Andrew Howard, Paige Howard, Leah Faulk, and Emily Faulk, who continue to bring so much love, joy, and happiness into our lives.

TABLE OF CONTENTS

INTRODUCTION

This resource book has been written to make teaching kindergarten a little easier for all of you who have been staying up late at night writing lesson plans. When we first started teaching five-year-olds in public school, we had a hard time finding a workable lesson plan format. We also had a hard time writing the lesson plans and preparing activities because the process was so time consuming. There were many resource books, but almost all of them were organized according to subjects, such as math and reading, rather than by units, such as forest animals and nutrition. Since the kindergarten program in our school was organized around the learning-center approach based on a unit of study for each week, it was necessary for us to spend hours looking for and thinking of activities to incorporate into our daily lesson plans. We couldn't find one resource book that met our needs, so we decided to write our own curriculum.

We developed a lesson-plan format, and for seven and one-half years, we wrote and rewrote these teaching plans. The ideas in this resource book have been used with thousands of children and have stimulated their interest and thinking. We hope this resource will be a valuable one for you while continuing to grow as a teacher. We also hope that since we've put it all together, you'll have more time to enjoy yourself, the children, and the teaching process.

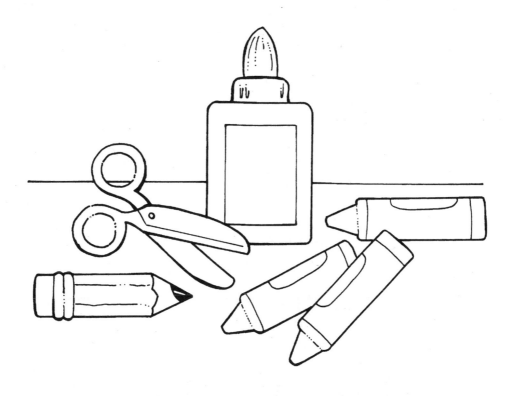

Description of Weekly Units

Each of the units in this book have been written for a week of instruction. The plans include a variety of activities that focus on a weekly theme. The well-balanced units can be followed step-by-step or adapted to meet your needs. Draw from your background, interest, and abilities to add enthusiasm to the plans. Throughout this book, the following skills are used in the weekly units:

▶ counting

▶ fine motor

▶ gross motor

▶ listening (sound discrimination)

▶ perceptual motor

▶ seriation

▶ sorting and classifying

▶ spatial relations

▶ time

▶ visual discrimination

▶ visual perception

The following content areas are included:

▶ art

▶ health

▶ language arts

▶ mathematics

▶ music

▶ science

▶ social studies

Description of Daily Plans

Each daily plan focuses on one part of the weekly unit. These daily plans can be followed step-by-step or adapted to meet your needs. Children's ages, attention spans, and individual characteristics will vary. Consider the time allotted for each activity and the amount of help the children will need when you modify these plans for your class. Many of the lesson plans contain more suggestions than you will be able to use in one day. However, on those days, you can choose the activities that are most appropriate for your children and remember the other ideas for those "rainy days." The following daily schedules are suggested:

Half-Day Schedule

Morning class
8:00-8:15	Free Time
8:15-8:45	First Group Time
8:45-9:45	Learning Centers
9:45-10:15	Outside Play
10:15-10:30	Snacks
10:30-11:00	Second Group Time
Evaluation	
Dismissal	

Afternoon class
12:00-12:15	Free Time
12:15-12:45	First Group Time
12:45-1:45	Learning Centers
1:45-2:15	Outside Play
2:15-2:30	Snacks
2:30-3:00	Second Group Time
Evaluation	
Dismissal	

Full-Day Schedule

8:00-8:15	Free Time
8:15-8:45	First Group Time
8:45-9:45	Learning Centers
9:45-10:15	Outside Play
10:15-10:30	Snacks
10:30-11:00	Second Group Time
11:00-11:30	Lunch
11:30-12:00	Story Time
12:00-12:30	Rest Time
12:30-1:45	Learning Centers
1:45-2:15	Outside Play
2:15-3:00	Third Group Time
Evaluation	
Dismissal	

Free Time

Free time is a free-play period at the beginning of each day. Place activities or toys to be used that day in the appropriate learning centers before children arrive. Encourage children to become involved in these activities as soon as they enter the room. Allowing children to engage in activities from the moment they walk into the classroom will assure that there are no wasted moments of learning time. This will also encourage children to ask "What will we learn today?" However, one rule we enforced in our classrooms was that if a new activity was presented in a learning center, the children could not interact with that activity until after group time.

Group Time

Group time is simply the lesson for the day. Each lesson is designed to broaden the children's base of experience with an understanding of the weekly theme. New concepts and new activities are taught to the whole group. During group time, you must explain to the children what they will be doing in the learning centers each day. If there are new games and activities presented on a given day, use part of group time to teach the children how to play those activities. This will be very time consuming at the beginning of the year, but as the children become familiar with the materials in your classroom, this procedure will become routine. In this resource book, the descriptions of group time are very brief. You must be creative in taking these brief descriptions and making them come alive for your children. Group time should

include songs, rhymes, plays, stories, and anything else you can think of that will make the lesson interesting and real for the five-year-olds. Here's one example of making a brief group-time outline into a creative detailed lesson.

Group Time
1. Song: "Good Afternoon."
2. Review the words *sea* and *ocean*.
3. Song: "My Bonnie Lies Over the Ocean."
4. Discuss sea horse and shark.
5. Game: "Fishing." Cut out several paper fish, write a letter on each one, and attach paper clips. Each child uses a fishing pole with a magnet on the end to catch a fish and name the letter.

Sing "Good Afternoon" together. Tell children to listen for words that begin with *Ss* when you discuss the sea. Print these words on the board, and discuss them as they arise—sea, shark, sea horse, swims, scales. Review the definitions of *sea* and *ocean* and point them out on the map. Sing "My Bonnie Lies Over the Ocean." Ask children how they know which animals in the sea are fish. Discuss backbones and gills. Tell children that you will discuss two fish living in the sea whose names begin with *Ss*. "What has the head of a horse, the tail of a monkey, and a pouch like a kangaroo?" (Sea horse.) Explain that the sea horse is a fish with a bumpy body that swims upright. The mother sea horse lays eggs in the father's pouch. Then explain the art project.

Pass around a piece of sharkskin. Ask if anyone can guess what it is. Use pictures of various sharks. Explain that a shark is a fish whose skin is covered with millions of triangular-shaped teeth. Some sharks are harmful and others aren't. The great white shark isn't white. The tiger shark has a striped body like a tiger. The hammerhead shark has a hammer-shaped head.

Pass around the fishing pole, and let each child catch a fish with the magnet.

Next, explain learning centers.

Learning Centers

Learning centers are designated subject areas within the classroom where activities are provided for children to be directly involved in the learning process. Centers usually planned for young children include art, science, math, language arts, blocks, dramatic play, and music. Other possible learning centers include woodworking, cooking, sand, and water. Sometimes a subject area may be incorporated into more than one center. For example, language arts are incorporated in all learning centers in this book. You will also notice that subject areas are sometimes moved to other learning centers. Don't let the designated learning centers limit your activities. Make your classroom arrangement a manageable environment that will provide the most inviting situation possible for children to learn.

The learning-center approach is a valuable teaching technique. It allows you to meet individual needs, develop the children's creative potentials, promote the development of positive self-concepts, create an environment to ensure intellectual growth, and broaden the children's experiences. Through learning centers, you can provide opportunities that will help to increase competence and skills in communication, physical coordination, independence, and social development.

Here are some suggestions for using learning centers:

1. Start the year using only independent activities that most five-year-olds can do without or with very little teacher direction (puzzles, housekeeping, books, sand, coloring, and manipulatives).

2. Teach learning-center rules at the beginning of the year. These rules are the guidelines children must remember in order to work in the centers independently. Review these rules from time to time.

3. Center activities do not need to be changed daily. Be flexible to meet the needs of the children. Make sure children know how to use each learning center before you introduce a new one.

4. After learning the classroom rules, children should be able to work in the learning centers independently. As they work, you can move around the room and ask children questions to guide their play. Conduct special projects that require your assistance with one small group of children at a time. The rest of the class can work independently at another learning center.

5. Limit the number of children at each center. Consider the available space and amount of materials when deciding how many children can work together cooperatively in each area. Post a sign with a numeral and a picture of the learning center to identify the number of children permitted there. Or, provide a set of clothespins or necklaces equal to the number of children permitted at a center. Children take a clothespin or necklace as they enter the center, wear it until their work is completed, and then put it back in the designated place to show that someone else can now play in that area.

6. Teach children to choose a center, complete the activity, and then choose another center. Children will be moving about the room more, but they will be on

tasks for longer periods of time and will also become more independent in their work habits. Allow and encourage children to move from center to center at their own pace as they complete each experience. Some children will spend thirty minutes at the art table and others may only work there for ten minutes.

7. Encourage children to explore all learning centers throughout the year. However, don't require that every child work in every center each day.

8. Too many children in a center, all children wanting to go to dramatic play first, and children going from center to center without completing the tasks are problems that will undoubtedly arise. So, start slowly and establish routines and guidelines. And remember, young children need to be guided in their play and reminded regularly in a positive manner of expectations and limits.

Blocks

Blocks can be the prime instructional material in a kindergarten classroom. Guide children during group time to think of activities that can be done with the block materials relating to the unit of interest. Always provide pictures, books, and other materials about the unit of study for children to use as they build. You will be amazed and impressed at their creations. Your children will not always build a structure that relates to the weekly theme, but this is acceptable and encouraged. Provide enough space in the block center for several children to work together. An area rug will provide a good surface for construction and keep down the noise level.

Listening/Music/Reading

The listening center develops competence in communication skills. Specific activities in the center promote listening skills, speaking skills, and reading-readiness skills. Children can listen to and sing along with records, listen to recorded stories, or even invent and record their own stories. Make a variety of books available on the weekly theme so that children are free to discover learning through books.

The listening center should consist of a record player and records, a cassette player and cassette tapes, headsets and jacks, a radio, and programmed materials. You may not always be able to provide a commercial record or tape of books and songs that relate to your weekly theme. For this reason, be sure to keep blank cassettes at school so that you can make tapes of your own voice singing appropriate songs or reading selected books. Provide a copy of the recorded books for children to "read" along as they listen. As in all learning centers, children need to be able to work independently. Therefore, teach your children how to operate the record and cassette players.

Art

The art center encourages children to express themselves through a variety of materials. Children can make the art projects simple or elaborate depending on their abilities. *Remember that the process is more important than the finished product.* Provide materials and give some guidance, but let the children do the rest. An easel is also used as much as possible. Changing the type of paints and colors as well as the paper will keep children interested.

Woodworking/Sand/Water

To generate interest and enthusiasm from children, we recommend that you rotate these three centers. The activity selected for the weekly unit or daily plan is determined by the relevance of one of these subjects to the topic. For instance, use a water learning center the week you're studying the ocean. Be creative. To add more variety and interest to the lessons, substitute other dry materials in the sand box, such as corn, beans, rice, or cornmeal, or use the surface of the water table for fingerpaints and playdough.

Printing

The printing center is a place for children to explore the writing process. Provide materials, such as chalk, pencils, crayons, markers, salt trays, clay trays, and typewriters. *Allow children to work at their own levels of ability.* Always have the key words from group time printed on the board for children to observe. The printing center is a learning center that is automatically individualized. For example, some children will only scribble. Other children may only go to the printing center and write the first letters of their names. There will also be children who copy all of the key words for the day to make a booklet that is complete with their own drawings.

Math/Language Arts

This center can be separate if there is adequate classroom space. Use teacher-made or commercial materials that emphasize math and language arts concepts. *Activities should also be appropriate for more than one level of ability.* Active participation in the math and/or language arts center makes learning more meaningful to young children. Teaching letters and numbers an also be included here, thus making them an integral part of the daily topic.

A wonderful project to incorporate throughout the year for language arts is a Language Experience Notebook. Buy or put together a notebook with plain white paper for each child. At least once a week, invite children to draw pictures about what was studied. Children can tell you about their pictures and you can write down their words. This Language Experience Notebook can be named *My Kindergarten Year.* This activity can be done at group time or at one of the learning centers. At the end of the school year, send the notebooks home. Parents will treasure their children's diaries of school activities.

Science/Social Studies

Separate this center if there is adequate classroom space. In the science and social studies center, children can manipulate objects, make discoveries, and examine books and pictures. Encourage children to draw conclusions, record their thoughts on paper if possible, and share ideas with their friends. The statement "Let's try this and see what happens" should be heard often.

Dramatic Play

The dramatic-play center is for pretending and make-believe. It is more than just a "housekeeping center." Arrange the center so that the children's make-believe is related to the weekly theme. For example, set up a grocery store during the unit on nutrition or a fire station during the unit on community.

Second Group Time/ Third Group Time

The number of group times incorporated into a daily plan is determined by the length of the school day. The activities presented for second group time may be expanded to cover a third group time as well. During this time, have the whole class sit down together, preferably in a carpeted area, and review the day's objectives or concepts. Use this time for musical activities, stories, dramatizations, games, and films. At the end of the day, allow some time for a closure period—a time to summarize what was accomplished that day and how well it was done. You can then make decisions as to how the next day's plan should be adjusted.

School Parties

School parties have been integrated into these daily lesson plans. We suggest that the daily schedule not be changed for school parties. Instead, include learning centers as usual and the actual party (eating) can take place at snack time.

Field Trips

Field trip suggestions are provided. However, complete lesson plans are also provided for each field trip day because you must always be prepared in case the field trip is cancelled for any reason.

Notes

1. In the lesson plans, games, toys, and puzzles that are commercial products are marked with a (C). You may not have all of the commercial materials we have suggested in this book. Therefore, you will need to substitute these suggestions with what is available to you.

2. Activities from the book *Workjobs* will have a (W) noted after them and activities from *Workjobs II* will have a notation of (WII). Both books are written by Mary Baratta-Lorton (see page 139).

3. Activities with an asterisk (*) require special supervision.

September
Week 1

Preparation:

▶ Schedule a small number of children to attend school each day for one or two hours this first week.

PRIMARY SCHOOL

Orientation to School

Group Time Activities

1. Introduce yourself.
2. Print each child's first name on a card and meet each child when you hold up his or her name.
3. Song: "Special"
4. Game: "Do As I Do." Do an action and children copy it.
5. Nursery Rhymes: "Jack Be Nimble," "Humpty Dumpty," and "Little Jack Horner." Children dramatize the rhymes.
6. Introduce the centers by walking around the room and showing the children the activities they will be doing.

Learning Centers

Blocks

Provide safety signs, toy cars and trucks, and cardboard streets.

Listening/Music/Reading

Provide a nursery rhyme record for children to listen to as they look at nursery rhyme books.

Art

Easel Paint: lavender and blue.

Leaves: Children cut green, brown, or orange leaves. Write each child's name on a leaf. Hang the leaves on a tree that is painted on the wall.

Woodworking/Sand/Water

Provide different-sized containers and strainers for free play in the sand.

Printing

Provide an old typewriter or plain paper and crayons. Print these words on cards for children to copy—school, friends, kindergarten, and teacher.

Math/Language Arts

Three Billy Goats Gruff Puzzle (C)

Jack and the Beanstalk Puzzle (C)

Cookie Monster Puzzle (C)

Gingerbread Boy Puzzle (C)

Legos (C)

Shapes (W)

Science/Social Studies

Provide balancing scales, magnifying glasses, rocks, and shells.

Dramatic Play

Provide dress-up clothes, dolls, dishes, and housekeeping furniture. Leave out all week.

More Group Time Activities

1. Sing familiar songs.
2. Read and dramatize more fun nursery rhymes.

September
Week 2

Preparation:

▶ Prepare a bulletin board entitled "Our School" with buildings and streets on it. (Children will add pictures to it all week.)

Safety

Day 1: Safety While Walking or Riding

Group Time Activities

1. Use first name cards. Children jump up as soon as they see their names.
2. Song: "Special."
3. Discuss the crosswalk guard and rules. Introduce a puppet to stimulate the discussion.
4. Song: "Stop! Look! and Listen!"
5. Introduce the letter *Ss*. Have children look for the letter *Ss* in the room.

Learning Centers

Blocks

Provide toy vehicles, safety signs, and blocks.

Listening/Music/Reading

Make a cassette tape of songs about safety. Provide listening headsets. Leave out all week.

Art

Easel Paint: red, green, and yellow. (Leave out all week.)

Safety Pictures: Children draw and cut out safety signs, cars, and school buses to put on a bulletin board entitled "Our School."

Printing

Provide paper and crayons. Print the following words on the chalkboard for children to copy—crosswalk guard, street, stop, safety, bicycle, and police officer.

Math/Language Arts

School Bus Puzzle (C)	Crosswalk Guard Puzzle (C)
Police Officer Puzzle (C)	Legos (C)
Friends Puzzle (C)	Train Puzzle (C)
Sharing Puzzle (C)	Cars and Garages (W)

Science/Social Studies

Children cut pictures out of magazines showing safe travel. Ask children to look for pictures that show people wearing safety belts. Have children compare the number of pictures showing people wearing safety belts and not wearing them.

Dramatic Play

Provide teacher-made belts on four child-sized straight chairs. Arrange the chairs like seats in a car.

More Group Time Activities

1. Take children to the street and practice crossing. Sing "Stop! Look! and Listen!" while crossing.
2. Children make up a story about "Safe Sam." Write down their words.

Day 2: School Safety

Group Time Activities

1. <u>Song</u>: "Beautiful Day."
2. Use first name cards. Children stand when they see their names.
3. <u>Song</u>: "The Bus Song."
4. Take class on a tour of the school. Discuss what was seen on the tour and how to care for school property (playground, classrooms, cafeteria, library, and office).

Learning Centers

Blocks

Provide wooden block people.

Art

<u>Helping Hands Mobile</u>: Each child traces his or her hand, cuts it out, and writes name on it. Write what the child says he or she will do to keep the school safe and clean. Hang all paper hands on one coat hanger and hang the mobile in the classroom.

Printing

Provide plain paper and crayons. Print these words on cards for children to copy—office, cafeteria, school, library, hall, and playground.

Math/Language Arts

Safety Puzzle (C)   Cars and Garages Game (W)

Wooden Safety Signs (C)   Legos (C)

Science/Social Studies

Children draw, color, and cut out playground equipment. Add to the "Our School" bulletin board.

Dramatic Play

Set up a school classroom. Provide a table, desk, chairs, and chalkboard.

More Group Time Activities

1. <u>Film</u>: *I'm No Fool With Safety at School.*
2. Review familiar songs.
3. <u>Flannel Story</u>: *Three Little Pigs.*
4. Discuss safety concepts.

Day 3: Fire Safety

Group Time Activities

1. <u>Song</u>: "Beautiful Day."
2. Review yesterday's safety concepts.
3. Use a safety chart and a puppet to discuss fire drills.
4. Practice a fire drill.
5. <u>Song</u>: "We Must Use Our Safety Rules at Home and School" (Tune: "She'll Be Comin' Round the Mountain When She Comes").
6. Say a list of words. Children stand up when you say words that begin with *Ss*.

Learning Centers

Blocks

Provide flannel town layout, vehicles, and safety signs.

Art

<u>Traffic Lights</u>: Children use plastic lids to trace and cut three circles—yellow, green, and red. Staple to popsicle sticks or children can glue the circles in order on a black paper rectangle.

Printing

Provide an old typewriter or unlined paper and crayons. Print these words on cards for children to copy—fire, safety, and drill.

Math/Language Arts

Cars and Garages Game (W)

<u>Sorting</u>: Place three large paper circles on the floor. Children can sort Interlocking Cubes (C) into a red, green, or yellow group.

Science/Social Studies

Provide unlined paper and crayons for children to draw and color safety signs to add to the bulletin board.

Dramatic Play

Line up chairs to resemble car seats. Add a police officer's hat, dress-up clothes, and safety signs.

More Group Time Activities

1. Children take turns being drivers, police officers, crosswalk guards, and traffic lights. Use the traffic lights they made in art today. Have children dramatize street safety using a toy 3-wheeler or a tricycle.
2. Introduce the letter *Gg*.
3. Play the game "Red Light, Green Light."

Day 4: School Personnel

Group Time Activities

1. <u>Song</u>: "Beautiful Day."
2. Hold up the children's name cards to help them learn to read their first names.
3. Use wooden block people (C) to discuss important school personnel and their jobs (secretary, principal, janitor, librarian, cafeteria staff, nurse).
4. Meet the principal and secretary in the office.
5. Ask children to think of words that begin with *Ss* and list them on the chalkboard.

Learning Centers

Blocks

Provide block people and vehicles.

Art

<u>Clay Molding</u>: Children use clay to shape people and school buildings.

Printing

Provide old typewriters. Print these words on a poster for children to copy—principal, janitor, secretary, teacher, nurse, and librarian.

Math/Language Arts

School Puzzle (C)

Police Officer Puzzle (C)

Candy Land Game (C)

Pegs and Peg Board (C)

Hands and Feet Puzzles (C)

Science/Social Studies

Children draw pictures of school personnel to put on "Our School" bulletin board.

Dramatic Play

Set up chairs to resemble seats on a bus. Add coins, tickets, bus driver's hat, and dress-up clothes.

More Group Time Activities

1. Take class for a walk around the playground. Point out boundaries and discuss safety rules to remember.
2. Review safety dos and don'ts.
3. <u>Film</u>: *School Workers.*
4. <u>Flannel Story</u>: *Little Red Riding Hood.*
5. Discuss dangers of talking to strangers.

Day 5: Tornado or Earthquake Safety

Group Time Activities

1. <u>Song</u>: "Beautiful Day."
2. Review yesterday's concepts.
3. Use a puppet and safety chart to discuss emergency drills.
4. Practice a tornado or earthquake drill.
5. Review *Ss*. Children take turns making the letter *Ss* with their bodies.

Learning Centers

Blocks

Provide flannel town layout, vehicles, and safety signs.

Listening/Music/Reading

Read *Safety Can Be Fun* by Munro Leaf.
Provide a variety of books about safety.

Art

<u>Tornado or Earthquake Safety</u>: Provide paper and crayons for children to draw pictures of what to do during a tornado or earthquake.

Printing

Provide old typewriters or plain paper and crayons. Print these words on cards for children to copy—tornado, fire, safety, and earthquake.

Math/Language Arts

Cars and Garages Game (W)

<u>Sorting</u>: Children sort Interlocking Cubes (C) according to the colors red, green, and yellow.

Science/Social Studies

Provide books with pictures of different kinds of weather.

Dramatic Play

Provide a large box to simulate a cellar, storm shelter, or closet. Also provide housekeeping materials.

More Group Time Activities

1. Read *Safety Can Be Fun* by Munro Leaf.
2. Each child acts out a safety rule while others guess the rule.

September
Week 3

Preparation:

▶ Prepare a bulletin board entitled "My Family is Special." Ask children to bring pictures of their families or pets to add to it.

▶ Prepare a bulletin board entitled "Our Kindergarten Neighborhood." (Children will add drawings to it on Day 1.)

▶ Invite mothers to visit on Day 1; fathers on Day 2; brothers and sisters on Day 3; grandparents on Day 4; and pets on Day 5.

Families and Pets

Day 1: Mothers

Group Time Activities

1. Print each child's last name on a card. Work with children on recognizing their last names.
2. Read *I Love My Mother* by Paul Zindel.
3. Discuss things mothers do and how we can help. Use a poster, made from magazine pictures, showing mothers involved in many tasks.
4. Song: "The Mulberry Bush." Dramatize actions with children.
5. Give clues about a secret letter and let children guess which one it is. Introduce secret letter *Dd*.

Learning Centers

Blocks

In addition to the blocks, provide large flat pieces of cardboard bricks (C). Leave materials out all week.

Listening/Music/Reading

Record the song "The Mulberry Bush," or another song about helping, on a cassette tape. Provide headsets. Leave this activity out all week. As an alternative, record the story *On Mother's Lap* by Ann Scott or *Love You Forever* by Robert Munsch.

Art

Easel Paint: brown and white. (Leave these colors out all week.)

My Home: Children draw their homes. Write children's names and addresses on the houses or apartment buildings. (Be sensitive to children's different living situations.) Help each child to begin remembering this important information. Place these drawings on a bulletin board entitled "Our Kindergarten Neighborhood."

Woodworking/Sand/Water

Sand: Provide construction trucks (C).

Printing

Provide unlined paper and crayons. Ask each child to make a book about his or her mother. (Be sensitive to children's different family situations.) Print these words on the chalkboard— Mother, Momma, Mom, and I love you.

Math/Language Arts

Find a Pair: Families, Houses (C)   Lincoln Logs (C)

My First Lotto (C)   Octons (C)

Science/Social Studies

Cut a variety of roofing shingles in half so that each one has a match. Children match pairs according to color, texture, size, and shape.

Dramatic Play

Provide housekeeping furniture, dress-up clothes, dolls, dishes, empty food containers, telephones, magazines, and newspapers.

More Group Time Activities

1. Game: "Lost and Found." One child pretends to be the police officer and another child pretends to be lost. Lost child tells his or her address to police officer.
2. Flannel Story: *Three Bears*. Discuss important safety rules.

Day 2: Fathers

Group Time Activities

1. Hold up last name cards. Children stand up when they see their last names.
2. Read *Daddy Makes the Best Spaghetti* by Anna Grossnickle Hines.
3. Discuss fathers' tasks and how we can help them.
4. Game: "Do As I Do." Do an action and children copy it.
5. Review *Dd*.
6. Write *Bb* on the board. Illustrate how *Bb* resembles bubbles. Think of other words that begin with *Bb*.

Learning Centers

Listening/Music/Reading

Make a recording of the story *Let's Play House* by Lois Lenski. Add the story *Daddy Makes the Best Spaghetti* by Anna Grossnickle Hines.

Art

My Family: Provide watercolor paints at a table. Children paint pictures of their families. Display pictures in the hall on the wall.

Woodworking/Sand/Water

Woodworking: Provide screws, bolts, wood pieces, screwdrivers, and bolt boards.

Printing

Children make books about fathers. (Be sensitive to children's different family situations.) Print these words on a poster—Father, Pop, Daddy, Dd, Dad, and I love you.

Math/Language Arts

Find a Pair: Families, Houses (C)

My First Lotto (C)

Lincoln Logs (C)

Octons (C)

Science/Social Studies

Children look at pictures of classmates' families. Encourage children to discuss how they are alike and different. (Be sensitive to children's different family situations.)

Dramatic Play

Add typewriter, a variety of work hats, and men's ties.

More Group Time Activities

1. Game: "Lost and Found."
2. Read *The Little Brute Family* by Russell Hoban and *People in My Family* by Jeffrey Moss.
3. Discuss the meaning of *one*. Children find things in the room of which there is only one.

Day 3: Brothers and Sisters

Group Time Activities

1. Hold up last name cards for children to recognize.
2. Show posters of brothers and sisters and discuss working together as a family.
3. Discuss being an only child.
4. Discuss new baby brothers and sisters.
5. Read *Rosa-Too-Little* by Sue Felt or *Tom in the Middle* by Bertha Amos.
6. With children standing, slowly say a list of words. Instruct children to jump when they hear words that begin with *Dd* and sit down when they hear words that begin with *Bb*.

Learning Centers

Listening/Music/Reading

Provide *Nobody Listens to Andrew* by Elizabeth Guilfaire.

Art

People in My Family: Precut paper dolls, which are connected hand in hand. Children color the paper dolls to look like people in their families.

Woodworking/Sand/Water

Woodworking: Provide screws, bolts, wood pieces, screwdrivers, bolt boards for fine-motor experimentation.

Printing

Children make booklets about their families. (Be sensitive to children's different family situations.) Print the following words on a poster that displays the meaning of each word—brother, sister, baby, family, and I love you.

Math/Language Arts

Find a Pair: Dolls (C)   The Safety Pin Game (W)

My First Lotto (C)   Go-Together Bottles (W)

Three Billy Goats Gruff Puzzle (C)

ABC Board: Glue large paper alphabet letters on a board and laminate. Make matching letters out of paper. Children match them by placing paper letters on top of the letters on the board.

Science/Social Studies

Children cut pictures from magazines about helping.

Dramatic Play

Add toys, a sleeping bag, and children's magazines.

More Group Time Activities

1. Game: "Lost and Found."
2. Flannel Story: *Three Billy Goats Gruff.* Talk about brothers and sisters.
3. Read *Babykins and His Family* by Richard Scarry or *Peter's Chair* by Ezra Jack Keats.
4. Discuss how *Bb* and *Dd* are alike and different.

Day 4: Grandparents and Other Relatives

Group Time Activities

1. Use last name cards.
2. Read *I Have Four Names for My Grandfather* by Kathryn Lasky.
3. Discuss grandparents: where they live (use map), why we call them "grand," what they do for us, and what we can do for them. (Be sensitive to children who do not have grandparents.)
4. Song: "Over the River and Thro' the Woods."
5. Introduce Grandparent's Day (September 11).
6. Review *Dd*.

Learning Centers

Listening/Music/Reading

Add the book *My Aunt Rosie* by Syd Hoff.

Art

Cards: Children make "Happy Grandparents' Day" cards.

Woodworking/Sand/Water

Woodworking: Provide screws, bolts, wood pieces, screwdrivers, and bolt boards.

Printing

Children make booklets about grandparents. (Be sensitive to children who do not have grandparents.) Print these words on cards—Grandparent, Gramma, Grandmother, Papa, Grandfather, Gramps, and Granny. Use string to hang the cards on a tree branch. Children can remove any of the cards from the "family tree" to copy in their booklets.

Math/Language Arts

Lacing Cards (C)	Tinker Toys (C)
Opposite Game (C)	Snap and Play (C)

Letter Boxes: Use a divided box and label each section with a letter. Provide pictures that begin with the letters in the sections. Children put pictures in the boxes according to beginning sounds.

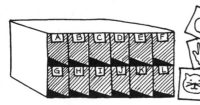

Science/Social Studies

Children work in Language Experience Notebooks. Children draw pictures of family members and favorite things they do together. Take dictation or let children write.

Dramatic Play

Provide household items and an unbreakable mirror.

More Group Time Activities

1. Read *My Aunt Rosie* by Syd Hoff.
2. Each child can contribute to the story "Why I Love My Family." (Be sensitive to each child's feelings about his or her family. Do not force a child to participate if he or she is uncomfortable with the activity.)

Day 5: Pets

Group Time Activities

1. Use last name cards.
2. Read *Pet Show* by Ezra Jack Keats.
3. Discuss pets and how to care for them. List what children say about caring for pets on a language chart.
4. If any pets are brought to school, let parents or children tell the class about their pets.
5. Song: "I Heard My Dog Bark."
6. Write names of pets that begin with *Dd* on the chalkboard.

Learning Centers

Blocks

Add plastic farm animals and stuffed animals to the block center.

Listening/Music/Reading

Provide book and recording of *Pet Show* by Ezra Jack Keats.

Art

My Pet: Children draw and color pictures of their pets or pets they would like. Write what children tell you about their pictures.

Folded Paper Puppy: Children make paper puppies with folded ears out of triangular pieces of paper.

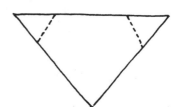

Woodworking/Sand/Water

Sand: Provide small farm animals.

Printing

Print the following words on chart paper with a picture for each word—dog, cat, pets, bird, and goldfish. Children can copy words and draw pictures.

Math/Language Arts

Cat and Goldfish Puzzle (sequence puzzle) (C)

Animal Puzzles (C)

Winnie the Pooh Game (C)

Find a Pair: Puppies (C)

Science/Social Studies

Children draw about families or pets in Language Experience Notebooks. Set up a puppet stage and allow children to use animal puppets to tell pet stories.

Dramatic Play

Set up pet shop with stuffed animals, cash register, and play money.

More Group Time Activities

1. Read *Can I Keep Him?* by Steven Kellogg.
2. Discuss which animals make good pets.

September
Week 4

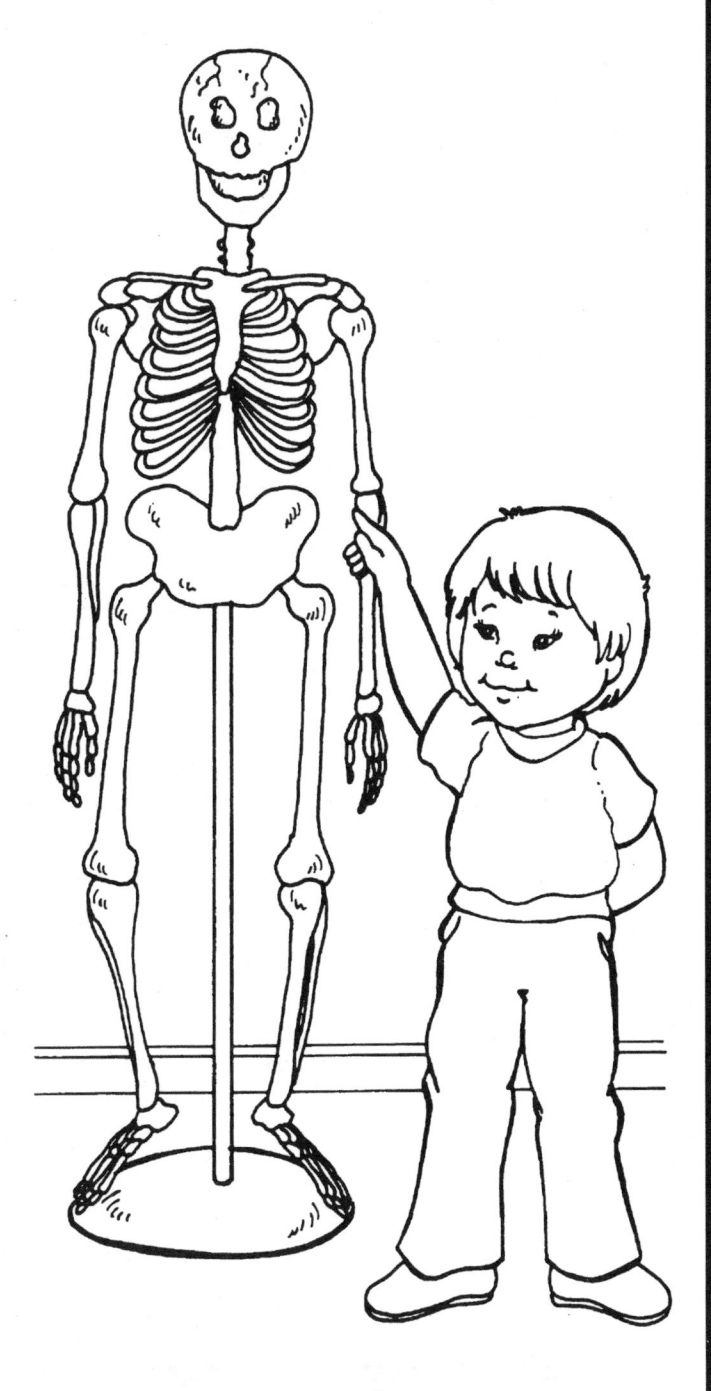

My Body

Day 1: Shape and Weight

Group Time Activities

1. Song: "Head, Shoulders, Knees, and Toes."
2. Discuss the word *me*.
3. Read *Smallest Boy in the Class* by Jerrold Beim.
4. Measure height and weight of each child. (Be sensitive to each child's feelings about his or her height and weight. Do not force a child to participate if he or she is uncomfortable with the activity.)
5. Have children lay on the floor. Put down masking tape the length of each child. Discuss longest and shortest.
6. Introduce the letter *Mm*. Discuss what the word *me* means and how we are all different.

Learning Centers

Blocks

Use masking tape to outline a hopscotch game. Close the blocks center this week so that children can play hopscotch.

Listening/Music/Reading

Make a cassette recording of these songs for children to sing along with or dramatize—"Head, Shoulders, Knees, and Toes," "Marching Song," "Touch," and "Turn Around" from the Hap Palmer record *Getting to Know Myself*.

Art

Body Prints: On large sheets of paper, outline each child's body. Children cut out bodies and color hair, eyes, lips, and clothes.

Body Chains: Children make paper chains the length of their bodies.

Woodworking/Sand/Water

Sand: Provide rulers. Wet the sand slightly. Children make handprints in sand and measure hands and fingers.

Printing

Provide alphabet stamp set and ink pads. Print these words on cards for children to copy—me, height, weight, short, and tall.

Math/Language Arts

Doctor Puzzle (C)	Snap and Play (C)
Dentist Puzzle (C)	Birthday Cakes (W)
Brushing Teeth Puzzle (C)	Hair Puzzle (C)
Hand Puzzle and Foot Puzzle (C)	

Science/Social Studies

Provide many pairs of socks. Children match the socks or place them in sets according to size, color, smell, or design.

Dramatic Play

Provide housekeeping furniture, dress-up clothes, dolls, telephone, and tape measures. Leave out all week.

More Group Time Activities

1. Give each child a string, and tell them to find an object that is longer, same length as, or shorter.
2. Children make an *Mm* out of blocks.
3. Weigh and measure each child. Put the information on a chart to compare to an April measurement. Make graphs. (Be sensitive to each child's feelings about his or her height and weight. Do not force a child to participate if he or she is uncomfortable with the activity.)

Day 2: Body Parts

Group Time Activities

1. <u>Song</u>: "Put Your Finger in the Air."
2. <u>Fingerplay</u>: "Hands" from *My Big Book of Fingerplays* by Daphne Hogstrom. (For other fingerplay ideas, see bibliography on p. 139.)
3. Discuss main parts of the body.
4. <u>Game</u>: "Simon Says."
5. <u>Song</u>: "The Body Rock" from the cassette *Kidding Around with Greg and Steve.*
6. <u>Game</u>: "Opposites." Child says the opposite word of what's called out, such as fingers, toes, hands, feet, and so on.

Learning Centers

Listening/Music/Reading

Make a recording of the songs "The Body Rock" and "The Hokey Pokey" from the cassette *Kidding Around with Greg and Steve.*

Art

Children may need to finish body prints from yesterday. Have children add the main parts of the body discussed at group time.

"Me" Mobile: Each child draws a face and traces around hands and feet. Help each child cut and attach body parts with string to coat hangers.

Woodworking/Sand/Water

<u>Sand</u>: Provide a balance scale and containers.

Printing

Provide stamp set and ink pads. Print these words on cards—head, foot, toe, hand, arm, and elbow.

Math/Language Arts

ABC Board (p. 18)   Feet Puzzle (C)

Hand Puzzle (C)   Let's Make Faces (C)

What's Missing? (C)

Science/Social Studies

Children trace hands and feet to measure and compare. Display tooth chart, skeleton, and teeth models.

More Group Time Activities

Make toasted people. Provide bread, milk, food coloring, paintbrushes, toaster, and a people-shaped cookie cutter. Each child cuts bread with cookie cutter and paints parts of the bread body with different colors of milk. Toast and eat.

Day 3: Stages of Growth

Group Time Activities

1. <u>Song</u>: "Sing After Me."
2. Use pictures, clothes, and books to discuss stages of growth.
3. Read *The Very Little Boy* by Phyllis Krasilovsky or *Peter's Chair* by Ezra Jack Keats.
4. Show clothes ranging from baby to adult sizes.
5. Discuss heights and skeletons. Show pictures.
6. Discuss and compare heights.
7. Introduce the letter *Ll*. Children make the letter with their bodies.

Learning Centers

Listening/Music/Reading

Add the song "If You're Happy And You Know It" to the cassette tape.

Art

Finish the "Me" Mobiles.

Woodworking/Sand/Water

<u>Sand</u>: Children use rulers to measure handprints and fingerprints.

Printing

Provide stamp kit and ink pads for children to copy the following words from a labeled poster—baby, child, adult, grown-up, big, and little.

Math/Language Arts

ABC Board (p.18)

<u>Sorting</u>: Children arrange Legos (C) according to size or sort buttons by likenesses and differences. Provide pairs of shoes for children to arrange in order from smallest to largest.

Science/Social Studies

Children cut out magazine pictures of people from babies to adults and glue them on construction paper in order from smallest to largest.

More Group Time Activities

1. Review the letter *Mm*. List foods that begin with *Mm* on chalkboard. Give each child some miniature marshmallows. Children can arrange the marshmallows into *Mm's* and then eat them.
2. Talk about the meaning of *two*. Use marshmallows.
3. Read *Time to Get Out of the Bath, Shirley* by John Burningham.

Day 4: Muscles and Bones

Group Time Activities

1. Discuss muscles and bones using pictures.
2. Pantomine being a rag doll without joints or muscles.
3. Do body exercises, and let children demonstrate "shorter," "longer," and "wider."
4. Discuss and show skeleton.
5. Song: "The Body Rock."

Learning Centers

Listening/Music/Reading
Add "Wiggle Wobble" from *Greg and Steve: We All Live Together, Vol. 1.*, to the cassette tape.

Art
Skeletons: Children glue toothpicks on black construction paper to make skeletons.

Woodworking/Sand/Water
*Woodworking: Provide small hammers, large tree stump, and large-headed nails. Two children can work at a time.

Printing
Provide stamp kit and ink pads for children to copy these words, that have been stamped on cards—muscle, bone, and skeleton.

Math/Language Arts
Lemonade Stand Game (C)

Alphabet Soup Game (C)

Sesame Street Puzzles (C)

How Tall Are You? (W)

Beanbag Face Game: Cut facial features out of the side of a box. Toss beanbags in the spaces.

Science/Social Studies
Display skeleton model and pictures of skeletons.

More Group Time Activities

1. Game: "Alike and Different." Show pairs of pictures. Children suggest how they are alike or different.
2. Review songs that have been in the listening center all week.

Day 5: Alike and Different

Group Time Activities

1. Discuss likenesses and differences between children. Use peanuts to demonstrate how things that look alike still have differences. Each blade of grass is also different.
2. Read *When You Were a Baby* by Ann Jonas.
3. Song: "Marching Around the Alphabet" from *Hap Palmer: Learning Basic Skills Through Music—Volume 1.* Let children dramatize the song.

Learning Centers

Listening/Music/Reading
Children can listen to all of the songs from the week.

Art
Fingerprint Pictures: Provide ink pads and construction paper for children to make fingerprint shapes. Provide *Ed Emberley's Great Thumbprint Drawing Book* and crayons to make pictures from fingerprints.

Woodworking/Sand/Water
Sand: Provide clean turkey bones and rulers. Children can discover the bones, measure, and compare them.

Printing
Provide stamp kit and ink pads for children to copy these words, which have been stamped on cards—hands, lips, fingers, hair, and eyes.

Math/Language Arts
Mosaics (C)

Peg Board and Animal Pegs (C)

The Paper Clip Game (W)

Science/Social Studies
Using an ink pad and ink, children put their handprints on one large sheet of paper. Children can compare the prints. Hang the handprint mural in the hall.

More Group Time Activities

1. Provide a lipstick sample for each child. Each child can make lip prints on his or her own sheet of paper.
2. Review songs of the week.
3. Have children work in their Language Experience Notebooks. Children draw pictures in the notebooks about what they like best about themselves or what they learned this week.

September—
Additional Activities

▶ Discuss the "911" emergency phone number. Explain the purpose of 911, the situations which might warrant an emergency call, and have each child find and practice dialing 911 on a telephone. Explain the importance of staying on the phone until the dispatcher hangs up, so the call can be traced if necessary.

▶ Make a class booklet illustrating and describing school personnel. Create two or three interview questions which will help children gain additional information about school personnel. Model the interview process, and have children work in pairs to practice before actual interviews. Share information at next group time and compile into a class booklet with illustrations.

▶ Share *The Giving Tree* by Shel Silverstein. Compare families to the "Giving Tree." Have children share examples of how family members give to one another. Introduce the term "family tree." Create very simple family trees by making branches for each family member's name and illustrating how these family members are "connected"— for example, how family members help each other or are dependent upon each other, and so on.

▶ Read *Louanne Pig in the Perfect Family* and *A Visit to Grandma's* by Nancy L. Carlson.

▶ Write a class story about an imaginary pet.

▶ Read *Arthur's Pet Business* by Marc Brown.

▶ Make bar graphs on chalkboard depicting class heights, weights, ages, eye color, hair length, and so on. (Be sensitive to each child's feelings about his or her height and weight. Do not force a child to participate if he or she is uncomfortable with the activity.) Make graph markers by collecting gallon milk tops, taping each child's picture or name on flat side, and attaching magnet to underside. Keep these markers in a designated space in classroom, to be used throughout the year.

▶ Have children make length comparisons of common objects. Have children take three objects from their desks, such as scissors, a crayon, and a ruler. Compare each object's length to find which is the longest and the shortest object. Have the children arrange the objects in order from shortest to longest. Discuss concepts of long, longer, longest and short, shorter, shortest.

▶ Read *The Magic School Bus: Inside the Human Body* by Joanna Cole. Discuss the book. Encourage the children to explore the book on their own.

▶ Create an estimation activity that can continue throughout the year. Fill a large jar with a variety of objects, such as superballs, erasers, rulers, and jelly beans. Encourage the children to make simple estimates of the number of objects or the biggest or smallest objects in the jar at any one time. Have the children record their estimates on paper posted near the jar. Each week discuss the children's different estimates. Change the objects in the jar frequently.

▶ <u>Songs</u>: "Five People in My Family."
*The Sesame Street Song Book-64
Favorite Songs*. New York, NY: Macmillan
Publishing Co., 1992.

"Reach Your Hand Up High." *The Sesame
Street Song Book-64 Favorite Songs*. New
York, NY: Macmillan Publishing Co., 1992.

"Tall Enough." *The Sesame Street Song
Book-64 Favorite Songs*. New York, NY:
Macmillan Publishing Co., 1992.

"Skin!" *The Sesame Street Song Book-64
Favorite Songs*. New York, NY: Macmillan
Publishing Co., 1992.

"Growing." *Hap Palmer Favorites-Songs
for Learning Through Music and
Movement*. Sherman Oaks, CA: Alfred
Publishing Co., 1981

"Rise and Shine." *The 2nd Raffi Songbook*.
New York, NY: Crown Publishers, Inc., 1986.

October
Week 1

Preparation:

▶ Prepare a bulletin board entitled "Where Do Our Foods Come From?" Put a map of North America or the World in the center of the bulletin board. Place pictures of foods around the map. Connect a string from each picture to the area on the map it comes from.

▶ Ask children to bring empty food cartons from home for a play grocery store.

▶ Plan a field trip for Day 5 to the grocery store or other food-related location.

▶ Discuss the six food groups that make up the food pyramid—fats, oils, and sweets; milk, yogurt, and cheese; meat poultry, fish, and eggs; vegetables; fruits; and breads, cereals, rice, and pasta.

Nutrition

Day 1: Dairy Products

Group Time Activities

1. Discuss dairy products using flannelboard pictures.
2. Discuss how chocolate milk is made. (Not from brown cows!)
3. Film: *Breakfast Gives You Bounce.*
4. Nursery Rhyme: "Little Miss Muffet." Discuss curds and whey.
5. Make chocolate milk or chocolate pudding.
6. Song: "The Milkman."

Learning Centers

Blocks

Provide plastic farm animals and Fisher Price Barn Set (C).

Listening/Music/Reading

Make a cassette recording of the songs "Alice's Restaurant" from *Hap Palmer: Learning Basic Skills Through Music—Health and Safety* and "Kinds of Food" from *Hap Palmer: Learning Basic Skills Through Music—Vocabulary.* Provide children with pictures of the foods mentioned in these songs to hold as they are named.

Art

Cow Mural: Provide a large cardboard cow. Children cut out pictures of dairy products from magazines to glue on cow.

Woodworking/Sand/Water

Sand: Provide various-sized plastic containers for measuring.

Printing

Provide real fruits and vegetables cut in half to make paint prints. Children dip the fruits and vegetables in a paper plate filled with paint and make prints on paper. Print these words on the chalkboard—milk, ice cream, cheese, cow, butter, and dairy.

Math/Language Arts

Nutrition Game (C)

The Food Game (W)

Flannelboard and dairy food pictures

Count the Milk Bottles: Glue paper houses on a posterboard. Write a numeral on each house. Make many small paper milk bottles. Children put the correct number of milk bottles by each house.

Science/Social Studies

Bring several kinds of cheese for children to taste on crackers. Provide books and pictures about cheese making.

Dramatic Play

Set up a grocery store. Provide cash register, paper grocery bags, play money, and empty food cartons. Leave out all week.

More Group Time Activities

1. Film: *The Cow Who Fell in the Canal.*
2. Read *The Supermarket* by Anne Rockwell.
3. Make butter by pouring 1/4 c whipping cream into each of four baby food jars. Add a dash of salt and shake until butter forms. Pour off any liquid. Serve on bread.
4. Introduce *Nn.* Give each child a newspaper. Ask children to look for food pictures or words that begin with *Nn.*

Day 2: Fruits and Vegetables

Group Time Activities

1. Use flannelboard and flannel-backed pictures of fruits and vegetables to discuss differences between them.
2. Let children name favorite fruits and vegetables. List the fruits and vegetables on butcher paper.
3. Discuss how fruits and vegetables are two separate groups in the food pyramid.
4. Provide precut fruits and vegetables. Encourage children to arrange the pieces into faces on plates and then eat them.
5. Film: *Lunch: Trying New Foods.*
6. Song: "Where Is Thumbkin?"

Learning Centers

Blocks

Add plastic fruits and vegetables.

Listening/Music/Reading

Provide the Hap Palmer record *Learning Basic Skills Through Music—Health and Safety.*

Art

Plates of Food: Children cut out pictures of fruits and vegetables from magazines and glue them on paper plates.

Clay Fruits and Vegetables: Children shape fruits and vegetables from clay.

Woodworking/Sand/Water

Sand: Provide different-sized containers for measuring.

Printing

Children continue making fruit and vegetable print designs and shapes. Print these words on the board—fruits, plums, vegetables, corn, cherries, grapes, potatoes, and carrots.

Math/Language Arts

Nutrition Puzzles (C)   Count the Milk Bottles

Nutrition Game (C)   Trees and Apples (W)

Counting Straws: Write numerals on painted cans. Children count the correct number of straws to put in each can.

Science/Social Studies

Children sort pictures of fruits and vegetables into correct boxes.

More Group Time Activities

1. Read *The Tale of Peter Rabbit* by Beatrix Potter.
2. Using fruits and vegetables, discuss the concept of large and small.
3. Make cooked playdough with the class. Explain that the dough will be ready for use tomorrow.
   Playdough Recipe:
   1 c flour   1/2 c salt
   2 tsp cream of tartar   1 c water
   1 T oil and food coloring
   Combine ingredients in a large skillet and cook on hot plate until mixture forms a dough. Constantly stir the mixture while it is cooking. Knead. Store in airtight container. Add spices, if desired, to give playdough a scent.

Day 3: Meat and Poultry

Group Time Activities

1. Discuss meats and poultry. Show pictures.
2. Film: *Dinner: A Time for Sharing.*
3. List favorite meats on butcher paper as children name them.
4. Make Pigs-in-Blankets with the group. Roll Vienna sausages in crescent roll dough. Use a microwave, toaster oven, or bring class to the cafeteria to bake the dough. Eat at snack time.

Learning Centers

Blocks

Add small toy tractors.

Listening/Music/Reading

Provide *Three Little Pigs* record and book.

Art

Q-Tip Art: Provide three colors of paint. Children use Q-Tips as brushes and paint on construction paper.

Woodworking/Sand/Water

Sand: Provide a variety of empty food containers for measuring and comparing. Make sure there are no sharp edges and are safe to use.

Printing

Children continue to use fruits and vegetables cut in half for printing. Print these words on the board—meats, eggs, poultry, chicken, ham, and bacon.

Math/Language Arts

Chicken and Egg Puzzle (C)

Bacon and Eggs (WII)

Sorting: Fill a grocery buggy with empty food containers. Provide grocery bags labeled with alphabet letters. Children put the food containers into the appropriate grocery bags.

Science/Social Studies

Provide playdough (homemade).

Provide sorting boxes for the children to sort pictures of different foods into the appropriate food groups.

More Group Time Activities

1. Review the six food groups in the food pyramid.
2. Film: *The Three Little Pigs.*
3. Children write the letters on the board that have been studied so far. Ask children to think of foods that begin with each letter.
4. Talk about the meaning of *four*. Use food containers to make this discussion concrete.

Day 4: Breads and Cereals

Group Time Activities

1. Discuss the characteristics of breads, cereals, and grains using a flannelboard and flannel pictures.
2. Children name the cereals they ate for breakfast. Make a class graph of favorite breakfast cereals.
3. Film: *Smart Snacks*.
4. Give each child 1/2 c of alphabet cereal. Children name the letters as they eat them. Children may also find the letters to make their names.
5. Show the differences in a variety of grains, such as corn, popcorn, wheat, and rice.

Learning Centers

Blocks

Provide pictures of farms as models for building.

Listening/Music/Reading

Provide *The Little Red Hen* record and book.

Art

Cereal Jewelry: Children string cereal on yarn for necklaces or bracelets.

Woodworking/Sand/Water

Provide corn kernels to use with the measuring containers.

Printing

Provide a jelly-roll pan with a shallow layer of wheat in it. Children use their fingers to copy these words in the tray of wheat—bread, wheat, cereal, grain, beans, and corn.

Math/Language Arts

Lincoln Logs (C)   Clocks (C)

Pegs and Peg Board (C)

Addition Box: Use any shoebox. Cut two holes in the lid. Make addition cards (1+1= 2). A child puts addition card on top of box so that the numerals are in line with the holes in lid. Provide something for child to manipulate while adding, such as marbles. For example, if the problem is 1+2, the child puts 1 marble in the first hole and two marbles in the second hole. The child then removes the box lid and counts how many marbles are in the box all together.

Science/Social Studies

Provide sorting boxes for children to sort pictures of food into the appropriate food groups.

More Group Time Activities

1. Film: *The Little Red Hen*.
2. Children make letters out of blocks.
3. Review the letter *Nn*.

Day 5: Fats, Oils, and Sweets/Field Trip

Group Time Activities

1. Discuss how too many sweets and fatty foods, such as corn chips and french fries, are not good for our bodies.
2. Show the children a picture of the food pyramid. Point out that the fats, oils, and sweets group is at the top of the pyramid because you should only eat a small amount of foods containing fats, oils, and sweets each day.
3. Discuss behavior on the field trip—in the cars and in the store.

Learning Centers

Blocks

Provide pictures of grocery stores for children to observe as they build.

Listening/Music/Reading

Provide Hap Palmer's record *Learning Basic Skills Through Music—Health and Safety*.

Art

Drawing: Allow free drawing or creative art with an assortment of materials. Encourage children to draw pictures of their favorite foods. Sort the children's favorite food pictures into the six food groups—fats, oils, and sweets; milk, yogurt, and cheese; meat, poultry, fish, eggs, and nuts; fruits; vegetables; and bread, cereal, rice, and pasta.

Woodworking/Sand/Water

Provide dried beans instead of sand for children to use while measuring with food containers.

Printing

Children continue to print with vegetables and fruits. Print these words on the board—nutrition, dairy products, fruits, vegetables, meats, fats, sweets, and breads.

Math/Language Arts

Nutrition Game (C)   Science/Social Studies

Nutrition Card Game (C)

Science/Social Studies

Provide sorting boxes for children to sort pictures of foods into the appropriate food groups.

More Group Time Activities

1. Review the letter *Nn*.
2. Write a thank-you letter with the class on butcher paper to the store, bakery, or cafeteria personnel you visited. Let each child sign the letter.
3. Read *I Want to Be a Storekeeper* by Carla Greene or *Bread and Jam for Frances* by Russell Hoban.

October
Week 2

Preparation:

▶ Ask each child to bring a bar of Ivory soap for art on Day 1

▶ Paint or draw a large tree and put it on the wall. (Children will add leaves to it during the week.)

Fall Season

Day 1: Columbus Day

Group Time Activities

1. Poem: "12 October" by Myra Cohn Livingston.
2. Discuss the ships, wind, and interesting problems of Columbus' voyage.
3. Show ships' routes on globe, and discuss globe concepts.
4. Introduce the letters *Kk* and *Qq* while talking about the King and Queen.
5. Have a discussion about Christopher Columbus using the book *Christopher Columbus: A Great Explorer* by Carol Greene. Present an accurate and truthful portrayal of this famous explorer.

Learning Centers

Blocks

Children can enjoy free play with the blocks all week.

Listening/Music/Reading

Provide a cassette recording of the songs "He Knew the Earth Was Round-O," "It's All Wrong," and "My Spanish Guitar."

Art

Ivory Soap Boats (special project): Children carve out the inside of the Ivory soap bars, using teaspoons. Attach sails to the boats. Some teacher assistance may be needed. Work with a small group of children on this project while the other children work independently in other learning centers.

Woodworking/Sand/Water

Water: Provide playdough, small wooden pieces, and aluminum foil for children to construct boats. They can see which material makes the best boat.

Printing

Spread a thin layer of blue clay on a cookie sheet. Children print these words from chalkboard in clay using a pencil or crayon—Columbus Day, October, America, Nina, Pinta, and Santa Maria.

Math/Language Arts

Deck of Cards (C)   Go Fishing Game (C)

Puzzle of the World (C)

Science/Social Studies

Sink/Float Experiment: Provide a variety of objects and water. After predicting and experimenting, children can divide the objects according to sink or float characteristics.

Dramatic Play

Put a blue blanket on the floor. Using a rocking boat (C), children can dramatize Columbus' voyage.

More Group Time Activities

1. Discuss things that come in threes or have three identical parts (triplets, tricycle, tripod). Talk about the meaning of *three*.
2. Listen to a recording of the ocean. Encourage children to imagine and then dramatize what sea voyages might have been like.
3. Film: *Here Comes Columbus Day*.

Day 2: Signs and Activities of Fall

Group Time Activities

1. List signs of fall on chalkboard as children name them. Discuss plants, animals, cooler temperatures, and changes in clothing. Show pictures.
2. Name and discuss family activities in the fall.
3. Make a recording of fall sounds, such as leaves falling, animals, birds flying south, and so on. Children pantomime a leaf falling to the ground.
4. Read *Now It's Fall* by Lois Lenski.

Learning Centers

Listening/Music/Reading

Provide recording and book *The Stranger* by Chris Van Allsburg.

Art

Easel Paint: brown, red, and yellow.

Fall Leaves: Children trace and cut out leaves on orange and brown paper. Tape leaves on a tree painted or taped on wall.

Woodworking/Sand/Water

Sand: Wet the sand and provide a variety of kitchen utensils.

Dramatic Play

Provide warm dress-up clothes, a rake, and a football.

Printing

Put these words on slips of paper in a bag—fall, leaf, school, football, orange, gold, and brown. Have children pick words out and then copy them.

Math/Language Arts

Holly Hobbie Game (C)

What Goes Together: Provide cards with pictures of fall items—leaves, football helmet, child, desk, rake, football, sweater, and books. Children group cards that go together.

Science/Social Studies

Provide leaves, nuts, and other fall items for children to examine and observe.

Snack Ideas

Pop popcorn with children.

More Group Time Activities

1. Give each child a paper bag. Take the class on a nature walk and collect acorns, leaves, and rocks. Be careful not to disturb the natural environment.
2. Language Experience Notebook: Children draw pictures of what was seen on the nature walk.

Day 3: Animals Prepare for Winter

Group Time Activities

1. Discuss different animals and how they prepare for winter—frogs (bottom of pond), bears (hibernate), birds (migrate to south), and squirrels (gather nuts).
2. Read *The House of Four Seasons* by Roger Duvoisin.
3. Discuss fall clothing and show examples.
4. Show pictures of children dressed for different seasons.

Learning Centers

Blocks

Add tractors, wooden-block farmer, and plastic animals.

Listening/Music/Reading

Provide a cassette recording of the songs "Furry Squirrel" and "Animals Are My Friends."

Art

Leaf Rubbings: Provide real leaves. Children place paper on top of leaves and color.

Woodworking/Sand/Water

Sand: Let children find buried sweet potatoes.

Printing

Print these words on the chalkboard and on slips of paper—frogs, winter, bears, clothing, birds, fall, and squirrels. Place the papers in a bag. Children pick a word out of the paper bag to copy.

Math/Language Arts

Animal Puzzles (C)   Safety Pin Game (W)

ABC Mailbox: Use a divided box and label each section with a different letter. Write names of objects on the outside of envelopes. Children sort envelopes according to the beginning letter of each word.

Science/Social Studies

Language Experience Notebook: Children draw a picture of animals preparing for winter.

Dramatic Play

Provide stuffed animals, blankets, and large boxes.

More Group Time Activities

1. Game: "Fishing for Letters." Write a different letter on each paper fish and tape a paper clip to each fish. Attach a magnet to the end of a stick for a pole. Each child catches a fish and names the letter.
2. Film: *How Animals Get Ready for Winter.*
3. Read *We're Going on a Bear Hunt* by Michael Rosen and Helen Oxenbury. Encourage dramatization and actions.

Day 4: Leaves

Group Time Activities

1. Using food coloring and water, demonstrate how to make orange and brown.
2. Show pictures and samples of leaves in the fall.
3. Explain why leaves change colors.
4. Play music and let children pretend to be falling leaves.
5. Film: *Autumn*.
6. Review the letter *Nn*.

Learning Centers

Blocks

Provide Fisher Price Farm (C)

Art

Torn Paper Trees: Children make fall trees using only torn pieces of paper (no scissors).

Woodworking/Sand/Water

Sand: Children continue to find sweet potatoes.

Printing

Children pick a word out of a paper bag to copy—leaf, yellow, red, orange, and brown.

Math/Language Arts

Season Puzzles (C)   Apple Tree Game (C)

Farmer Puzzle (C)

Acorn Tray: Provide a sorting tray (try one that apples are packed in). Write a different numeral in each section. Children put the right number of acorns in each space.

Science/Social Studies

Display an autumn harvest of cotton, pumpkin, or soybeans.

Dramatic Play

Provide fall dress-up clothes and books about fall activities.

More Group Time Activities

1. Crayon Shavings (special project): Children scrape crayon shavings on waxed paper with the edge of blunt scissors. Help children place crayon shavings and pressed leaves between two pieces of waxed paper. Place waxed paper between newspapers. Adult irons at low heat until crayon shavings are melted. These projects are beautiful displayed in windows.
2. Read *Mighty Tree* by Dick Gackenbach.
3. Fingerplay: "Autumn Leaves" from *Mitt Magic*.

Day 5: Nuts

Group Time Activities

1. Review the words *fall* and *harvest*.
2. Explain that a nut is a type of seed that grows in a shell.
3. Show leaves and nuts from several trees and discuss their uses. Crack nuts and let children taste. Mention that some nuts don't taste good.
4. Discuss what animals do with nuts in the fall.
5. Read *A Tree Is Nice* by Janice Udry.
6. Song: "Furry Squirrel."

Learning Centers

Blocks

Provide tractors, wooden farmer, and plastic animals.

Listening/Music/Reading

Provide recording and book *The Tiny Seed* by Eric Carle.

Art

My Favorite Football Team: Draw football jerseys on large sheets of paper. Each child decorates a jersey for his or her favorite football team.

Woodworking/Sand/Water

Sand: Children hide nuts, then dig them up, count the different kinds, and decide which type of nut they have the most of.

Printing

Print these words on the board and on cards—pecan, walnut, and hickory. Children pick a word or words out of a basket to copy.

Math/Language Arts

Acorn Tray: Count acorns.

Apple Tree Game (C)   Light Bright (C)

Season Puzzle (C)   Farmer Puzzle (C)

Science/Social Studies

Provide sorting tray and bucket of nuts for children to sort. Children crack and eat nuts. Display autumn harvest products, such as cotton, pumpkin, and sweet potatoes.

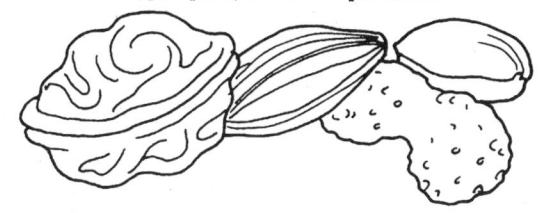

Dramatic Play

Provide dress-up clothes, housekeeping furniture, and magazines about fall.

More Group Time Activities

1. Discuss nuts. Review the life cycle of a peanut.
2. Make peanut butter by blending one large jar of unsalted peanuts, 1/2 tsp salt, and 3 T cooking oil in a food processor. Serve on bread or celery.
3. Song: "Peanut Butter" from *Chants for Children*.
4. Review the letter *Nn*.

October
Week 3

Preparation:

▶ Encourage children to wear clothes that are the color being studied each day. Encourage parents to send snacks that are also that color. (Day 1, blue; Day 2, yellow; Day 3, green; Day 4, purple; and Day 5, red.)

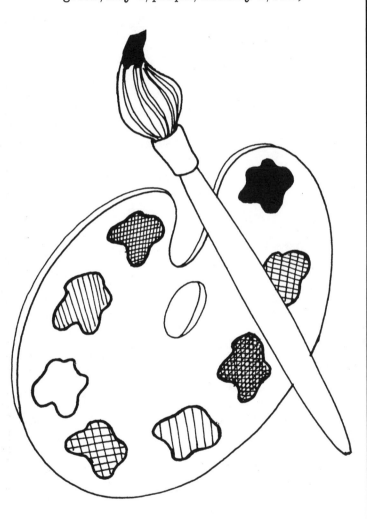

Colors

Group Time Activities

1. Show pictures and have children identify blue items.
2. Discuss Blue Grass music. Explain that the word *blue* can mean feeling sad.
3. Discuss prisms. Use a prism to make rainbows.
4. Read *The Great Blueness and Other Predicaments* by Arnold Lobel.

Learning Centers

Blocks

Provide a large box, a flashlight, and a ruler. Children experiment with light and shadows.

Listening/Music/Reading

Provide a record of Blue Grass music and encourage free dancing and moving.

Art

The Great Blueness: Each child draws on a large sheet of paper with only black crayons. Then every child paints over the paper with very thin blue tempera. Hang the pictures up and title them "The Great Blueness."

Woodworking/Sand/Water

Water: Provide blue water and water toys.

Printing

Spread a thin layer of blue clay on a cookie sheet. Children print these words from the chalkboard in the clay using a crayon or stick—blue, sad, blueberries, rainbow, and prism.

Math/Language Arts

Color Bingo (C)   Light Bright (C)

Colorama (C)

Sorting: Provide blue objects for sorting and counting.

Science/Social Studies

Place flowers or celery stalks in blue water. Children observe and draw pictures of how it looks each day. Children experiment with water and blue food coloring. Provide paper towels.

Dramatic Play

Children play in "blue land." Add as many blue objects as possible.

More Group Time Activities

1. Film: *Blueberries for Sal.*
2. Songs: "Parade of Colors" from *Hap Palmer: Learning Basic Skills Through Music—Volume 2* and "Colors," from *Hap Palmer: Learning Basic Skills Through Music—Volume 1.*
3. Language Experience Notebook: Colors.

Day 2: Yellow, Mixing Colors

Group Time Activities

1. Show objects and pictures of things that are yellow.
2. Discuss feelings associated with yellow.
3. Read *The Color Kittens* by Margaret Wise Brown.
4. Demonstrate mixing colors with water and food coloring.
5. Give clues about a secret letter, *Rr.*

Learning Centers

Blocks

Hang up a large sheet and have children use a flashlight to make shadows on it.

Listening/Music/Reading

Provide cassette and book of *Seven Diving Ducks* by Margaret Friskey.

Art

Easel Paint: yellow.

Macaroni Necklaces: Children string macaroni on yarn.

Woodworking/Sand/Water

Water: Provide yellow water and kitchen utensils. Add liquid detergent to the water.

Printing

Spread a thin layer of yellow clay on a cookie sheet. Children print in the clay using a crayon or stick. Display pictures of these words—yellow, color, blue, corn, and duck. Print the words on the pictures.

Science/Social Studies

Children continue to examine celery stalks in blue water. Place one stalk in yellow water. Children can experiment with water and yellow food coloring. Also, place blue water and red water in windows with thermometers in them. Children observe and make notes or drawings about observations.

Dramatic Play

Children play in "yellow land." Add as many yellow objects as possible, such as yellow sheets, a yellow duck, and a yellow toothbrush.

More Group Time Activities

1. Read *Yellow, Yellow* by Frank Asch.
2. Game: "Yellow Jell-O." Tell children they have been changed into a bowl of banana Jell-O and that the bowl is beginning to shake. Children wave hands, jiggle, and wiggle like Jell-O. (*The Outrageous Outdoor Game Book* by Bob Gregson.)

Day 3: Green, Rainbow

Group Time Activities

1. Read *Little Blue, Little Yellow: A Story for Pippo and Ann and Other Children* by Leo Lionni.
2. Let children name green things, such as Kermit the Frog, grass, and trees.
3. Discuss how a rainbow is made and point out the colors contained in one. Use posters of rainbows.
4. Write *Rr* on the board. Make pictures out of the letter *Rr.*

Learning Centers

Blocks

Children use blocks and flashlights to make shadows.

Listening/Music/Reading

Provide the cassette and book *Green Eggs and Ham* by Dr. Seuss.

Art

Easel Paint: green.

Drawing: Children do free drawings of Kermit the Frog, puppets, and rainbows. Place a stuffed Kermit (C) in the middle of the table.

Woodworking/Sand/Water

Water: Provide green water, kitchen utensils, and liquid soap.

Printing

Spread a thin layer of green clay on a cookie sheet. Children print in the clay using a nail. Display pictures of these words—green, blue, and yellow. Print the words on the pictures.

Math/Language Arts

Candy Land Game (C)   Snap and Play (C)

Color Dominoes (C)

Science/Social Studies

Provide three jars of water with blue, red, and yellow food coloring. Children use medicine droppers to mix colors in sections of an egg carton. Place celery stalk in green water.

Dramatic Play

Children play in "green land." Provide as may green objects as possible.

More Group Time Activities

1. Use food coloring to dye raw eggs green, then scramble, and cook them on a hot plate. Give green eggs to the children as a snack.
2. Show children how to make a Kermit the Frog paper-bag puppet. Color a white bag green. Use white styrofoam packing pieces for the eyes. Glue on long green paper arms and legs.
3. Song: "Bein' Green."

Day 4: Purple

Group Time Activities

1. Children name things that are purple, such as eggplant or grapes.
2. Discuss warm and cool colors.
3. Check thermometers in colored water on the windowsill.
4. Hold up alphabet cards. Ask children to hold up their arms when they see an *Rr*.

Learning Centers

Blocks

Children use blocks and flashlights to make shadows.

Listening/Music/Reading

Provide the cassette and book *Harold and the Purple Crayon* by David Johnson Leisk.

Art

Purple Cows:
Children draw and cut out purple cows. Give children copies of the poem "The Purple Cow" by Gelett Burgess, to glue on their cows.

Woodworking/Sand/Water

Water: Provide purple water and water toys.

Dramatic Play

Children play in "purple land." Provide many purple objects.

Printing

Spread a thin layer of purple clay on a cookie sheet. Provide a nail for children to print in clay. Print these words on the chalkboard for the children to copy—purple, cow, yellow, green, red, and blue.

Math/Language Arts

Candy Land Game (C)	Geozello Gears (C)
Color Dominoes (C)	Octons (C)
Purple Slime and Worms (C)	Legos (C)

Science/Social Studies

Provide food coloring in the three primary colors, medicine droppers, and white egg cartons for children to mix colors. Put different colors of construction paper in front of a sunny window, place objects on top of the paper. Children observe what happens to the paper.

More Group Time Activities

1. Review "The Purple Cow" poem. Write the poem on chart paper and read together. Discuss the meaning of this poem.
2. Read *Growing Colors* by Bruce McMillan or *Colors* by Heidi Goennel.

Day 5: Red, Light and Shadow

Group Time Activities

1. Discuss things that are red.
2. Discuss how red is associated with being angry.
3. Discuss natural light, artificial light, fireflies, and the sun (a mixture of colors).

Learning Centers

Blocks

Children use blocks and flashlights to make shadows.

Listening/Music/Reading

Distribute color signs and let children march around or hold up appropriate color signs as they listen to songs about colors.

Art

Tie-Dye (special project): With teacher's assistance, children can tie-dye T-shirts.

Red Collage: Children make red collages using red beans, red sparkles, red scrap paper, and red sequins.

Woodworking/Sand/Water

Water: Provide red water and sponges of different shapes.

Printing

Spread a thin layer of red clay on a cookie sheet. Children print in the clay using a crayon or pencil. Print these words on the chalkboard—red, light, shadow, stop, and mad.

Math/Language Arts

Color Bingo (C)	Apple Tree Game (C)
Colorama (C)	Apple Tree (W)

Science/Social Studies

Place one stalk of celery or a white carnation in red water. Children cut out magazine pictures of things that are red and glue on a mural.

Dramatic Play

Children play in "red land" with many red objects.

Outside Play Idea

Game: "Shadow Tag." When a child who is "It" steps on another child's shadow, he or she shouts "Sun Tag." The person tagged becomes the next "It." (*The Outrageous Outdoor Games Book* by Bob Gregson.)

More Group Time Activities

1. Film: *The Red Balloon.* Afterward, give each child a red balloon to take home.
2. Read *How the World Got Its Color* by Marilyn Hirsh.

October
Week 4

Preparation:

▶ Plan a field trip to a fire station for Day 5.

Fire Safety

Group Time Activities

1. Film: *Firefighters.*
2. Use a puppet and discuss the role of a firefighter and firefighter's equipment and clothes.
3. Poem: "Fire, Fire! Said Mrs. McGuire" from *Chants for Children.*
4. Introduce the letter *Ff.*

Learning Centers

Blocks

Provide fire hats, fire trucks, and hoses. Leave out all week.

Listening/Music/Reading

Provide recording and book *I Want to Be a Fire Fighter* by Edith Kunhardt.

Art

Easel Paint: red and orange. (Leave out all week.)

Fire Trucks: Children make fire trucks out of red construction paper and add black paper wheels and white paper ladders.

Woodworking/Sand/Water

Water: Provide red water, rubber tubes, hoses, and sponges.

Printing

Provide red paper and white crayons. Display pictures with these words printed on them—Sparky, fire truck, hose, firefighter, water, and fire safety.

Math/Language Arts

Go-Together Bottles (W)   Pegs and Peg Board (C)

Find a Pair: Houses (C)   Fire Truck Puzzle (C)

Weight Boxes (W)

Science/Social Studies

Provide Fisher Price Fire Station (C). Display a real firefighter's hat and fire safety books.

Dramatic Play

Set up a fire station. Provide hats, truck, bell, boots, jacket, and sleeping bags. Leave out all week.

More Group Time Activities

1. Read *Coyote Goes Hunting for Fire; A California Indian Myth* by Margery Bernstein and Janet Kobrin.
2. Create a song titled "The Wheels on the Fire Truck Go Round and Round" (Tune: "The Bus Song").

Day 2: Fire Truck and Fire Station

Group Time Activities

1. Read *The First Book of Firemen* by Benjamin Brewster.
2. Discuss the fire truck and the station. Use the Fisher Price Fire Station (C) to demonstrate.
3. Song: "I Am a Fireman" (Tune: "I'm a Little Teapot").

Learning Centers

Listening/Music/Reading

Provide recording and book *Firefighters A to Z* by Jean Johnson.

Art

Red Collage: Children make collages with an assortment of red items, such as glitter, kidney beans, and paper.

Woodworking/Sand/Water

Water: Provide red water and a variety of plastic bottles with caps, lids, and pumps.

Printing

Provide red paper so that children can copy these words from the chalkboard—Sparky, water, hose, fire truck, and firefighter. Children can make a book about fire safety.

Math/Language Arts

Go-Together Bottles (W)   Pegs and Peg Board (C)

Weight Boxes (W)   Firefighter Puzzle (C)

Science/Social Studies

Provide Fisher Price Fire Station (C).

Provide firefighter boots and other kinds of boots for children to examine and compare.

More Group Time Activities

1. Review the letter *Ff*. Children shape a garden hose into different letters.
2. Read *Fire Engines* by Anne Rockwell.

Day 3: Fire Safety

Group Time Activities

1. Gather literature from your local fire station to discuss a plan of escape, fire extinguishers, smoke detectors, and safety rules.
2. Children pretend to report a fire by using a play telephone.
3. Place a jar over a burning candle. Watch and discuss how a fire will not burn without oxygen.
4. Song: "Firefighters" (Tune: "Pop Goes the Weasel").

Learning Centers

Listening/Music/Reading

Children continue to listen to *Firefighters A to Z*. Children can create their own illustration of one letter of the alphabet as modeled in *Firefighters A to Z*. Compile all illustrations into a class book.

Art

Fire Murals: Children make murals about fire safety on large sheets of bulletin-board paper.

Woodworking/Sand/Water

Water: Provide red water, and discuss the boats that put out fires. Provide plastic boats and rubber tubing.

Printing

Provide red paper and crayons for printing. Display pictures of these words—extinguisher, smoke alarm, burn, and fire. Print the words on the pictures.

Math/Language Arts

What's Cooking Game (C)   Write On Wipe Off Cards-ABC (C)

Fire Truck Puzzle (C)   Hearts Card Game (C)

Hard/Soft Sort: Provide a variety of objects. Children sort according to hardness or softness.

Science/Social Studies

Display a firefighter's coat.

More Group Time Activities

1. Read *The Little Fireman* by Margaret Wise Brown.
2. Discuss different situations children may encounter in dealing with fire. Let children demonstrate and verbalize safety actions in these situations.
3. Discuss the meaning of *seven* using paper firefighter hats or something related to fire safety.
4. Song: "Safeway" from *Hap Palmer: Learning Basic Skills Through Music—Health and Safety*.

Day 4: Fire Prevention

Group Time Activities

1. Use a puppet or a fire safety poster to discuss safety rules to remember in preventing fires. Read portions of *Safety Can Be Fun* by Munro Leaf. Discuss pot handles, heaters, outlets, cigarettes, trash, flammable liquids, fireplaces, doors, and matches.
2. List rules as you discuss.
3. Show pictures of Smokey the Bear and Sparky.
4. Films: *Rescue Rangers Fire Safety Adventures* and *Donald's Fire Drill.*

Learning Centers

Listening/Music/Reading

Provide books about fire safety.

Art

Firefighter Hats: Children make firefighter hats out of paper bags (figure A) or red construction paper (figure B).

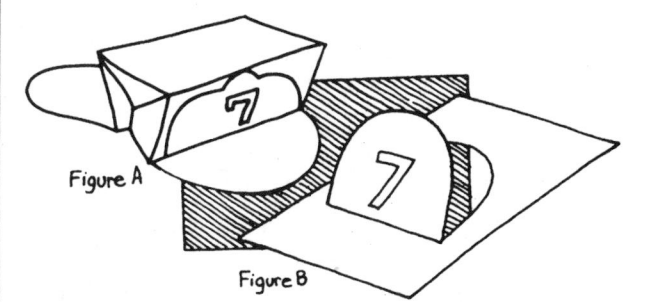

Figure A

Figure B

Woodworking/Sand/Water

Water: Provide red water and sponges.

Printing

Provide red paper and crayons for drawing. Display pictures of these words—Smokey, fire prevention, smoke, fumes, and safety. Print the words on the pictures.

Math/Language Arts

Birthday Cakes (W)   Stringing Beads (or buttons) (C)

Firefighter Puzzle (C)   Rubber Letters (C)

Science/Social Studies

Have children try on a real firefighter's suit.

More Group Time Activities

1. Review the songs learned this week.
2. Read *Save That Raccoon!* by Gloria P. Miklowitz.
3. Children draw and write in their Language Experience Notebooks.

Day 5: Field Trip

Group Time Activities

1. Discuss rules for behavior at fire station.
2. Read *The Fire Cat* by Esther Averil.
3. Review the letter *Ff.*
4. Film: *Hook and Ladder, The Fire Department Story.*

Learning Centers

Listening/Music/Reading

Provide a recording of the songs "Fire Down Below," "Firefighters," and "I Am a Fireman."

Art

Fingerpaint: Children use red fingerpaint.

Woodworking/Sand/Water

Water: Provide red water and plastic boats.

Printing

Provide red paper and crayons so children can print these words from chalkboard—Smokey, fire prevention, smoke, fumes, and safety.

Math/Language Arts

Birthday Cakes (W)   Rubber Letters (C)

Firefighter Puzzle (C)   Word Puzzle (C)

Stringing Beads (C)

Science/Social Studies

Provide pocketscopes (C) for children to observe water taken from several locations, such as pond, bathroom sink, and water fountain.

More Group Time Activities

1. Write a thank-you letter to the firefighters. Have each child sign the letter.
2. Read *A Visit to the Fire Station* by Dotti Hannum. Write a true class story about the field trip to the fire station. Have children work in pairs to illustrate the story.

October

Week 5

Preparation:

▶ Have children wear their Halloween costumes for the party on Day 5.

Halloween

Group Time Activities

1. Song: "Eensy-Weensy Spider."
2. Discuss spiders (eight legs, webs, life cycle). Show spider collection.
3. Read *Spiders in the Fruit Cellar* by Barbara Joosse.
4. To introduce the letter *Hh*, have many letters on the board. Children point to the *H's*. Children make pictures out of the letter.
5. Talk about the meaning of *eight*. Use a spider in the discussion.

Learning Centers

Blocks

Provide small plastic spiders. Leave out all week.

Listening/Music/Reading

Spooky Special Project: In a closet or dark corner of your room, provide a black light. Give children fluorescent paint to paint on black paper. Children can listen to a cassette of Halloween songs while they paint. The musical piece "Danse Macabre" by Saint-Saens creates an "eery" mood that would be appropriate for this activity. Leave out all week.

Art

Easel Paint: White paint on black paper. (Leave out all week.)

Spiders: Use garden nets to put up a giant spider web in the classroom. Children can make spiders out of paper or egg-carton sections and add eight legs. Hang spiders on spider web.

Woodworking/Sand/Water

Provide orange clay and kitchen utensils.

Printing

Children use chalk to print on black paper. Display pictures of these words—spiders and eight. Print the words on the pictures.

Math/Language Arts

Pegs and Peg Board (C)   Light Bright (C)

Match the Pumpkin Faces: Make matching pumpkin faces on construction paper. Cut out pumpkins. Have children find matching pumpkin faces.

Science/Social Studies

Provide spider collection, magnifying glass, and Fisher Price Scientist Set (C).

Dramatic Play

Set up the Count's haunted house. Provide black capes, housekeeping furniture, and Halloween objects for counting.

More Group Time Activities

1. Cassette: "Danse Macabre" by Saint-Saens. Check with local music store. Discuss the story. Children act out the story.
2. Read *A Woggle of Witches* by Adrienne Adams.
3. Fingerplay: "Little Witches" from *Mitt Magic*.

Day 2: Bats

Group Time Activities

1. Song: "There Was an Old Witch."
2. Discuss bats (babies, radar, sleeping habits).
3. Read *Hattie the Backstage Bat* by Don Freeman.
4. Talk about the meaning of *five*. Use Halloween candy.
5. Introduce the letter *Pp*.

Learning Centers

Art

Bats: Children trace and cut out black bats. Use string to hang the bats.

Drawing: Children draw with chalk on black paper.

Leaf Witches: Children glue pressed leaves on construction paper for witch bodies. Children add the rest of the body parts and brooms.

Woodworking/Sand/Water

Provide cookie cutters, kitchen utensils, and orange clay.

Printing

Children print with white crayons on black paper. Print these words on the chalkboard for the children to copy—bat, mammal, radar, and milk.

Math/Language Arts

Halloween Puzzles (C)

Pumpkin Sequence: Make construction-paper pumpkins for children to arrange from smallest to largest.

Haunted House Math: Color and cut out construction-paper haunted houses. Write a numeral on each one. Children count the correct number of pieces of Halloween candy for each haunted house.

Science/Social Studies

Provide a pumpkin that has been cut open. Children examine pumpkin seeds with magnifying glass.

Dramatic Play

Add books about Halloween to the Count's house. Add small plastic pumpkins.

More Group Time Activities

1. Film: *A Spooky Tale for Halloween.*
2. Game: "Ghost Robber." "It" sits in a chair. The rest of the class sits on the floor behind "It." Place a container of candy behind "It." Point to one child at a time who tries to be a ghost and take the candy without being heard by "It."
3. Fingerplay: "Five Little Ghosts" from *Mitt Magic*.

Day 3: Pumpkins

Group Time Activities

1. Song: "Have You Seen the Ghost of John?" from *Chants for Children*.
2. Discuss life cycle of a pumpkin.
3. Discuss the difference between jack-o'-lanterns and pumpkins.
4. Name foods and show pictures of foods made from pumpkins.
5. Estimate the circumference of a pumpkin. Each child cuts a piece of yarn they think will fit around the outside of the pumpkin. Have each child come up and use his or her piece of yarn to measure around the pumpkin. Compare children's estimates to see who came the closest to the actual circumference of the pumpkin. Measure the length of the yarn that was closest.
6. Carve a jack-o'-lantern, clean out the inside, and put seeds out for the birds.

Learning Centers

Listening/Music/Reading

Provide a cassette of *Halloween Night*.

Art

Halloween Night: Children glue popsicle sticks on black paper to make a fence. Then children add paper pumpkins, cats, or a moon.

Woodworking/Sand/Water

Sand: Provide wet sand and cookie cutters or kitchen utensils.

Printing

Children print on orange paper. Print these words on the appropriate pictures—pumpkin, orange, and seeds.

Math/Language Arts

Haunted House Math (W)   Light Bright (C)

Halloween Puzzles (C)

Halloween Word Match: Write Halloween words on one set of construction-paper cards. Draw Halloween pictures on another set of cards. Children make matches.

Science/Social Studies

Provide pocketscopes (C) for children to examine pumpkin flesh.

Dramatic Play

Add orange and black objects to the Count's house for children to count.

Snack Idea

During snack time, toast pumpkin seeds in a toaster oven. Add butter and salt. Let children taste them.

More Group Time Activities

1. Fingerplay: "Five Little Pumpkins" from *Mitt Magic*.
2. Using magic markers, color styrofoam cups to look like monsters. When all children have finished, take the class and their cups to the lunchroom. Place the cups in the oven (200° F) for a few seconds to shrivel. Hang the monster cups from the ceiling in the classroom.

Day 4: History and Superstitions

Group Time Activities

1. Read *Humbug Witch* by Lorna Balian.
2. Song: "There Was an Old Witch."
3. Discuss history of Halloween and superstitions (good luck—horseshoe, rabbit's foot, knock on wood, silver dollar, four-leaf clover; bad luck—ladder, black cat, broken mirror, Friday 13th).
4. Discuss date of Halloween.

Learning Centers

Listening/Music/Reading

Provide cassette and book *The Thirteen Days of Halloween* by Carol Greene.

Art

Trick-or-Treat Bags: Provide large paper bags. Fold the top down twice, staple handle on, and let children decorate front and back.

Woodworking/Sand/Water

*Woodworking: Children construct simple wood monsters, using an assortment of wood pieces, nails, hammers, and glue.

Printing

Children use chalk to print on black paper. Print these words with chalk on black construction-paper cards—Halloween, witches, ghosts, goblins, black cats, and superstitions.

Math/Language Arts

Pegs and Peg Board (C)

Pumpkins: Make paper pumpkins of different sizes. Children arrange them in order from smallest to largest.

Candy Count: Provide small plastic pumpkins (C). Write a numeral on each one. Children count correct number of pieces of candy to go in each pumpkin.

Science/Social Studies

Display cleaned turkey bones and posters of skeletons. Children examine bones with magnifying glasses.

Dramatic Play

Add plastic spiders to the Count's house.

More Group Time Activities

1. Children work in groups of four or five to make Halloween murals to hang in the hall.
2. Read *Witches' Holiday* by Alice Low.
3. Introduce the letter *Jj*.
4. Fingerplay: "Five Little Goblins" from *Mitt Magic*.

Day 5: Halloween Party

Group Time Activities

1. Discuss history of Halloween. Review the date and customs of Halloween.
2. Discuss safety rules for trick-or-treating.
3. Children wear costumes on a parade around school.
4. Game: "Guess Who?" Children guess who is in each costume.

Learning Centers

Listening/Music/Reading

Continue listening to the cassette of Halloween songs.

Art

Party Placemats: Using black paper, children make their own placemats for the party. Punch holes around the edges and let children lace with orange yarn.

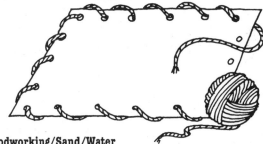

Woodworking/Sand/Water

*Woodworking: Encourage children to continue making Halloween wooden monsters.

Printing

Children print with white crayons on black paper. Print these words on black construction paper—Halloween and disguise.

Math/Language Arts

Light Bright (C)   Halloween Word Match

Haunted House Math   Halloween Puzzles (C)

Science/Social Studies

Language Experience Notebook: Halloween.

Provide apples cut in half for children to examine.

Dramatic Play

Add more Halloween objects to the Count's house. Provide containers for sorting.

Snack Ideas

Halloween Party

More Group Time Activities

1. Children find something in the *Hh* box, tell what the object is, and what letter it begins with.
2. Read *Georgie's Halloween* by Robert Bright.
3. Stick a popsicle stick through an apple for each child. Tie strings to the sticks and hang the apples in the room. Children try to take bites from the apples while keeping both hands behind their backs.

October—
Additional Activities

- Make a class poster of healthy vs. unhealthy foods. Have each child cut out one or two pictures of food from a magazine. As a class, vote on which side of the poster each food belongs on and tell why. Glue pictures under appropriate heading.

- Make a "lunch box" by folding a large piece of construction paper in half. Glue on handles. Have children create a "healthful lunch" from magazine pictures of foods studied during the week. Glue the pictures inside the lunch box. Children can decorate outside of lunch box. Hang lunch boxes from ceiling.

- Game: "What Am I?" Each child pretends to be a certain food. Class members ask yes or no questions to figure out what food each child is. After a specific number of questions, have a different child be "It."

- Make a "trunk" from a shoebox or brown construction paper. Discuss Christopher Columbus' voyage. Have children "pack" 3 items they would have taken on this voyage. Children can create these items from construction paper. Have class work in pairs to tell each other which items they have packed and why.

- Design a class ocean mural. Discuss what may be found in an ocean using various books. Talk about Columbus' ocean voyage. Each child can complete one piece of the ocean by drawing their ocean scene using very dark crayon. Then paint over the scene with very thin blue tempera paint.

- Read *A Picture Book of Christopher Columbus* by David A. Adler.

- Create adjective posters. Have children describe various fall things, such as leaves, trees, animals, and so on. Draw the item in the center of the poster and write describing words around it. Display adjective posters during fall unit. Encourage children to use adjectives.

- Make a fall mural by having each child draw one fall thing they see, or one fall activity their family participates in, on a large piece of butcher paper displayed in the classroom.

- Read *Once There Was a Tree* by Natalia Romanova.

- Read *When Autumn Comes* by Robert Maass.

- Read *A Book of Seasons* by Alice and Martin Provensen.

- Read *What's the Matter With Carruthers?* by James Marshall.

- Read *Has Winter Come?* by Wendy Watson.

- Write a class story modeled after *Harold and the Purple Crayon* by David Johnson Leisk. Have children decide on a main character, a setting, and events in the story. Make the story into a big book and have children illustrate pages or record on cassette.

- Color Word Collage: Have children brainstorm as many objects as possible that are a certain color. Write or draw answers in the given color.

- Encourage children to discuss fire safety at home. Discuss the importance of having a family plan in place in case of fire, such as exits from the house, a meeting place outside of the house, and be familiar with the "stop, drop, and roll" procedure.

- Read *Fighting a Fire* by Brenda Williams.

- Read *When There is a Fire Go Outside* by Dorothy Chlad.

- Have a spooky story day. Encourage children to bring stuffed animals and blankets. Gather in a circle. Turn out all the lights except for a flashlight. Tell ghost stories or use stories from *Scary Stories to Tell in the Dark* by Alvin Schwartz.

- Make bats to hang in the room. Have each child bring in an empty toilet-paper roll. Color or cover with black construction paper. Glue on construction-paper wings and yellow eyes. Make this an activity in following directions by giving one directive at a time.

- Read *Let's Find Out About Halloween* by Paulette Cooper.

- Read *Halloween Cookbook* by Susan Purdy.

- Read *How Spider Saved Halloween* by Robert Kraus.

- Read *Cats and Bats and Things with Wings* by Conrad Aiken.

- Songs: "Captain Vegetable." *The Sesame Street Song Book: 64 Favorite Songs.* New York, NY: Macmillan Publishing Co., 1992.

  "Breakfast Time." *The Sesame Street Song Book: 64 Favorite Songs.* New York, NY: Macmillan Publishing Co., 1992.

  "Bein' Green." *The Sesame Street Song Book: 64 Favorite Songs.* New York, NY: Macmillan Publishing Co., 1992.

  "Colors." *Hap Palmer Favorites-Songs for Learning Through Music and Movement.* Sherman Oaks, CA: Alfred Publishing Co., 1981

  "All the Colors of the Rainbow." *Hap Palmer Favorites-Songs for Learning Through Music and Movement.* Sherman Oaks, CA: Alfred Publishing Co., 1981

November
Week 1

Preparation:

▶ Dye some rice red and some rice blue. If you live in Canada, dye some rice red and leave some rice white. Add food coloring to rubbing alcohol. Leave the rice in the colored alcohol until the desired color is achieved. Drain the rice and spread it on newspaper to dry.

Patriotism

Day 1: North America Today

Group Time Activities

1. <u>Song</u>: "Happy Birthday to America" (Tune: "Oh Christmas Tree") or "O Canada."
2. Show pictures of past presidents or prime ministers. Explain a president or prime minister's job.
3. Show pictures of the current president or prime minister, and tell about his or her family life and his or her special interests.
4. Show pictures of important government buildings in the capital city, such as the White House or the Canadian parliament buildings.
5. Discuss and show pictures of American or Canadian symbols, such as the Statue of Liberty, the Bald Eagle, or the Canadian Coat of Arms.

Learning Centers

Blocks
Children use blocks in free construction all week.

Listening/Music/Reading
Record the songs "Happy Birthday to America," "You're a Grand Old Flag," "Yankee Doodle," "O Canada," and "God Save the Queen."

Art
<u>Easel Paint</u>: red, white, and blue. (Leave out all week.)

<u>Government Monuments</u>: Children make Washington monuments or a Canadian parliament building by cutting shapes out of white styrofoam meat trays and gluing them on dark blue construction paper.

Woodworking/Sand/Water
Provide measuring containers and red, white, and blue rice. Leave out all week.

Printing
Provide a clay tray for children to write on. Print these words on the chalkboard—president, White House, prime minister, and provinces.

Math/Language Arts
Ring Toss (C)   Rhyming Words Match (C)

<u>Patriotic Concentration</u>: Draw patriotic symbols or place stickers on small construction-paper cards. Make two of each picture. Children turn all cards over, face down. Children take turns turning two cards up. If they match, that child keeps them. If cards don't match, both are turned back over. The child with the most cards at the end is the winner.

Science/Social Studies
<u>Language Experience Notebook</u>: The president or the prime minister.

Encourage children to make models of the White House or Canadian House of Commons out of shoeboxes. Provide books and pictures of the White House or Canadian House of Commons for reference. Use materials, such as styrofoam packing pieces, pipe cleaners, and construction paper.

Day 1: North America Today

Dramatic Play

Set up a representation of the White House or Canadian parliament buildings. Provide a small desk, chair, telephone, paper, pencils, newspapers, and an American or a Canadian flag.

More Group Time Activities

1. As a class, write a letter to the president of the United States or the prime minister of Canada.
2. Sing patriotic songs.
3. Use small American or Canadian flags in a discussion of the meaning of *six*.
4. As class write a book called "If I Were President" or "If I Were Prime Minister." Have each child dictate one thing he or she would do if he or she were president or prime minister. Have each child illustrate his or her page.
5. Share information from the book *Canada* by Jack Brickendon.

Day 2: Our Flag

Group Time Activities

1. Discuss the importance of the Pledge of Allegiance.
2. Repeat the pledge together.
3. Show pictures of flags from different countries.
4. Discuss the history of the American flag. Count the stars and stripes. Discuss the history of the Canadian flag. Count the points on the maple leaf.
5. Give each child strips of paper. Discuss how the paper strips are like the stripes on the flag. Each child makes an *A* using strips of paper.
6. Song: "American Flag" (Tune: "Frere Jacques").

Learning Centers

Blocks

Provide pictures of the American or Canadian flags as well as some actual flags, too.

Listening/Music/Reading

Provide Hap Palmer's record *Patriotic and Morning Time Songs* and a variety of musical instruments.

Art

Flags: Provide red construction paper. Children glue on precut white stripes and blue squares. Children color in 50 white stars or stick on star stickers. For a Canadian flag, provide red and white construction paper. Children cut out and glue big red stripes on both ends of a white flag. Have children color a red maple leaf in the center of the flag.

Torn Paper Flags: Children work together on one giant flag. Mark off sections for stripes and stars, and color in areas ahead of time. This will take two or three days but will be beautiful. To make a Canadian flag, mark the areas for the two red stripes and the red eleven-pointed maple leaf on a white background.

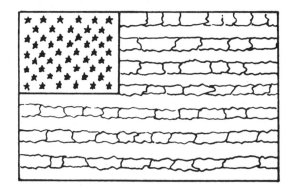

Printing

Provide letter stencils. Print these words on the chalkboard or on picture posters—flag, stars, stripes, America, red, white, blue, or Canada, red, white, maple leaf, and flag.

Day 2: Our Flag

Math/Language Arts

Patriotic Puzzle (C)   Puzzle of USA (C)

Children of the World Floor Puzzle (C)

Sorting: Provide objects for children to sort into red, white, and blue groups.

Washington Face Puzzle: Laminate and cut a silhouette of President Washington into a puzzle.

Canadian Coat of Arms Puzzle: Laminate and cut a picture of the Canadian Coat of Arms into a puzzle.

Science/Social Studies

Display pictures of presidents, books about America, American flags, and money. If you live in Canada, display pictures of past and present prime ministers and other leaders of Parliament, books about Canada, Canadian flags, and money.

Dramatic Play

Provide housekeeping furniture, American or Canadian flag, and a rocking chair.

Outside Play Idea

Go to the flag pole and say the Pledge of Allegiance together.

More Group Time Activities

1. Language Experience Notebook: Our Flag.
2. Film: *America The Beautiful*.
3. Share information from the book *Canada, Good Neighbor to the World* by Adam Bryant.

Day 3: Independence

Group Time Activities

1. Discuss patriotism (love of country).
2. Tell a brief history of the United States. (England, war, independence, 13 colonies, Paul Revere, first president, freedom). Use pictures, map or globe. Or, tell a brief history of Canada.
3. Review or teach patriotic songs.
4. Show pictures of famous people and places in America, such as George Washington and Paul Revere statues, Independence Hall, and so on. Or, show pictures of famous people and places in Canada, such as the Canadian Parliament or House of Commons buildings, and so on.
5. Review letter *Aa*.

Learning Centers

Listening/Music/Reading

Provide cassette of patriotic songs and musical instruments.

Art

Clay: Children use clay to mold figures of famous Americans or Canadians.

Paul Revere Hats: Children make three-cornered hats out of three pieces of black paper or newspaper.

Blow Painting: Children use medicine droppers to drop drops of very thin red and blue paint on construction paper. Children blow air through straws to scatter paint. Discuss how paint resembles bombs bursting in air.

Printing

Provide paper and pencils or a tray of red clay. Print these words on laminated pictures—independence, Washington, and White House or independence, Canada, parliament.

Math/Language Arts

Patriotic Puzzles (C)   USA Puzzle (C)

Lincoln Logs (C)

Sorting: Children sort red, white, and blue objects.

Science/Social Studies

Children use the mosaics (C) to make replicas of the American or Canadian flags.

Dramatic Play

Add a stick horse to the housekeeping center. Children can use the stick horse to pretend to be Paul Revere.

Outside Play Idea

Children play relay games on stick horses.

More Group Time Activities

1. Film: *The Star-Spangled Banner*.
2. Have a patriotic parade. One child carries the flag. The others sing and play musical instruments as they march around the room.
3. Read *Paul Revere's Ride* by Henry Wadsworth Longfellow.

Day 4: Election Day

Group Time Activities

1. Discuss election day and point out the date on the calendar.
2. If the year is an election year, show pictures of the candidates.
3. Have a mock election. Declare a winner. Watch TV for results in an election year.
4. March to patriotic music.

Learning Centers

Listening/Music/Reading

Provide a cassette of "The Star-Spangled Banner" or "America."

If you live in Canada, provide a tape of "O Canada" or "God Save the Queen."

Provide paper and crayons for children to draw while listening.

Art

Patriotic Creations: Provide red and white yarn, pipe cleaners, construction paper, and styrofoam pieces. Children can create flags or other patriotic symbols. Encourage creativity.

Printing

Provide old typewriters for children to type these words—election, ballots, November, voting, president, prime minister, and winner.

Math/Language Arts

Flag: Children count the stars and stripes on a flag. Children can count the points on the red maple leaf on the Canadian flag.

Star Sequence: Provide paper stars of different sizes. Children arrange them in order from smallest to largest. In Canada, provide children with paper maple leaves of different sizes.

Stripe Sequence: Provide strips of paper. Children arrange the strips in order of shortest to longest.

Same As: Provide paper parts of stars and pairs of stripes that are the same size. Children find matching pairs. Cut different-sized paper maple leaves in half. Children find matching pairs.

Science/Social Studies

Children continue to use mosaics (C) to make replicas of the American or Canadian Flags.

Dramatic Play

Set up a voting station. Provide paper ballots, sign-in book, pencils, and desk. Make ballots so that children can vote on a class bird or a class color.

Outside Play Idea

Provide hoola hoops.

More Group Time Activities

1. Listen to patriotic songs. Children sing along and use musical instruments.
2. Children dramatize waiting in line to vote. Talk about who is first, second, and third in line.

Day 5: The Alphabet (Just for fun!)

Group Time Activities

1. Song: "ABC song."
2. Read *Dr. Seuss's ABC* by Dr. Seuss.
3. Children use ropes to make letters *Uu*, *Vv*, and *Ww* on the floor.
4. Play Alphabet Bingo (C).

Learning Centers

Blocks

Children enjoy free construction.

Listening/Music/Reading

Provide cassette of *Dr. Seuss's ABC* by Dr. Seuss.

Art

Playdough: Children use playdough to make *ABCs*.

Woodworking/Sand/Water

Wet Sand: Provide large hollow *ABCs* (C). Have printed words nearby. Children can mold names and words using the hollow *ABCs*.

Printing

Provide a stamp set and ink pads.

Math/Language Arts

ABC Stencils (C)   ABC Puzzles (C)

ABC Train (W)

Science/Social Studies

Children cut *ABCs* out of newspaper and make names, words, or pictures on construction paper.

Dramatic Play

Set up a school classroom. Provide small chalkboards, chalk, table, chairs, paper, pencils, and books.

Outside Play Idea

Children try to step on their own shadows and on their classmates' shadows.

More Group Time Activities

1. Talk about the letters *Xx*, *Yy*, and *Zz*.
2. Play Alphabet Bingo (C) as a group.
3. Read *Anno's Alphabet* by Mitsumasa Anno.

November
Week 2

Preparation:

▶ Prepare a bulletin board, entitled "Can You Make a Shape Picture?

Shapes

Group Time Activities

1. Read *Everything Has a Size* by Bernice Kohn.
2. Use an overhead projector to cast shadows on the wall. Children guess what the objects are.
3. Game: "Grab Bag Guessing." Place a variety of objects in a bag. Blindfold a child. The child takes one object out of the bag and tries to guess what it is by feeling its shape.
4. Demonstrate how letters and words have shapes. Also, discuss the shapes of traffic signs.
5. Make large masking-tape shapes on the floor. Instruct children to stand inside the square, sit in the triangle, and so on.

Learning Centers

Blocks

Children enjoy free construction all week.

Listening/Music/Reading

Provide cassette and book of *The Shape of Me and Other Stuff* by Dr. Seuss.

Art

Sponge Shape Paint: Children dip sponge shapes in paint and make prints on paper.

Woodworking/Sand/Water

Wet Sand: Children draw shapes and pictures with their fingers and let friends guess what they are.

Printing

Children use small, individual chalkboards to copy these words—shape, square, club, circle, and diamond.

Math/Language Arts

Mosaics (C)   Design Cubes (C)

Rubberband Board (C)

Paper Shape Puzzles: Laminate and cut large construction-paper shapes into puzzles. Make each shape puzzle a different color.

Shape Bingo (C)

Science/Social Studies

Language Experience Notebook: Shapes.

Children find objects in the room and trace their shapes on paper.

Dramatic Play

Provide housekeeping furniture and the "Grab Bag Guessing" game.

More Group Time Activities

1. Game: "Color and Shape Bingo" (C).
2. Read *The Shape of Me and Other Stuff* by Dr. Seuss.

46

Day 2: Rectangle, Square, and Triangle

Group Time Activities

1. Discuss the differences between a square, a rectangle, and a triangle. Have children name things that are in these shapes. Encourage children to find these shapes in the room.
2. Read *Circles, Triangles and Squares* by Tana Hoban.
3. Song: "Triangle, Circle, Square" from *Hap Palmer: Learning Basic Skills Through Music—Volume 2.*

Learning Centers

Listening/Music/Reading

Children continue to listen to *The Shape of Me and Other Stuff* by Dr. Seuss.

Art

Toothpick Art: Children glue toothpicks on construction paper.

Woodworking/Sand/Water

*Woodworking: Draw shapes on wooden boards. Provide small hammers and nails with large heads. Children hammer nails on lines.

Printing

Print these words on the chalkboard and draw shapes to match—rectangle, shape, triangle, and square. Children copy words on small individual chalkboards.

Math/Language Arts

Triominoes (C)   Dominoes (C)

Octons (C)   Interlocking Cubes (C)

Science/Social Studies

Give children several construction-paper shapes to make pictures. Display pictures on a bulletin board titled "Can You Make a Shape Picture?"

Dramatic Play

Provide rocking boat, fishing pole, and construction-paper shapes with paper clips attached to them. Put a magnet on the fishing pole. Children fish for shapes. Leave out all week.

Outside Play Idea

Children draw shapes using sticks in the dirt.

More Group Time Activities

1. Song: "The Hokey Pokey" from Random House Recording.
2. Game: "Fish for Shapes." Have children sit on the floor in a large circle. Place paper shapes with paper clips attached in the center of the circle. Pass fishing pole with a magnet on the end and let each child catch a shape.

Day 3: Oval and Circle

Group Time Activities

1. Discuss how a circle and an oval are different.
2. Children draw circles and ovals on the board and in the air.
3. Find circles and ovals in the room and name others.
4. Game: "Shape Basket Turnover." Tape construction-paper shapes in a circle on the floor. There should be one shape per child. Play a record. When the music stops all the children must find a shape to stand on.
5. Read *The Sesame Street Book of Shapes.*

Learning Centers

Listening/Music/Reading

Provide a recording of the song "How Many Ways" from *Hap Palmer: Creative Movement and Rhythmic Exploration.* Children can move their bodies as they listen.

Art

Shape Pictures: Provide children with paper shapes to make pictures on construction paper.

Woodworking/Sand/Water

Wet Sand: Children can mold shapes.

Printing

Children use small chalkboards to write these words— circle, rectangle, shape, oval, and square.

Math/Language Arts

Rubberband Boards (C)   Tinker Toys (C)

Octons (C)   Mosaics (C)

Science/Social Studies

Provide different-shaped objects. Children trace objects on paper.

Shape Beanbag Game: Cut a square, rectangle, triangle, and circle out of the side of a cardboard box. Children stand back and try to throw beanbags in the shape holes.

More Group Time Activities

1. Game: "I Spy." "It" looks around the room and picks an object. "It" then says "I spy something (names color)." Children try to guess what "It" picked. The child who guesses correctly is the next "It."
2. Read *Shapes and Things* by Tana Hoban.
3. Song: "Circles Everywhere."

Day 4: Pyramid, Cube, Cone, Sphere, and Cylinder

Group Time Activities

1. Introduce three-dimensional shapes. Show shapes and words to match.
2. Show three-dimensional objects (picture of pyramid, can, cup, ice-cream cone, ball, and candle).
3. Take a walk outside, and point out shapes.
4. Song: "Marching Song" (Tune: "Frere Jacques").

Learning Centers

Listening/Music/Reading

Make a recording of "Marching Song" on a cassette tape.

Art

Peanut Butter Clay Shapes: Provide peanut butter clay. Children form shapes with the clay and then save them to eat at snack time.

Peanut Butter Clay:

1/2 c peanut butter   1/4 tsp honey

1/2 c powdered milk

Mix all ingredients. Add more honey if too dry. Add more powdered milk if too wet.

Woodworking/Sand/Water

Wet Sand: Provide objects that are shaped like pyramids, cubes, cones, and spheres.

Printing

Provide paper and crayons. Print these words on the chalkboard—pyramid, cone, cylinder, cube, and sphere.

Math/Language Arts

Shapes: Provide ropes to make shapes.

Lincoln Logs (C)   Birthday Cakes (W)

Go-Together Jars (W)

Science/Social Studies

Provide nature objects, such as leaves, nuts, or tiny rocks. Allow children to make shape pictures with nature objects on posterboards.

More Group Time Activities

1. Read *Shapes* by Jan Pienkowski.
2. Song: "One Shape, Three Shapes" from *Hap Palmer: Learning Basic Skills Through Music—Volume 2.*

Day 5: Shapes that Change

Group Time Activities

1. Ask children to think of things that change shape.
2. Demonstrate how objects can change shape, such as balloons, water, foods, plants, people, and sand.
3. Read *It Looked Like Spilt Milk* by Charles Green Shaw. (This book can easily be made into a flannelboard presentation.)

Learning Centers

Listening/Music/Reading

Provide a recording of the song "Just Like Yours" from *Hap Palmer: Math Readiness, Vocabulary and Concepts.*

Art

Playdough: Children use playdough to make shapes and then change the shapes.

Shape Mobile: Children cut out construction-paper shapes. Each child uses yarn to tie shapes to a coat hanger.

Woodworking/Sand/Water

Wet Sand: Children make shapes.

Printing

Provide a tray with a thin layer of salt in it. Children print these words with their fingers—circle, rectangle, oval, square, and diamond.

Math/Language Arts

Flannel Shapes (C) and flannelboard.

Snowmen (W)

Science/Social Studies

Children continue to make shape pictures on construction paper using objects from nature.

More Group Time Activities

1. Sing children's favorite songs.
2. Song: "Circle Game" from *Hap Palmer: Getting to Know Myself.*
3. Read *Shapes, Shapes, Shapes* by Tana Hoban.

November
Week 3

Preparation:

▶ Invite a guest speaker from the Native American Culture to come in and share experiences and answer questions from the children. Plan for Day 2.

Native American Culture

Group Time Activities

1. Begin with a class discussion reviewing several explorers' experiences with the native people in America. Review and discuss the history of the term "Indian." For example, when Columbus landed in America, he thought he was in the West Indies and began to call the people he met "Indians."
2. Discuss and explain the term "Native American." Use this term when appropriate throughout the unit.
3. As a class, make a "K-W-L" poster to be displayed throughout the unit (K-What we think we know about Native Americans, W-What we would like to know, L-What we have learned). Use pictures from the past and the present to encourage discussion. Fill in the K and W sections. Add to this chart throughout the unit. Save for Day 5.
4. Briefly explain the existence of many different Native American tribes. Discuss how tribes vary in locations, way of life, customs, and language. Be sure to include the Native Americans of Alaska.
5. Read *Indian Two Feet and the Wolf Cubs* by Margaret Friskey.
6. Discuss the meaning of *ten*. Use cultural objects to illustrate the number ten, such as ears of corn, feathers, drums, totem poles, and so on .
7. Introduce the letter *Ii*. Use Form-a-Sound Cards (C).

Learning Centers

Blocks

Provide various pictures positively portraying the Native American culture.

Listening/Music/Reading

Provide a cassette tape of different Thanksgiving and Native American songs. Also, provide cassette and book of *Indian Two Feet and His Horse* by Margaret Friskey.

Art

Easel Paint: brown and yellow. (Leave these colors out all week.)

Native American Cultural Dress: Provide children with pictures of Native Americans in traditional dress, as well as contemporary dress. Be respectful of the culture. Point out that Native American tribes dressed differently based on the climate and cultural traditions. Show the children examples of Native American clothing from different areas of North America. Encourage children to compare likenesses and differences. Point out that special clothing was worn for ceremonies and celebrations. Invite the children to try drawing an item of Native American clothing.

Woodworking/Sand/Water

Sand: Provide plastic figurines.

Printing

Print *I's* on construction paper. Children glue corn on the preprinted *I's*. Print these words on the chalkboard—corn, Sioux, canoe, totem pole, Inuit, and Native American.

Day 1: Background Information

Math/Language Arts

Lincoln Logs (C)

Inuit Girl Puzzle (C)

Trees and Leaves (W)

Apache Girl Puzzle (C)

Science/Social Studies

Explain to the children that teepees were primarily used by the Plains tribes because they were easy to pack up and move from place to place. Set up a teepee using sheets and wooden poles. Provide sticks or wooden blocks, dishes, dolls, towels, and an inflatable canoe. Leave materials out all week.

More Group Time Activities

1. Film: *Woodland Indians of Early America* and *The Hopi Indian.*
2. Read *Corn Is Maize: The Gift of the Indians* by Aliki.
3. Discuss how Native Americans used corn. Discuss the time needed to crush corn. Let children continue trying to crush corn, using a rock.

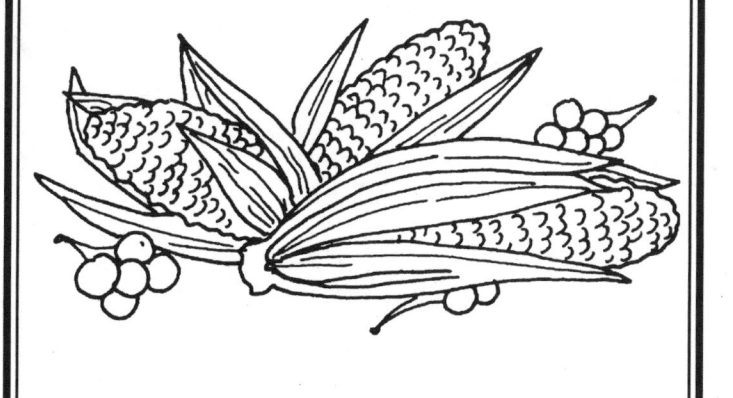

Day 2: Guest Speaker

Group Time Activities

1. Review K-W-L chart. Discuss any fallacies in the K column. Encourage children to think of one thing for the W column. They can save this question for the guest speaker.
2. Have guest speaker share some basic cultural information and their experiences living as a Native American today. Ask the guest speaker to briefly talk about the many different tribes and famous cultural figures, such as Pocahontas, Squanto, Samoset, and Sequoyah. Also, have the speaker go over the K-W columns on the class chart. This is an ideal time to discuss stereotyping and correct any misconceptions. Allow time for questions from the class.
3. Begin a "Then and Now" chart. As the topics of housing, transportation, and hunting are discussed, make comparisons of the past and the present through pictures, discussion, stories, and so on. Add new information to the K-W-L chart.
4. Discuss and show pictures of cone-shaped teepees, dome-shaped wigwams, rectangular long houses, and 8-sided hogans. Explain that the type of house the Native Americans used depended on the season of the year and the materials available.
5. Children find ways to make the letter *Ii* with their bodies.

Learning Centers

Blocks

Provide pictures of Native American homes.

Listening/Music/Reading

Provide the cassette and book of *Indian Two Feet and His Horse* by Margaret Friskey.

Art

Dream Catchers: Children make dream catchers from pipe cleaners, yarn, large beads, and paper feathers. Hang dream catchers in bedroom to catch dreams.

Woodworking/Sand/Water

Wet Sand: Provide sticks and samples of different Native American designs and pictographs. Let children draw in the sand.

Printing

Provide stamp set and ink pads. Print these words on the chalkboard—hogan, wigwam, adobe, and teepee.

Math/Language Arts

Mosaics (C) to make Indian designs

Small Pegs and Pegboard (C)

More Group Time Activities

1. Practice skipping and hopping on one foot with the children.
2. Read *Pueblo Boy: Growing Up in Two Worlds* by Marcia Keegan.

Group Time Activities

1. Discuss how Native Americans hunted. Various tribes used different methods—bow and arrow, sling, spears, disguises, and traps. Contrast with present day means of obtaining food.
2. Show pictures and objects demonstrating how animals provided skins for clothing, blankets, food, shelter, jewelry, and utensils.
3. Discuss how Native Americans traveled—using rafts, canoes, boats, horses, sleds (in places where it snowed), and often just walking. They had no wheeled vehicles. Transportation varied with the location of the tribe. Contrast this with present day means of transportation.
4. Read *Three Little Indians* by Gene S. Stuart. This is a book about three children from different Native American tribes.

Learning Centers

Blocks

Provide pictures of rafts, canoes, horses, boats, and sleds.

Listening/Music/Reading

Add the song "Navajo Happy Song" to the cassette tape.

Art

Animal Skins: Children make dried animal skins out of paper bags. Provide precut "animal skins." Show children examples of Native American pictographs. Have children write their names on the paper skins and then wrinkle them as much as possible. Spread "skins" out flat again and hang them up on the wall.

Totem Poles: Children make totem poles from paper bags. Have children color the bags, stuff bags half-full with newspaper, and close them by folding down the tops. Place bags on top of each other in the corners of the classroom.

Woodworking/Sand/Water

Sand: Provide sifters, baskets, and measuring cups.

Printing

Provide clay trays with large nails. Print these words on the chalkboard—buffalo, bows, arrows, club, slings, canoes, and horses.

Math/Language Arts

Indian Puzzles (C)

Number Peg Boards and Pegs (C)

Matching: Draw and cut Native Americans and horses out of construction paper. Write capital letters on the Native Americans and lower-case letters on the horses. Have children match them.

Science/Social Studies

Language Experience Notebook: Native Americans.

Provide a display of books, pictures, and objects to encourage ideas for this activity.

More Group Time Activities

Discuss the uses of pottery in the Native American culture. If possible, have examples to show children. Make salt clay for children to use to mold pottery. Combine 1 c flour and 1 c salt. Add cool water and mix to proper consistency. Add more flour if too sticky.

Day 4: Group Time Activities

Group Time Activities

1. Discuss and show pictures of Native American art, designs, wall paintings, and sand paintings.
2. Show pictures of Native American writings and drawings. Discuss how the Native Americans used art for communication.
3. Draw a series of pictures on the chalkboard and let children interpret the meaning.

Learning Centers

Listening/Music/Reading

Provide the musical instruments for children to use as they listen to the cassette of songs.

Art

Drums: Children can make drums out of coffee cans or round oatmeal boxes. Provide construction paper to cover and decorate the drums.

Woodworking/Sand/Water

Sand: Provide sifters, baskets, and measuring cups.

Printing

Provide clay trays and large nails. Print these words on the chalkboard—designs, symbols, drum, sand painting, and shaker.

Math/Language Arts

Design Cubes (C)   Animal Puzzles (C)

Lincoln Logs (C)   Inuit Girl Puzzle (C)

Apache Girl Puzzle (C)

Science/Social Studies

Provide blank paper and pictures of Native American rug designs. Have children try drawing the Native American designs on their papers. Display books and pictures about Native American life, arrowheads, and wooden bowls.

More Group Time Activities

1. Review the K-W-L chart. Add things that have been learned throughout this week. Correct any misconceptions or fallacies in the K column.
2. Review the "Then and Now" chart. Add information from this week's experiences. Continue to make comparisons of the past to present day in order to present an accurate and true portrayal of the Native American culture.

Day 5: Dances, Games, and Songs

Group Time Activities

1. Review songs from this unit.
2. Discuss information learned about Native American life. Be respectful of the culture.
3. Explain reasons for the Native American dances, such as rain, thanks, and answers.
4. Game: "Bean Toss." Use five dried butterbean seeds. Color one side of each bean black. Place all beans in a wooden bowl. A child gives a quick lift to the bowl and gets one point for every bean that is color-side up after the quick lift.

Learning Centers

Listening/Music/Reading

Provide cassette and book of *Indian Two Feet and His Horse* by Margaret Friskey.

Art

Lacing Canoes: Children lace precut, prepunched paper canoes and color with crayons.

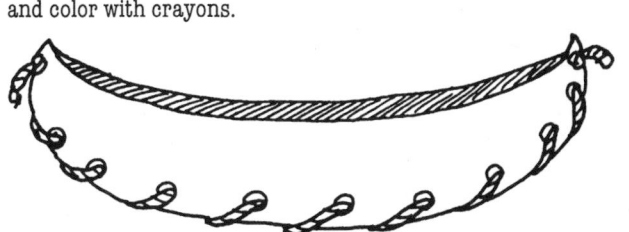

Woodworking/Sand/Water

Sand: Provide sifters, baskets, and measuring cups.

Printing

Provide clay trays and large nails. Print these words on the chalkboard—bean toss, drum, and dance.

Math/Language Arts

Mosaics (C)   Pentalbi (C)

Indian Puzzles (C)   Inuit Girl Puzzle (C)

Apache Girl Puzzle (C)

Science/Social Studies

Display Native American items, such as arrowheads, dolls, and bowls.

More Group Time Activities

1. Play games and watch video tapes of Native American children dancing.
2. Read *Knots On a Counting Rope* by Bill Martin, Jr.
3. Language Experience Notebook: Native Americans.
4. K-W-L Chart: Complete chart by adding what was learned (L) during this unit.

November
Week 4

Preparation:

▶ Ask each child to bring a bar of Ivory soap for art on Day 1.

▶ Paint or draw a large tree and put it on the wall. (Children will add leaves to it during the week.)

▶ Thanksgiving Day in Canada is celebrated on the second Monday in October.

Thanksgiving Celebrations

Group Time Activities

1. Create a class poster titled "Thanksgiving is..."
2. Read *How Many Days to America?* by Eve Bunting. Discuss how the people leaving their homes and country must have felt.
3. Discuss the many people that continue to come to America and Canada from other countries today. Use appropriate newspaper articles to illustrate.
4. Share the picturebooks *Anno's USA* by Mitsumasa Anno. Read the "Afterword" to the children and encourage discussion.
5. Discuss the Mayflower and its voyage.
6. Discuss the difference between *T* and *Th* sounds.

Learning Centers

Blocks

Children enjoy free construction all week. Display pictures of ships.

Listening/Music/Reading

Record the Thanksgiving songs "Over the River and Thro' the Woods," "Things I'm Thankful for," and "Thanksgiving at Grandma's" on a cassette tape and leave out all week.

Art

Pilgrim Puppets: Children use construction paper to draw and cut out pilgrims. Children glue pilgrims on popsicle sticks to make puppets.

Woodworking/Sand/Water

Water: Provide plastic boats.

Printing

Provide old typewriters for children to type these words— Mayflower, Thanksgiving, pilgrim, Native American, harvest, and so on.

Math/Language Arts

Indian Puzzles (C)   Thanksgiving Puzzles (C)

Counting: Provide plastic figurines. Children make sets of ten.

Measuring: Provide scales and whole kernel corn. Children weigh and balance containers of corn.

Science/Social Studies

Display globe, books, and pictures of pilgrims.

Dramatic Play

Provide rocking boat and dress-up clothes. Spread a blue sheet or blanket on the floor. Encourage children to dramatize the Pilgrims' voyage.

More Group Time Activities

1. Briefly discuss celebrations of thanks in other countries.
2. Read *Cranberry Thanksgiving* by Wende Devlin.
3. Song: "Turkey in the Straw."
4. Discuss turkeys. Show turkey pictures.
5. Write a large *T* on the board. Draw a large turkey around the *T*.
6. Read *Arthur's Thanksgiving* by Marc Brown.

Day 2: The First Thanksgiving

Group Time Activities

1. Read *Squanto and the First Thanksgiving* by Joyce K. Kessel and Lisa Donze. Emphasize the key role the Native Americans played in the pilgrims' survival.
2. Discuss the Native American custom of giving thanks (having a feast). Discuss and show pictures of the joint celebration of the pilgrims and Native Americans in 1621.
3. Song: "The Turkey."
4. Review *T* and *Th* sounds.

Learning Centers

Blocks

Display pictures of pilgrim homes. Provide Lincoln Logs (C).

Art

Pinecone Turkeys: Children make pinecone turkeys. Use baking cups or construction paper for feathers and turkey head.

Woodworking/Sand/Water

Sand: Provide sifters, funnels, and containers.

Printing

Children use tracing stencils to write these words—Native Americans, winter, wild, pilgrims, and turkey.

Math/Language Arts

Indian Puzzles (C)   Thanksgiving Puzzles (C)

Measuring: Children weigh corn on scales.

Counting: Children count sets of ten using plastic figurines.

Science/Social Studies

Place a variety of feathers and magnifying glasses. Also, display books and pictures about pilgrims and Thanksgiving.

Dramatic Play

Children dramatize the voyage of the pilgrims. Provide rocking boat, blanket, dolls, towels, and dishes.

More Group Time Activities

1. Help children make pilgrim collars and hats.
2. Read *Three Young Pilgrims* by Cheryl Harness.
3. Re-enact the first Thanksgiving. Have some children pretend to be pilgrims and some Native Americans. Use the book *Squanto and the First Thanksgiving* by Joyce K. Kesel and Lisa Donze (p. 26 to the end) as a guide.

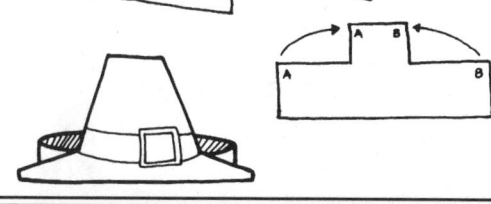

Day 3: Food and Family Celebrations

Group Time Activities

1. Read *Thanksgiving Day* by Gail Gibbons.
2. Discuss family traditions. Have each child draw one symbol that represents Thanksgiving in his or her family on a class poster. Have children explain what they drew and why. Title the poster "How We Celebrate Thanksgiving."
3. Discuss various Thanksgiving foods, such as turkey, dressing, cranberry sauce, potatoes and gravy, pumpkin pie, corn, and fruit. Explain the origins of these foods (the Native Americans introduced these foods to the pilgrims).
4. Make cranberry sauce with the class. Dissolve 2 c sugar in 2 c water and heat to boiling. Boil 5 minutes. Add 4 c cranberries and cook until skins pop, approximately 5 minutes. Serve warm or chilled.

Learning Centers

Art

Paper-Plate Thanksgiving: Children cut out pictures of foods they eat at Thanksgiving. Paste pictures on a paper plate.

Woodworking/Sand/Water

Sand: Children use sifters and strainers to find corn kernels.

Printing

Print these words on the chalkboard for children to trace using stencils—turkey, corn, cranberry sauce, and pumpkin pie.

Math/Language Arts

Food Puzzle (C)   Thanksgiving Puzzles (C)

Indian Puzzles (C)   Horse Puzzle (C)

Lincoln Logs (C)

Science/Social Studies

Provide seeds from Thanksgiving foods, such as cranberries, pumpkins, grapes, and apples.

Dramatic Play

Provide housekeeping furniture, dishes, empty food containers, spoons, recipe books, and aprons.

More Group Time Activities

1. Introduce the letter *Ee*.
2. Review all Thanksgiving songs.
3. Make a class bar graph titled "My Favorite Thanksgiving Food." As a class, narrow choices to 4 or 5 different foods.
4. Children share what their families do on Thanksgiving.

November—
Additional Activities

▶ Hold a class election. Talk about what qualities are important in a leader like the president or prime minister. Have children vote (heads down, hands up) for a class president for the day. Talk about what it would be like to be the President of the United States or the Prime Minister of Canada (be sure to present not only the positives, but the negatives as well).

▶ Discuss rules with the children. Talk about why rules are important. Brainstorm rules of society, such as speed limits, traffic signals, laws, and so on. As a class, decide on a new rule. Have the children talk about what is good or bad about the new rule. Pair the children and have them try to convince their partners to see their points of view. Vote on the rule. Sample rules might include chocolate milk every day, gum chewing allowed in school, or no talking in school.

▶ Have children research their ethnic background and share this information at group time. Discuss our common bond in being Americans or Canadians. Write a class book titled "I Like Being an American Because..." or "I Like Being a Canadian Because..."

▶ Read *And Then What Happened, Paul Revere?* by Jean Fritz.

▶ Read *Great American Heroes* by Jean Fielder.

▶ Read *Pop! Goes the Weasel* and *Yankee Doodle-New York City in 1776 and Today, with Songs and Pictures* by Robert Quackenbush.

▶ Read *Have You Ever Seen...? An ABC Book* by Beau Gardner.

▶ Have children work in pairs to write a letter on the board. Have the class choose a letter. Then write that letter on the board. Divide the class into teams. As a team, have the children form the chosen letter using just their bodies.

▶ Identify letters in the room. Start at any place in the alphabet and have children find the given letter somewhere in the room (children may not use the alphabet posted in the room). Identify an answer by a raised hand. Have children keep their own record of how many times they found the given letter first. Go through the entire alphabet. Explain to children that this is an eyes only game (letter must be seen without touching anything) and that all letters may not be visible.

▶ Discuss shapes in our world, such as circles in stoplights, rectangles in billboards, diamonds in baseball fields, and so on. Use one of Tana Hoban's shape books to help illustrate this concept. Have children work in teams to brainstorm as many shapes in our world as they can. Combine ideas on a class poster titled "Shapes in Our World."

▶ Have children identify shapes in the classroom. One child can name the shape as the rest of the children try to find the shape. Identify the shape by standing next to it or pointing to it.

▶ Children can make shape art by making pictures out of three or four shapes drawn on paper. Discuss how we can see shapes in objects, such as triangles could be cat ears, circles could be a snowman, and rectangles could be doors and windows. Use one of Tana Hoban's shape books to help illustrate this concept. Model a shape art drawing, if needed.

▶ Make a shape mobile. Have children bring a hanger from home. Have children cut out shapes from construction paper by tracing around patterns. Attach shapes to hanger using yarn.

▶ Pretend you are one of the children coming to America on the Mayflower. Make a suitcase from brown construction paper and "pack" three items that you would bring with you. Share what you have "packed" with a partner.

▶ Pretend you are one of the pilgrims. Write a letter or draw a picture for one of your friends in England. Tell them what it is like in America.

▶ Make turkeys using paper plates for the body and construction paper for the head, feathers, eyes, beak, and feet. On the body of each turkey, write the turkey's name. Have children dictate a short story about how their turkey feels on Thanksgiving Day.

▶ Write a class Thanksgiving story. Talk about characters, setting, beginning, middle, and end. Have each child add a line to the previous story. Tape record or write and illustrate the story.

▶ Share Thanksgiving songs and dances: "Creek Ribbon Dance" and "Turkey In The Straw" from *Holiday Singing & Dancing Games* by Esther L. Nelson (pp. 49-54).

▶ Read *Songs of the Chippewa* by John Bierhorst.

▶ Read *A Visit to Grandma's* by Nancy L. Carlson.

▶ Read *1,2,3 Thanksgiving!* by W. Nikola-Lisa.

▶ Read *Sometimes It's Turkey-Sometimes It's Feathers* by Lorna Balian.

▶ Read *Merrily Comes Our Harvest In: Poems for Thanksgiving* by Lee Bennett Hopkins.

▶ Songs: "The Red, White, and Blue." *The Holiday Song Book*. New York, NY: Lothrop, Lee & Shepard Company, 1977.

"A Pocket Full of B's." *Hap Palmer Favorites-Songs for Learning Through Music and Movement*. Sherman Oaks, CA: Alfred Publishing Co., 1981

"AB-C-DEF-GHI." *The Sesame Street Song Book*. New York, NY: Simon & Schuster, 1971

"Circles." *The Sesame Street Song Book*. New York, NY: Simon & Schuster, 1971

"On the First Thanksgiving Day." *The Holiday Song Book*. New York, NY: Lothrop, Lee & Shepard Company, 1977.

"Let Us Give Thanks" (Tune: "Here We Go Round the Mulberry Bush). *More Piggyback Songs*. Everett, WA: Warren Publishing House, 1984.

December
Week 1

Preparation:

▶ Plan a field trip to an airport, bus station, or some other transportation-related location for Day 4.

Transportation

Group Time Activities

1. Discuss Native Americans and pioneers and their use of canoes and flat boats. Mention Mark Twain and Huck Finn. Show pictures.
2. Discuss the first steamboat.
3. Discuss modern transportation methods. Make a class chart listing the mode of transportation and number of children who have traveled by these methods. Continue to add to chart throughout the week.
4. Song: "Row, Row, Row Your Boat."
5. Read *If I Sailed a Boat* by Miriam Young. Review Christopher Columbus' voyage.

Learning Centers

Blocks

Allow free construction.

Listening/Music/Reading

Provide a cassette recording of "Row, Row, Row Your Boat." Children can illustrate a time they were in a boat or a picture of a boat they would like to travel in, as they listen to the song.

Art

Boats: Children use styrofoam meat trays to make boats. Provide clay for children to use as a stand for a popsicle-stick sail.

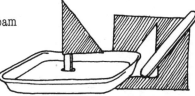

Woodworking/Sand/Water

*Woodworking: Provide wood scraps, glue, hammers, and nails for children to build boats.

Printing

Provide stamp set and ink pads for children to print these words—canoe, barge, water, steamboat, submarine, ship, tugboat, ocean liner, sailboat, and freighter.

Math/Language Arts

Mosaics (C)   Lacing Cards (C)

Transportation Puzzles (C)   Giant Transportation Puzzle (C)

Science/Social Studies

Make a set of pictures of transportation vehicles and a set of pictures of vehicle drivers. Children match drivers with vehicles.

Dramatic Play

Provide a rocking boat (or a large empty box), cardboard paddles, and a blue blanket to spread over the floor. Children pretend they are taking a water voyage.

More Group Time Activities

1. Film: *Goofy's Field Trips: Ships*.
2. Game: "Guess Who or What I Am." Give clues about some job or vehicle associated with transportation. Children guess what the job is.
3. Song: "She'll Be Comin' Round the Mountain."

Day 2: Land Travel

Group Time Activities

1. Discuss how children traveled to school today.
2. Discuss how Native Americans and early settlers traveled. Show a timeline of land transportation.
3. Game: "I'm Going on a Trip." One child names something to take on a trip. A second child says what the first child said and adds one more thing. Continue game in this manner until each child has had a turn.
4. Song: "She'll Be Comin' Round the Mountain."
5. Discuss modern transportation and driver's licenses.

Learning Centers

Blocks

Provide trucks, traffic signs, and streets out of heavy cardboard.

Listening/Music/Reading

Make a recording of *The Little Train* by Lois Lenski.

Art

Train Wheels: Children cut out black circles and glue white crosses on the wheels. Staple a rubberband to the back of the wheels. Put the wheels on the children's wrists. All children hook together by standing in a line. Each child holds the arms of the child in front of him or her. Children slide their feet and move around the room while making train sounds.

Woodworking/Sand/Water

Sand: Provide small plastic horses, wagons, and cowboys.

Printing

Provide stamp kits for children to write these words—horse, bus, motorcycle, bicycle, and car.

Math/Language Arts

Cars and Garages (W)

Magnetic Cars and Trucks (C)

Giant Transportation Puzzle (C)

Transportation Puzzles (C)

Science/Social Studies

Label three boxes with a picture of land, air, and water. Provide various pictures of transportation vehicles. Children place the pictures in the correct boxes.

Dramatic Play

Set up chairs as a train. Provide paper tickets, dress-up clothes, suitcases, and dolls.

More Group Time Activities

1. Exercise with the group.
2. Film: *Goofy's Field Trips: Trains.*
3. Review *Tt.* Think of transportation words that begin with *Tt.*
4. Read *Big Red Bus* by Ethel Kessler.
5. Song: "Motorcycle Racer."

Day 3: Air Travel

Group Time Activities

1. Discuss hot air balloons.
2. Show a picture of the first airplane.
3. Use a record or a cassette of transportation sounds. Children identify the sounds.
4. Discuss modern jets and airplanes.
5. Film: *Goofy's Field Trips: Planes.*
6. Take an imaginary trip around the world. Use a globe.
7. Song: "Riding in an Airplane."

Learning Centers

Blocks

Provide model airplanes, Fisher Price Airplane (C), and Fisher Price Airport (C).

Listening/Music/Reading

Provide a recording of transportation sounds. Encourage children to draw pictures while listening.

Art

Airplanes: Children make paper airplanes. Have children fold paper in a variety of ways to discover what makes the airplanes fly best.

Woodworking/ Sand/Water

Sand: Provide plastic construction vehicles and dump trucks.

Printing

Provide stamp kits and paper for children to make these words—helicopter, spaceship, airplane, and hot air balloon.

Math/Language Arts

Alphabet Soup(C)   Transportation Puzzles (C)

The Safety Pin Game (W)   Airplanes and Hangers (W)

Science/Social Studies

Language Experience Notebook: Children draw pictures of modes of transportation, such as airplanes or hot air balloons. Children categorize transportation pictures into land, water, and air vehicles.

Dramatic Play

Children pretend they are going on a hot air balloon ride using a large box or large basket. Provide small cars, trucks, and houses to place on the floor around the box or basket.

More Group Time Activities

1. Ask children to name all the modes of transportation studied this week. Add to class chart begun on Day 1.
2. Give a problem situation about transportation. Let children think of solutions.
3. Introduce the letter *Oo.* Use the words *ocean* and *over* in the discussion.

Day 4: Field Trip

Group Time Activities

Discuss rules children should remember while on this trip.

Learning Centers

Blocks

Provide trucks, traffic signs, Fisher Price Airport (C), and wooden block people.

Listening/Music/Reading

Provide a cassette recording of the songs "Motorcycle Racer," "Row, Row, Row Your Boat," "She'll Be Comin' Round the Mountain," and "Riding in an Airplane."

Art

Creative Art: Provide construction paper, bottle caps, yarn, and styrofoam meat trays for children to create.

Woodworking/Sand/Water

Water: Provide meat trays, aluminum foil, clay, and pieces of wood so that children can make boats.

Printing

Provide stamp kits and paper for children to make these words—water, land, and air.

Math/Language Arts

Cars and Garages (W)   Magnetic Cars and Trucks (C)

Transportation Puzzles (C)

Train Cars: Cut off the tops of 1/2-pint milk cartons. Cover the cartons with construction paper. Write a letter of the alphabet on each one. Children put the train cars in order, starting with A.

Science/Social Studies

Provide a display of toy vehicles, transportation pictures, and books. Provide an old radio from a car or an old tire for children to examine.

Dramatic Play

Children can take a pretend train ride.

More Group Time Activities

1. Write a class thank-you letter to the transportation personnel you visited.
2. Read *Davy Goes Places* by Lois Lenski.
3. Song: "Working on the Railroad."

Day 5: Numbers (Just for a break!)

Group Time Activities

1. Songs: "Five Little Ducks" and "Numbers Tell a Lot about You."
2. Read *Rooster's Off to See the World* by Eric Carle. (This can easily be made into a flannelboard activity.)
3. Read *Bears on Wheels* by Stanley and Janice Berenstain.
4. Fingerplays: *My Big Book of Fingerplays* by Daphne Hogstrom.

Learning Centers

Blocks

Children enjoy free construction.

Listening/Music/Reading

Provide the recording and book *Rooster's Off to See the World* by Eric Carle.

Art

Playdough: Children make numerals out of playdough and then make a corresponding number of dough objects.

Woodworking/Sand/Water

Wet Sand: Provide large plastic hollow numerals (C).

Printing

Provide Write On Wipe Off Cards (C). Print these words on the chalkboard—numbers, adding, counting, and zero.

Math/Language Arts

Number Bingo (C)   Dominoes (C)

Science/Social Studies

Language Experience Notebook: Children write numerals or cut numerals out of newspapers and glue on construction paper.

Dramatic Play

Set up a school classroom. Provide a table and chairs, books, small chalkboard, ruler, paper, and pencils.

More Group Time Activities

1. Read *Richard Scarry's Best Counting Book Ever* by Richard Scarry.
2. Play Number Bingo (C) with the whole class.
3. Game: "Hopscotch." Make a hopscotch game on the floor using masking tape. All children take turns.
4. Make a recording of the songs "Countdown," "Movin' by Numerals," and "Move Around the Room," from the book *Hap Palmer Favorites—Songs for Learning Through Music and Movement.*

December
Week 2

Preparation:

▶ Ask a parent to provide a live tree for the classroom. (For the next two weeks, children will be making decorations to hang on the tree.)

▶ Dye macaroni red and green for an art project. Place the macaroni in rubbing alcohol with food coloring added. After the macaroni has absorbed the color, drain it, and let it dry on newspaper.

Christmas Around the World

Group Time Activities

1. Find Germany on the globe and talk about that country.
2. Discuss Kris Kringle and other German Christmas customs.
3. Read *May I Stay?* by Harry Allard.

Learning Centers

Blocks

Children enjoy free construction. Provide pictures of Germany, Kris Kringle, and Christmas trees to encourage children's play.

Listening/Music/Reading

Provide Christmas music for listening.

Art

Apples: Children cut out paper apples to hang on the tree.

Wreaths: Provide paper plates with the centers cut out. Children decorate the plates with yarn and red and green macaroni.

Christmas Chains: Use red and green strips of construction paper for children to make chains. Hang chains on tree or from ceiling.

Candles: Children cover toilet-paper rolls with construction paper and add a paper flame to the top.

Woodworking/Sand/Water

Provide playdough for children to make cookies, apples, and candles. Leave out all week.

Printing

Print these words on paper Christmas symbols and on the chalkboard—Germany, Kris Kringle, and Christmas tree.

Math/Language Arts

Apple Tree Game (C)

Sorting: Provide candles. Children arrange candles according to height, thickness, or color.

Science/Social Studies

Point out Germany on the globe. Display items from Germany.

Dramatic Play

Provide a small (two foot) tree. Provide plastic decorations, wrapping paper, tape, boxes, housekeeping furniture, and dishes.

More Group Time Activities

1. Film: *Twas the Night before Christmas*.
2. Have a candlelight procession as German children do. Use flashlights or paper candles made in the art center.
3. Song: "Oh Christmas Tree."
4. Read *The Little Man in Winter* by Walburga Attenberger or *The Queen Who Couldn't Bake Gingerbread* by Dorothy Van Woerkom.

Day 2: Christmas in Italy

Group Time Activities

1. Show Italian flag. Show pictures of the country and talk about its customs.
2. Talk about *La Befana*. Read *Befana* by Anne Rockwell.
3. Introduce *Cc*. Use the words *candy* and *carolers* in the discussion.

Learning Centers

Blocks

Provide pictures of Italy and Italian customs to stimulate the children's block play.

Listening/Music/Reading

Provide a recording of Christmas carols.

Art

Spaghetti Art: Children glue uncooked spaghetti lengths on construction paper in sequence from shortest to longest or in a design.

Woodworking/Sand/Water

Water: Provide yellow water and kitchen utensils. Add liquid detergent to the water.

Printing

Spread a thin layer of yellow clay on a cookie sheet. Children print in the clay using a crayon or stick. Display pictures of these words—yellow, color, blue, corn, and duck. Print the words on the pictures.

Math/Language Arts

Christmas Puzzles (C)

*Christmas Rope: String styrofoam packing pieces for the Christmas tree. Children use large crewel needles (dull points) and thread. Some teacher assistance may be needed.

Fractions Puzzles: Cut out pictures of pizza from frozen pizza boxes. Cut each pizza into fraction puzzles. For example, cut one pizza in half, cut one in fourths, and so on.

Acorn Tray: Provide an apple-packing tray and a variety of nuts. Children sort nuts.

Science/Social Studies

Display Italian items, books about Italy, and a globe with a marker pointing to Italy.

Dramatic Play

Provide cardboard bricks (C) and a few small logs for children to construct a fireplace. Provide wrapping paper, tape, boxes, and tree decorations.

More Group Time Activities

1. Film: *Christmas Time in Europe*.
2. Have children act out the custom of *La Befana* in Italy.
3. Read *Anno's Italy* by Mitsumasa Anno.

Day 3: Christmas in England

Group Time Activities

1. Discuss England. Use globe, map, and items from England. Show England's flag.
2. Discuss Christmas customs in England, such as Father Christmas, top hats, carols, and plum pudding.
3. Review *Cc* for carolers.
4. Discuss the Kissing Bough (mistletoe) and the Yule Log.
5. Read *Plum Pudding for Christmas* by Virginia Kahl.

Learning Centers

Blocks

Provide pictures depicting Christmas in England.

Listening/Music/Reading

Provide a recording of Christmas carols.

Art

Christmas Puppets: Provide construction paper, glue, glitter, sequins, and popsicle sticks. Children make puppets of their choice. Provide a puppet stage for children to have puppet plays.

Pinecone Bird Feeders: Children put peanut butter all over pinecones and roll them in bird seed. Children hang their bird feeders.

Printing

Print these words on paper Christmas symbols and on the chalkboard— England, Father Christmas, holly, ivy, and plum pudding.

Math/Language Arts

Christmas Puzzle (C)

Top Hats: Make and cut out black paper top hats. Write a numeral on each one. Children arrange the top hats in order from one to ten.

Nut Sort: Provide assorted nuts and small plastic baskets. Children sort the nuts.

Light Bright (C)

Science/Social Studies

Display a globe, books on England, and items from England.

Dramatic Play

Add plastic holly and ivy.

More Group Time Activities

1. Make a paper chain out of construction-paper strips. Count down the days until Christmas. Remove one link for each day from now until Christmas.
2. Draw a large Christmas tree on the board with Christmas balls on it. Write the studied letters on Christmas balls. Children take turns coloring Christmas balls with colored chalk as you call out a letter that has been studied.
3. Discuss Charles Dickens. Read *Walt Disney's Christmas Carol*.

Day 4: Christmas in Holland

Group Time Activities

1. Count down days until Christmas.
2. Discuss Holland, using the globe, books, pictures, and wooden shoes.

3. Discuss Christmas in Holland, such as December 6, Saint Nicholas, Black Peter, boat, and white horse.
4. Song: "Jingle Bells." Let children use bells.
5. Review *Cc*.
6. Read *The Cow Who Fell in the Canal* by Phyllis Krasilovsky.

Learning Centers

Blocks

Instead of block play, encourage children to go "ice skating" on the carpet. Use waxed paper for skates. Children remove their shoes, place waxed paper under each foot, and then slide their feet. Use masking tape to outline a lake area on the carpet.

Listening/Music/Reading

Provide cassette and book *The Littlest Angel* by Charles Tazewell.

Art

Gingerbread People: Children make gingerbread people out of construction paper. Provide yarn and raisins for children to glue on their gingerbread people.

Printing

Print these words on paper Christmas symbols and on the chalkboard—Saint Nicholas, Black Peter, Sinter Klass, Santa Claus, and Holland.

Math/Language Arts

Christmas Puzzles (C)	Acorn Tray
Counting Nuts	Horse Puzzle (C)

*Christmas Rope: Children continue to string styrofoam packing pieces for tree in the classroom.

Science/Social Studies

Display globe, wooden shoes, books about Holland, and items from Holland.

Dramatic Play

Add a stick horse.

More Group Time Activities

1. Children make up a Christmas feast menu. Write on a chart what food each child describes for the feast.
2. Read *The Woman Who Lived in Holland* by Mildred Howells.

Day 5: Christmas in Mexico

Group Time Activities

1. Discuss Mexico and find it on a globe.
2. Show pictures of a piñata or show a real piñata. Show a poinsettia. Discuss Christmas customs in Mexico.
3. Children help fill piñata with candy to be used at next group time. Count the candy pieces with children as you add them to the piñata.
4. Talk about the meaning of *nine*. Use the Christmas candy for the discussion.

Learning Centers

Blocks

Provide pictures of a Mexican Christmas for children to observe as they play.

Listening/Music/Reading

Provide cassette and book *Nine Days to Christmas* by Marie Hall Ets.

Art

Poinsettias: Children cut out paper poinsettias, attach pipe cleaners for stems, and tie together. Children attach these stems to plastic cherry tomato boxes. Provide tissue paper for children to stuff in the cherry tomato boxes around the stems.

Printing

Print these words on paper Christmas symbols and on the chalkboard—Mexico, poinsettia, Magi, and piñata.

Math/Language Arts

Christmas Puzzles (C)	Lincoln Logs (C)

Addition Box: Use kidney beans.

Science/Social Studies

Display a globe, real poinsettias, books and pictures of Mexico, and items from Mexico.

Dramatic Play

Hang the piñata in the dramatic-play center until next group time.

More Group Time Activities

1. Give each child a chance to break the piñata.
2. Read *The Silver Whistle* by Ann Tompert.
3. Film: *Feliz Navidad*.

December
Week 3

Preparation:

▶ Invite any families of children in your class who are Jewish (or someone from the Jewish community) to come in and share their Hanukkah traditions. Plan for Day 1

Other Holidays and Holiday Symbols

Day 1: Hanukkah

Group Time Activities

1. Invite your guest speaker(s) to share his or her Hanukkah experiences. Encourage the guest speaker to explain the history of Hanukkah and the symbolism of the menorah.
2. Read *Hanukkah!* by Roni Schotter.
3. Discuss and explain the menorah, dreidel, latkes, and shamash. If possible, have these objects on hand to show to the class. (Use the book, *Hanukkah!* as a guide.)
4. Song: "Hanukkah Song."

Learning Centers

Blocks

Encourage free construction.

Listening/Music/Reading

Provide cassette and book *Happy Hanukkah Rebus* by David A. Adler.

Art

Menorah: Children trace menorah patterns on white construction paper. Cut out and glue on black construction paper background. Add yellow flames. Children can color the candles. Be sure to point out which candle is the shamash.

Egg Carton Decorations: Cut out egg carton sections. Children color, glue on sequins, and insert pipe cleaners. Hang decorations on the tree.

Woodworking/Sand/Water

Wet Sand: Provide holiday cookie cutters, plastic holly sprigs, and kitchen utensils.

Printing

Provide green construction paper. Print these words on the chalkboard—Hanukkah, eight, dreidel, shamash, latkes, menorah, light, and festival.

Math/Language Arts

Addition Box: Use holiday candy.

Light Bright (C)

Science/Social Studies

Language Experience Notebook: Each child draws a picture of a holiday celebrated at his or her home.

Display symbols of Hanukkah. Provide pictures and books for the children to learn about Hanukkah.

Dramatic Play

Provide housekeeping furniture, Hanukkah symbols, and plastic or paper decorations.

More Group Time Activities

*Have an adult make latkes by grating several peeled potatoes and 1 onion. Drain excess water. Then add 1 tsp salt, 1/4 tsp pepper, 1 T flour, 1/2 T baking powder, and 2 eggs. Drop mixture by the spoonful into hot oil and flatten each pancake with back of spoon. Flip when brown; serve with applesauce. Enjoy latkes at snack time.

Day 2: Kwanzaa

Group Time Activities

1. Discuss Africa and find it on a globe.
2. Introduce the African-American holiday Kwanzaa. Give a brief history.
3. Read *Kwanzaa* by A.P. Porter.
4. Discuss the bendera and the symbolism of the colors—red, green, and black.
5. Draw comparisons and contrasts between Kwanzaa, Hanukkah, and Christmas, such as holiday colors, menorah and kinara, special meals, gifts, and so on.

Learning Centers

Blocks

Allow free construction.

Listening/Music/Reading

Provide recording and book *Moja Means One: Swahili Counting Book* by Muriel Feelings.

Art

Mkeka: Have children practice weaving red, green, and black strips of paper. Once children have learned to weave, have them weave a small placemat called a *mkeka*. This center may require some parental assistance.

Bendera: Provide red, green, and black construction paper for children to make this special flag. Use straws for the flag pole. Provide a sample.

Woodworking/Sand/Water

Wet Sand: Continue using cookie cutters and kitchen utensils.

Printing

Provide red and green construction paper. Write the following words on the chalkboard—Kwanzaa, mkeka, kinara, Swahili, Africa, bendera, and mazao.

Math/Language Arts

Sorting: Provide red, green, and black objects for sorting.

Grouping: Separate objects, such as buttons, blocks, dice, and so on, into groups of seven.

Design Boards (C)   Etch-A-Sketch (C)

Science/Social Studies

Language Experience Notebook: One Thing I Learned About Kwanzaa.

Provide symbols, books, and pictures about Kwanzaa for children to explore.

Dramatic Play

Provide housekeeping furniture, Kwanzaa symbols, and red and green decorations.

More Group Time Activities

1. Read *Kwanzaa* by Deborah M. Newton Chocolate.
2. Assign pairs of children one Kwanzaa symbol. Have children illustrate or describe their Kwanzaa symbols. Compile the pages into a class Kwanzaa book.
3. Film: *Holidays Your Neighbors Celebrate.* (These holidays extend beyond the winter season.)

Day 3: Holiday Symbols

Group Time Activities

1. Discuss Christmas symbols, such as wreaths, holly, stars, angels, mistletoe, stockings, and candles. Show an example of each symbol and discuss its meaning. Use *Holly, Reindeer, and Colored Lights: The Story of the Christmas Symbol* by Edna Barth as a reference guide.
2. Review the custom of having a Christmas tree. Show and identify twigs from several evergreen trees, such as pine, cedar, magnolia, and holly. Show the children the written words, as well as the seeds, the leaves, or the needles of several evergreens.
3. Review the meaning and symbols of Hanukkah. Show a menorah and dreidel.
4. Song: "The Dreydl."
5. Hanukkah song and dance: "Hanukkah, Oh Hanukkah" from *Holiday Singing & Dancing Games* by Esther L. Nelson (pp. 56-60).

Learning Centers

Blocks

Encourage children to "ice skate" instead of block play.

Listening/Music/Reading

Provide a cassette of Christmas and Hanukkah songs.

Art

Stars: Children glue popsicle sticks in a star shape to make Christmas ornaments. Children paint stars when glue is dry. Hang ornaments on the Christmas tree.

Woodworking/Sand/Water

Wet Sand: Provide large plastic hollow letters.

Printing

Provide green paper. Print these words on the chalkboard—wreath, holly, menorah, angel, star, dreidel, and stocking.

Math/Language Arts

Sorting: Provide red and green objects for sorting.

Design Boards (C)   Etch-A-Sketch (C)

Memory Christmas Game   Light Bright (C)

Science/Social Studies

Provide quart jars with different levels of water in them and spoons for the children to experiment making different sounds.

Dramatic Play

Provide boxes, wrapping paper, a tree, and plastic decorations. Children can wrap boxes.

More Group Time Activities

1. Read *Christmas in Noisy Village* by Astrid Lindgren and Ilon Wikland and *I Love Hanukkah* by Marilyn Hirsh.
2. Talk about non-material gifts and homemade gifts. Focus on the spirit of the holiday season.
3. Film: *The First Christmas Tree.*

Day 4: Meaning of Christmas

Group Time Activities

1. Ask children to share what Christmas means to them.
2. Read *A Charlie Brown Christmas* by Charles Schulz.

Learning Centers

Blocks

Allow free construction.

Listening/Music/Reading

Provide the cassette and book *A Charlie Brown Christmas* by Charles Schultz.

Art

Creative Fun: Encourage creative art time using a variety of materials, such as construction paper, lace scraps, yarn, and glitter.

Woodworking/Sand/Water

Sand: Provide plastic farm animals.

Printing

Provide a tray of salt. Children write in the salt using their fingers. Print these words on the chalkboard—Christmas, Hanukkah, December, Kwanzaa, and giving.

Math/Language Arts

Christmas Puzzles (C)   Let's Make Faces (C)

Memory Christmas Game

Addition Box: Use Christmas candy.

Science/Social Studies

Display Christmas catalogs. Children cut out pictures of presents they might give for Christmas.

Dramatic Play

Add other manipulatives to Santa's toy shop for children to make toys.

More Group Time Activities

1. Film: *The Littlest Angel.*
2. Sing Christmas carols.

Day 5: Holiday Party

Group Time Activities

(Be sure to include any Hanukkah or other holiday activities, depending on the background of your children. This celebration should be inclusive of all children.)

1. Read *Bah Humbug?* by Lorna Babian.
2. Sing Christmas carols.
3. Children decorate butcher-paper murals to use as tablecloths for Holiday party.
4. Film: *How the Animals Discovered Christmas.*

Learning Centers

Blocks

Encourage free construction.

Listening/Music/Reading

Provide the cassette and book *A Charlie Brown Christmas* by Charles Schultz.

Art

Collages: Provide a variety of holiday wrapping papers. Children cut out different shapes and glue them on construction paper to make collages.

Woodworking/Sand/Water

Wet Sand: Provide Jell-O molds, cookie cutters, and kitchen utensils.

Printing

Provide green paper. Print these words on the chalkboard— tree, ball, string, and decoration.

Math/Language Arts

Light Bright (C)

Christmas Tree Size Sequence Puzzle (C)

Addition Box: Use Christmas candy.

Science/Social Studies

Have parent dressed as Santa at this center. Children talk to Santa.

Dramatic Play

Encourage children to dramatize their ideas about Christmas.

Snack Idea

Holiday Party

More Group Time Activities

1. Game: "Ho, Ho, Ho." Blindfold one child. Point to another child to say, "Ho, Ho, Ho." The blindfolded child guesses who said it.
2. Read *Arthur's Christmas Cookies* by Lillian Hoban.

December–
Additional Activities

▶ Make a transportation chart at the beginning of this unit. Have children brainstorm a list of as many methods of transportation as they can, such as bus, car, plane, horse, sailboat, and so on. Make bar graphs showing how many children in the class have traveled by each method.

▶ Write a class book titled "Places We've Been." Have the children dictate stories about places they have visited and how they traveled to these special places. Try to locate these special places on a globe or map.

▶ Have a mystery suitcase which is "packed" for a trip. Give clues about the objects in the suitcase and see if the children can guess where you are going, such as to the mountains, the ocean, the desert, a ranch, a farm, a lake, and so on.

▶ Read *Stringbean's Trip to the Shining Sea* by Vera B. Williams. Provide postcards at a writing station. Encourage children to write messages on postcards to send to family and friends. Have a completed card at this station as a model.

▶ Make class number books. Let children choose which number they would like to illustrate for the first book. Other variations might include counting by 2s, 5s, 10s, and 100s. This could also be adapted to be "My Favorite Number Is..." Encourage children to be able to tell why they have chosen their favorite numbers.

▶ Check to see if any families in your class have a German, English, Dutch, Italian, or Mexican background. Invite members of the children's families to come and share their special holiday practices and bring in pictures or special objects used during this season.

▶ Invite German, Italian, or Spanish language students from your local high school to come and share some of the holiday practices, songs, and pictures from these countries.

▶ Provide an assortment of holiday books depicting practices in other countries. Encourage children to explore these books at one of the centers. The book *Santa Claus Around the World* by Lisl Weil gives brief accounts of different customs from around the world.

▶ Share Christmas songs and dances, such as "Hurry Little Horsey!" and "Christmas Luau" from *Holiday Singing & Dancing Games* by Esther L. Nelson (pp. 61-69).

▶ Read *Polar Express* by Chris Van Allsburg.

▶ Read *Christmas in July* by Arthur Yorinks and Richard Egielski.

▶ Read *The Tree That Came to Stay* by Nancy Carpenter.

▶ Read *Looking for Santa Claus* by Henrik Drescher.

▶ Read *One Little Goat: A Passover Song* by Marilyn Hirsh.

Songs: "Let's Go Driving." *The Sesame Street Songbook: 64 Favorite Songs*. New York, NY: Macmillan Publishing Co., 1992.

"New Way to Walk." *The Sesame Street Songbook: 64 Favorite Songs*. New York, NY: Macmillan Publishing Co., 1992.

"Counting Is Wonderful." *The Sesame Street Songbook: 64 Favorite Songs*. New York, NY: Macmillan Publishing Co., 1992.

"Keep Christmas With You." *The Sesame Street Songbook: 64 Favorite Songs*. New York, NY: Macmillan Publishing Co., 1992.

"Five Beats to Each Measure." *Hap Palmer Favorites—Songs for Learning Through Music and Movement*. Sherman Oaks, CA: Alfred Publishing Co., 1981

"What a World We'd Have If Christmas Lasted All Year Long." *Hap Palmer Favorites—Songs for Learning Through Music and Movement*. Sherman Oaks, CA: Alfred Publishing Co., 1981

"Rock of Ages." *The Holiday Song Book*. New York, NY: Lothrop, Lee & Shepard Company, 1977.

"The Twelve Days of Christmas." *The Holiday Song Book*. New York, NY: Lothrop, Lee & Shepard Company, 1977.

"Jolly Old Saint Nicholas." *The Holiday Song Book*. New York, NY: Lothrop, Lee & Shepard Company, 1977.

"Go Down Moses." *The Holiday Song Book*. New York, NY: Lothrop, Lee & Shepard Company, 1977.

January
Week 1

Preparation:

▶ Ask each child to bring a food that is prepared and suitable to add to soup on Day 2.

▶ Plan a field trip for Day 5 to a weather station or a television station to talk to the weatherperson.

Winter Weather

Day 1: Introduction to Weather

Group Time Activities

1. <u>Song</u>: "Big Beautiful Planet."
2. Give an introduction to weather and the winter unit.
3. Write words for the four seasons on the chalkboard. Use pictures to compare.
4. <u>Song</u>: "Frosty the Snowman."
5. Review the letter *Ww*. Ask children to think of *Ww* words. Write these on butcher paper to be displayed all week.
6. <u>Fingerplay</u>: "This Is a Snowman as Round as a Ball" from *Chants for Children*.

Learning Centers

Blocks

Provide pictures of a weather station and weather instruments.

Listening/Music/Reading

Provide cassette and book *The Snowy Day* by Ezra Jack Keats.

Art

<u>Snowperson</u>: Children draw snow people on construction paper and add Cheerios, popcorn, or cotton to represent the snow.

Woodworking/Sand/Water

Lay a blanket in the bottom of the table to absorb noise. Provide white, uncooked rice, balance scales, and measuring cups.

Printing

Children print in a tray of salt with their fingers. Print these words on the chalkboard—weather, weatherperson, winter, wet, wind, and windy.

Math/Language Arts

Snowman (W)   Seasons Puzzle (C)

<u>Winter Words Poster</u>: Write weather words on a poster and write the same words on cards. Be sure to write the words exactly the same size. Cut cards into individual letters. Children arrange the letters on the poster to spell the words.

Science/Social Studies

Display winter clothes and books about winter.

Dramatic Play

Set up a weather station. Provide Flannel Board Weather Kit (C), telephone, weather chart, thermometer, and wind gauge. Leave out all week.

More Group Time Activities

1. Play Number Bingo.
2. Read *The Self-Made Snowman* by Fernando Krahn.
3. Read *Stone Soup* by Marcia Brown.
4. <u>Film</u>: *An Alphabet of Weather*.

Day 2: Winter Food and Clothing

Group Time Activities

1. Discuss winter foods using pictures, such as hot foods, nutritious foods, and canned foods.
2. Discuss the importance of winter clothing, such as hats, gloves, and scarves. Show clothing. Discuss the safety aspects of adequate clothing in winter.
3. Read *Stone Soup* by Marcia Brown.
4. Prepare stone soup using the food children brought to school at the appropriate time in the story. Cook on a hot plate. Plan to eat soup at snack time.

Learning Centers

Blocks

Instead of block play, encourage children to "ice skate" on rug. Children remove their shoes. Give each child two pieces of waxed paper. Children place the waxed paper under each foot and slide.

Listening/Music/Reading

Provide the cassette and book *Stone Soup* by Marcia Brown.

Art

Mittens: Children make mittens out of wallpaper samples and tie together with yarn. Label the right and left mittens.

Woodworking/Sand/Water

Provide uncooked white rice for measuring.

Printing

Children write in a salt tray using their fingers. Print these words on the chalkboard—coat, scarf, mitten, glove, and hat.

Math/Language Arts

Bacon and Eggs (WII)   Mousetrap Math (WII)

Science/Social Studies

Provide various zippers. Provide pictures of clothing to sort according to season. Add big boxes labeled with each season.

Snack Idea

Eat the stone soup.

More Group Time Activities

1. Song: "Looby Loo."
2. Game: "Simon Says." Tie a string on each child's right hand. Give instructions of things for children to do, such as rub their stomachs or pat their heads. If the statement begins with "Simon says," the children are to follow the directions.
3. Review *Zz*.
4. Read *I Like Winter* by Lois Lenski.

Day 3: Winter Activities, Animals, and Plants

Group Time Activities

1. Use a chart to review animals and winter activities, such as hibernation, fur, migration, and finding food. Place a bird feeder outside the classroom window.
2. Discuss plants in winter (dormant, appears dead, inside are roots, stems, and seeds).
3. Discuss winter activities and safety rules (skiing, playing hockey, ice skating, tobogganing).
4. Song: "Frosty the Snowman."
5. Show words written on cards that were used this week and group the words according to beginning sounds.

Learning Centers

Blocks

Display pictures of animals in winter.

Listening/Music/Reading

Provide the cassette and book *The Snowy Day* by Ezra Jack Keats.

Art

Chalk Drawings: Children dip chalk in water or milk before drawing on construction paper.

Woodworking/Sand/Water

Provide shaving cream for free play.

Printing

Children write in salt tray. Print these words on the chalkboard—hibernation, migration, fur, and evergreen.

Math/Language Arts

Mousetraps Math (WII)

Count the Snow: On construction paper, draw snow people that have numerals written on their hats. Children glue the correct number of styrofoam packing pieces on their snow people pictures.

Science/Social Studies

Display dormant grass and a branch. Talk with the children about what happens to grass and trees in the winter.

Provide several jackets and sweaters for children to practice zipping, snapping, and buttoning.

More Group Time Activities

1. Work with children on finding different ways to hold a tennis ball. Use a timer and have children squeeze the tennis balls between their knees and try to walk across the room. Have children roll the tennis ball to a jar lid and let the ball move the lid to the wall.
2. Read *I Hate to Take a Bath* by Judi Barrett.
3. Language Experience Notebook: Winter Weather.

Day 4: Meterologists

Group Time Activities

1. <u>Song</u>: "Big Beautiful Planet."
2. Discuss meteorologist's work, such as forecasting, study, reporting, making records, and keeping charts of the weather.

3. Read *Dan the Weatherman* by Jene Barr to explain what instruments a weatherperson uses and why.
4. Show weather instrument posters or pictures.
5. Review *Ww* and items that begin with this sound.
6. Children pretend to be mercury in a thermometer. Have the children stand up and sit down according to the weather picture you hold up.

Learning Centers

Blocks

Provide pictures of weather stations.

Listening/Music/Reading

As the children listen to *The Snowy Day* by Ezra Jack Keats on a cassette tape, ask children to draw pictures about the story.

Art

<u>A Snowy Day</u>: Children make snow pictures using cotton or styrofoam packing pieces on construction paper.

<u>Count the Snow</u>: Write a numeral on a paper for each child. Children draw winter pictures on their papers and glue the corresponding number of snowflakes as the numeral.

Woodworking/Sand/Water

Provide shaving cream for creative play.

Printing

Children write in a tray of salt with their fingers. Print these words on the chalkboard—weather, winter, wet, and wind.

Math/Language Arts

Snowmen (W)   Season Puzzles (C)

Weather Words Poster

<u>Mitten Match</u>: Cut matching mittens from a variety of materials or wallpaper samples. Children find the matching pairs.

Science/Social Studies

Display several pairs of boots. Children compare and arrange the boots in order according to size.

More Group Time Activities

1. Read *The Snow* by John Burningham.
2. Look at an ABC chart and decide which letters have been studied. Review these letters.
3. <u>Song</u>: "It Is Snowing" (Tune: "Frere Jacques").

Day 5: Field Trip

Group Time Activities

1. Discuss rules children need to remember on the trip.
2. Review weather instruments.
3. Read *Katy and the Big Snow* by Virginia Lee Burton.

Learning Centers

Blocks

Provide pictures of weather stations and weather instruments.

Listening/Music/Reading

Provide the recording and book *White Snow, Bright Snow* by Alvin Tresselt.

Art

<u>Snowflakes</u>: Children cut snowflakes from folded white paper.

Woodworking/Sand/Water

Provide uncooked white rice for measuring and balancing. Provide balancing scales and measuring cups.

Printing

Children print in a tray of salt with their fingers. Print these words on the chalkboard—weather, wind, winter, weatherperson, wet, and windy.

Math/Language Arts

Snowmen (W)   Season Puzzles (C)

Weather Words Poster

Science/Social Studies

Display newspaper pages that report the weather.

Display pictures of weather instruments.

More Group Time Activities

1. Write a thank-you letter with the class to the weather station personnel.
2. Read *White Snow, Bright Snow* by Alvin Tresselt.

January
Week 2

Preparation:

▶ Invite parents who are health-care professionals to come in and talk about their jobs on appointed days.

▶ Have children bring new toothbrushes from home and practice correct brushing techniques on Day 3.

▶ Plan a field trip to a doctor's office or hospital for Day 5.

Health Friends

Day 1: Optometrist

Group Time Activities

1. Introduce eye movement words, such as open, shut, blink, and wink.
2. Show the children an eye chart. Children use mirrors to look at their eyes and surrounding parts. Compare color and size.
3. Ask children to close their eyes and try to move around the room. Discuss with the children what it was like to not be able to see. Have reference books on Helen Keller available during this discussion. Remind children how important it is to take care of their eyes.
4. Discuss the optometrist's job and education. Invite any parent who is an optometrist to share his or her experiences.
5. Discuss and show pictures of eye parts.
6. Discuss glasses. Show samples and discuss use.

Learning Centers

Blocks

Allow creative play.

Listening/Music/Reading

Make a recording of "Grandma's Spectacles" and "I Know an Old Lady" on a cassette tape.

Art

Moveable Eyes: Children draw a face with two slits at each eye. Then children draw different eye patterns on two strips of paper and slide the strips through the slits in the face to show eye movements.

Woodworking/Sand/Water

Woodworking: Provide wood shavings, sawdust, small pieces of wood, string, and glue.

Printing

Provide Write On Wipe Off Cards (C) for children to copy these words—eyes, iris, lid, wink, eyebrow, blink, eyelash, shut, pupil, and open.

Math/Language Arts

Making Faces (C)	Tinker Toys (C)
Lacing Cards (C)	Picture Dominoes (C)
ABC Lotto (C)	

Science/Social Studies

Display models of the eye, body, and skeleton. Display books about eyes and posters about eye care.

Dramatic Play

Set up an optometrist office. Provide eye charts, white T-shirts, a toy telephone, chairs, and magazines.

More Group Time Activities

1. Read *I Wish I Was Sick, Too!* by Franz Brandenberg or *Teddy Bears Cure a Cold* by Susanna Alison Sage.
2. Game: "Guess What I Saw." Children sit in a circle. "It" sits in center. "It" says, "On my way to school this morning, I saw something." "It" imitates what he or she saw. Other children guess. The correct guesser can be the next "It."

Day 2: Nurse

Group Time Activities

1. Discuss the role of a nurse, such as the education needed and the many responsibilities of the job.
2. Have a parent who is a nurse talk to the children about his or her job and demonstrate the use of a few medical instruments, such as a stethoscope or a blood pressure cuff. Also, invite the school nurse to visit the classroom.
3. Discuss care of cuts, bruises, and insect bites with a safety chart.
4. Record: *Hap Palmer: Learning Basic Skills Through Music—Health and Safety.*
5. Read *I Hate to Take a Bath* by Judi Barrett.

Learning Centers

Blocks

Provide pictures of a hospital, Fisher Price Hospital (C), wooden block people, and traffic signs.

Listening/Music/Reading

Add "Are You Sleeping?" to the cassette tape.

Art

Create Your Own: Provide pipe cleaners, yarn, styrofoam meat trays, and construction paper for children to use in creative art.

Woodworking/Sand/Water

Water: Move the water table to the dramatic-play center. Provide a bowl of clean water, a bar of soap, and paper towels for children to use for hand washing between seeing patients while they dramatize being nurses.

Printing

Provide Write On Wipe Off Cards (C). Print these words on the board—nurse, friend, helper, exercise, and health.

Math/Language Arts

Health Friend Puzzle (C)   Alphabet Soup Game (C)

Nutrition Game (C)   Interlocking Cubes (C)

Octons (C)

Science/Social Studies

Display models of teeth and body, health charts, and thermometers.

Dramatic Play

Set up a doctor's office. Provide bandages, charts, scales, prizes, white shirts, Fisher Price Medical Bag (C), and water table.

More Group Time Activities

1. Sing favorite songs.
2. Language Experience Notebook: Health Friends.
3. Make crazy pictures out of the letter *Dd* on the chalkboard. Children make their own crazy pictures on paper.
4. Read *Doctors and Nurses: What Do They Do?* by Carla Greene.

Day 3: Dentist

Group Time Activities

1. Discuss the dentist's education and job. If possible, invite a parent to share his or her experiences as a dentist.
2. Discuss growth of teeth, caring for them, proper brushing, and flossing techniques. Show model of teeth and gum. Have children bring new toothbrushes to school and actually practice brushing using proper techniques.
3. Film: *Big Mouth Goes to the Dentist.*
4. Make a class bar graph titled "How Many Missing Teeth Do You Have?"

Learning Centers

Blocks

Provide pictures of the mouth, gums, and teeth.

Listening/Music/Reading

Provide a recording of the song "Brush Away" from *Hap Palmer: Learning Basic Skills Through Music—Health and Safety.*

Art

Toothpick Art: Children glue toothpicks on construction paper to make pictures of designs.

Woodworking/Sand/Water

Water: Provide two tubs of water, soap and paper towels. Children wash hands in water and dry them. Then children wash hands, using soap, and dry them. Compare paper towels.

Printing

Provide Write On Wipe Off Cards (C). Print these words on the chalkboard—teeth, tooth, dentist, floss, cavity, and filling.

Math/Language Arts

Pegs and Peg Board (C)   Mosaics (C)

Money Jars and Pennies: Put a numeral on each baby food jar. Children put the correct number of pennies in each jar.

Science/Social Studies

Display models of teeth and charts of brushing techniques. Provide toothbrushes and dental floss for children to use with the plastic teeth models.

Dramatic Play

Set up a dentist's office. Provide Doctor Drill'n Fill (Play-Doh Modeling Set by Kenner) (C).

More Group Time Activities

1. Film: *Teeth Are for Chewing.*
2. Record: "Brush Away" by Hap Palmer from *Learning Basic Skills Through Music—Health and Safety,* .
3. Game: "Who's Missing?" "It" closes eyes. Point to a child to leave the group. "It" opens eyes and tries to guess who is missing.

Day 4: Doctor

Group Time Activities

1. Discuss a doctor's education and job, such as diagnosis, treatment, and prevention. If possible, have a parent share his or her experiences as a doctor.
2. Discuss the importance of regular check-ups.
3. Discuss a pharmacist's job.
4. Introduce names of different types of doctors, such as surgeons and pediatricians.
5. Read *I Want to Be a Doctor* by Carla Green.
6. Ask children to think of words that begin with *Dd* and write the words on the chalkboard.

Learning Centers

Blocks
Provide pictures of hospitals.

Listening/Music/Reading
Provide the Hap Palmer record *Learning Basic Skills Through Music—Health and Safety*.

Art
Stethoscopes: Each child threads an empty thread spool on a piece of yarn and ties a knot in the string.

Woodworking/Sand/Water
Water: Provide egg beaters and Ivory soap.

Printing
Provide Write On Wipe Off Cards (C). Print these words on the chalkboard—doctor, hospital, medicine, and sick.

Math/Language Arts

Health Friend Puzzle (C)	Bacon and Eggs (WII)
Nutrition Card Game (C)	Go-Together Bottles (W)
Brushing Teeth and Hair Puzzles (C)	

Science/Social Studies
Provide Doctor Drill'n Fill (Play-Doh Modeling Set by Kenner) (C). Display models of eye, teeth, and human body.

Dramatic Play
Set up a hospital. Cover a table with a white sheet. Provide white jackets, Fisher Price Doctor Kits (C), bandages, crutches, ice bags, and a sling.

More Group Time Activities

1. Read *Rip Van Winkle* by Washington Irving.
2. Song: "Are You Sleeping?"
3. Read *Madeline* by Ludwig Bemelmans.
4. Film: *Sniffles, Sneezes and Contagious Diseases*.

Day 5: Field Trip

Group Time Activities

Discuss the field trip with children. Discuss what will be observed and the behavior expected.

Learning Centers

Blocks
Provide Fisher Price Hospital (C), traffic signs, wooden block figures, and toy cars and trucks.

Listening/Music/Reading
Add "Five Little Monkeys Jumping on the Bed" and "Go Tell Aunt Rhody" to the cassette tape.

Art
All Eyes: Children cut eyes out of magazines and glue them on construction paper.

Glasses: Cut the plastic off a beverage six pack into pairs of glasses. Children use pipe cleaners on the sides to hold the glasses on their heads.

Woodworking/Sand/Water
*Woodworking: Provide nuts, buttons, jar lids, wood shavings, glue, hammers, nails, and wood scraps.

Printing
Provide Write On Wipe Off Cards (C). Print these words on the chalkboard—eyes, iris, lid, wink, eyebrow, blink, eyelash, shut, pupil, and open.

Math/Language Arts

Making Faces (C)	Lacing Cards (C)
ABC Lotto (C)	Tinker Toys (C)
Picture Dominoes (C)	

Science/Social Studies
Display a real tooth that has been placed in a sealed jar of Coca Cola. Display a real tooth that has been placed in a sealed jar of water. Leave out to observe over the next several days.

Dramatic Play
Set up an optometrist's office. Provide eye chart, white shirts, paper, pencils, telephones, chairs, and magazines.

More Group Time Activities

1. Write a class thank-you letter to the health-care professional who conducted the tour on the field trip visit.
2. Read *Up Day, Down Day* by Jacquie Hann.
3. Film: *Why We Need Doctors: No Measles, No Mumps for Me*.
4. Review *Dd*.

January
Week 3

Our Five Senses

Day 1: Touch

Group Time Activities

1. Introduce the word *detective*. Talk about detective work.
2. Read *Let's Take a Walk in the Zoo* by Jane Bell Moncure and discuss what senses were used in the book.
3. Discuss the "Detective Agency" set up in the dramatic-play center. Give children a mystery to solve each day at the center.
4. Song: "Hand Jive" from *Greg and Steve—We All Live Together, Volume 4.*
5. Blindfold one child at a time, and ask him or her to touch and then identify sandpaper letters and numerals.
6. Use your finger to draw numbers, letters, or simple pictures on the children's backs. Have each child guess what you drew.
7. Film: *Bambi Learns about Touch.*

Learning Centers

Blocks

Blindfolded children guess the shapes of blocks.

Listening/Music/Reading

Provide a recording of the songs "Touch" from *Hap Palmer: Getting to Know Myself* and "Touch the World" from *Hap Palmer: The Feel of Music.*

Art

Texture Collages: Provide a variety of wallpaper samples.

Rubbings: Children make rubbings of objects in the classroom.

Woodworking/Sand/Water

Provide containers of several types of sand and dirt.
Provide magnifying glasses and pocketscopes (C).

Printing

Provide typewriters. Print these words on the chalkboard—touch, feet, hot, cold, soft, and rough.

Math/Language Arts

Math Rugs (W)   Puzzles (C)

Playdough (C)

Touch Board: Glue various materials on a piece of posterboard. Provide a blindfold. Have children touch the materials and then guess what they are.

Counting Objects Blindfolded: Provide small boxes that have objects in them. Ask blindfolded children to count the objects.

Science/Social Studies

Rough/Smooth Game: Provide a box of materials and two boxes labeled "Rough" and "Smooth." Children sort the objects according to texture.

Dramatic Play

Set up a detective agency. Be creative. Each day provide a mystery in a box. Children try to solve the mystery. Add books about detectives, magnifying glasses, paper, pencils, and toy telephones. Leave out all week.

More Group Time Activities

1. Blindfold a child. Have him or her touch another child and guess who it is.
2. Discuss Braille and show samples.
3. Discuss Martin Luther King, Jr., and why a day in January is set aside to honor him.
4. Solve the mystery of the day.

Day 2: Sight

Group Time Activities

1. Review a detective's job. Give clues about the mystery of the day.
2. Discuss the sense of sight.
3. Show eye charts, magnifying glass, and glasses.
4. Display a tray of objects. Remove one object at a time and children guess what's missing.
5. Read *Through Grandpa's Eyes* by Patricia MacLachlan.
6. <u>Film</u>: *Bambi Learns about Seeing*.

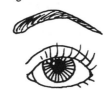

Learning Centers

Blocks

Provide posters of different designs to make using the unit blocks. Ask children to recreate the designs.

Listening/Music/Reading

Provide the cassette and book *Three Blind Mice*.

Art

<u>Frame It</u>: Use matboard scraps obtained free from local frame shops. Children draw pictures of something they love to see. Provide sticks or popsicle sticks to glue around the pictures to frame them.

Woodworking/Sand/Water

<u>Water</u>: Add bubble bath. Provide washcloths and sponges.

Printing

Provide typewriters. Print these words on the chalkboard—sight, see, and eye.

Math/Language Arts

What's Missing Lotto (C)   Dominoes (C)

Light Bright (C)

More Group Time Activities

1. <u>Game</u>: "Guess Who?" Children sit in a circle with "It" in the center. Describe another child. "It" tries to guess which child is being described.
2. Read *I See Something You Don't See* by Robin Michal Koontz.
3. Discuss the many accomplishments of Helen Keller.
4. Solve the mystery of the day.

Day 3: Hearing

Group Time Activities

1. Take children on a listening walk. Come back to the room and write a list of sounds heard.
2. Discuss how the ear works.
3. <u>Film</u>: *Bambi Learns about Hearing*.
4. Read *A Button in Her Ear* by Ada Bassett Litchfield.
5. Review the letter *Hh*.
6. Discuss the mystery of the day.

Learning Centers

Blocks

Provide a cassette player and cassette tape so children can record the sounds of the blocks as they play.

Listening/Music/Reading

Provide a recording of various common sounds. Children draw pictures of the sounds they recognize.

Art

<u>Name That Sound</u>: Each child decorates a soft drink can. Tell children to find something in the room to put in their cans and then tape up the hole. At next group time, challenge the other children to guess what each child put in his or her can by listening to the sound it makes.

Woodworking/Sand/Water

<u>Water</u>: Provide a variety of small objects for children to drop into the water and listen to the different sounds.

Printing

Provide typewriters. Print these words on the chalkboard—ears, sounds, and hearing.

Math/Language Arts

Colorama (C)   Rhyming Bingo (C)

Puzzles (C)   Sound Boxes (W)

Science/Social Studies

Provide several jars filled to different levels with water. Children tap jars with spoons. Provide tuning forks (C) and a small pan of water.

More Group Time Activities

1. <u>Game</u>: "Guess Who Made the Sound." The child chosen as "It" is blindfolded. Point to a child to say something. "It" tries to guess who spoke.
2. <u>Game</u>: "Simon Says."
3. Use an autoharp. Children sit when they hear low notes and stand when they hear high notes.

4. Children guess what is making the sound in each child's can.
5. Review the letter *Hh*.
6. Solve the mystery of the day.

Day 4: Smell

Group Time Activities

1. Discuss the saying "Follow your nose." Discuss smells and what they can tell us:
   a. Smoke tells us to take action.
   b. Food makes us hungry and tells us what's cooking.
   c. Medicine tells us that someone is sick.
   d. Unfamiliar smells make us curious.

   Discuss how smells vary:
   a. Same items may smell different, such as perfume in a bottle and on people.
   b. Different items may smell the same, such as lemon soap and lemon air freshener.
   c. Not everything has a smell.
   d. Smells can be changed, such as popped popcorn and burnt popcorn.
2. Game: "Smelling Fun." Children are blindfolded and then guess what they are smelling.
3. Film: *Bambi Learns about Taste and Smell.*
4. Discuss the mystery of the day.

Learning Centers

Blocks

Encourage free play.

Listening/Music/Reading

Provide the cassette and book *Three Blind Mice.*

Art

Shaving Cream Designs: Children fingerpaint with shaving cream.

Jell-O Smell: Children draw designs with glue on paper, sprinkle with Jell-O, shake off excess, and smell.

Woodworking/Sand/Water

Water: Add bubble bath and provide kitchen utensils.

Printing

Provide typewriters. Print these words on the chalkboard—smell, sense, and nose.

Math/Language Arts

Making Faces (C)   Rubber Band Boards (C)

Geozellos (C)

Science/Social Studies

Provide garlic bulb, apple, onion, orange, lemon, potpourri, scented votive candles, and small soaps for children to smell.

More Group Time Activities

1. Read *Smelling Things* by Allan Fowler.
2. Game: "Smelling Fun."
3. Read *The Barn* by John Carl Schoenherr.
4. Solve the mystery of the day.

Day 5: Taste

Group Time Activities

1. Read *My Five Senses* by Aliki.
2. Explain how the tongue works.
3. Discuss how taste may affect our behavior, such as the taste of lemon makes some people grimace.
4. Discuss how the same items may not always taste the same, such as different flavors of gum or cookies.
5. Discuss how different items may have the same flavor, such as lemon pudding and lemonade.
6. Discuss how some items that look the same may not always taste the same, such as vanilla and lemon pudding that are the same color.
7. Discuss how food flavors can be altered, such as bread and toast.
8. Film: *Our Senses Working Together.*
9. Discuss the mystery of the day.

Learning Centers

Blocks

Provide posters of designs made with building blocks. Children can copy the designs.

Art

Fingerpaint: Children fingerpaint with lemon pudding, coconut pudding, or whipped cream.

Food Collages: Provide macaroni, raisins, cereal, and marshmallows.

Woodworking/Sand/Water

Wet Sand: Children make mud pies.

Printing

Provide typewriters. Print these words on the chalkboard—taste, salt, tongue, lemon, sweet, sour, and bitter.

Math/Language Arts

Making Faces (C)   Rubber Band Boards (C)

Geozellos (C)

Science/Social Studies

Provide magazines for children to cut out pictures showing the five senses and glue on construction paper.

More Group Time Activities

1. Read *Fish for Supper* by M.B. Goffstein. Discuss the senses used when cooking fish or other foods, especially the sense of sight. For example, when we can see the food we begin to anticipate the taste.
2. Review the letter *Tt.*
3. Solve the mystery of the day.

January
Week 4

Preparation:

▶ Take candid shots of children ahead of time and display them around the room.

▶ Prepare a bulletin board of various pictures taken by photographers, including portraits, landscapes, silhouettes, and close-ups.

▶ Plan a field trip to a camera shop, photography studio, or darkroom for Day 5.

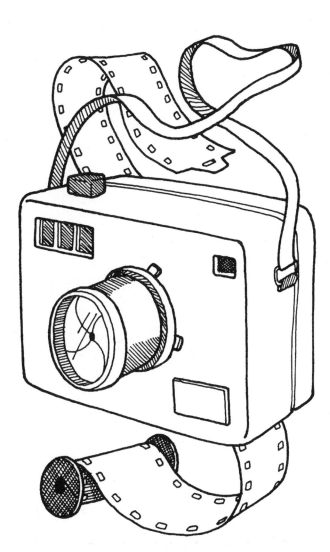

Photography

Day 1: Parts of the Camera

Group Time Activities

1. Introduce children to photography, and discuss the bulletin board you've prepared with pictures taken by photographers.
2. Discuss and show film, negatives, mounts, and gloves.
3. Discuss parts of a camera using posters and a camera.
4. Using a film projector, explain *focus* and *out of focus*.
5. Read *Simple Pictures Are Best* by Nancy Willard.

Learning Centers

Blocks

Instead of block play, provide two roller boards and rollers for children to use.

Listening/Music/Reading

Provide any favorite records or cassette tapes. Provide color advertising books, photography annuals, and magazines. Leave out all week.

Art

Milk Carton Cameras: Gather milk cartons from the lunchroom. Children cover milk cartons with black paper and add camera parts by gluing on buttons and thread spools. Children put hand-drawn pictures inside the milk cartons as negatives. As children take photographs, they take the hand-drawn pictures out of the cameras.

Woodworking/Sand/Water

Woodworking: Provide bolts, screws, hardware, locks and keys, screwdrivers, and wood.

Printing

Provide typewriters. Print these words on the chalkboard—photography, body, light, shutter, pictures, camera, and lens.

Math/Language Arts

Light Bright (C)   Snapshots (WII)
Estimating Jars and Beads (W)

Science/Social Studies

Set up a photography display showing black and white pictures, color pictures, film, negatives, slides, scrap books, and photography magazines.

Dramatic Play

Set up a photography studio and darkroom. Provide cut up comic strips for negatives, old cameras or toy cameras, toy telephone, and tubs to be used for "developer" solutions. Leave out all week.

More Group Time Activities

1. Film: *Hansel and Gretel*.
2. Discuss things that come in pairs. Make a list of ideas on chalkboard.
3. Read *Year After Year* by Bill Binzen.

Day 2: Taking Pictures

Group Time Activities

1. Demonstrate how to load a camera with film.
2. Demonstrate how to hold and focus a camera. Review parts of the camera.
3. Discuss lighting and the need for a flash indoors.
4. Discuss removal of film from camera and exposure to light.
5. Use pictures to discuss the saying "A picture is worth a thousand words." Show picture(s) and have children tell a partner how it makes them feel or what they see.

Learning Centers

Blocks
Encourage free construction.

Art
For My Friend: Each child draws or colors a picture for a friend and puts it in an envelope. All children put their pictures in a basket when they are finished. At next group time, each child takes an envelope out of the basket.

Woodworking/Sand/Water
Woodworking: Provide screws and screwdrivers, nuts and bolts, and wood scraps.

Printing
Provide typewriters. Print these words on the chalkboard—flash, pictures, snapshots, and cameras.

Math/Language Arts
Playdough (C)   Snapshots (C)

Button Sorting: Children sort buttons according to size, color, or holes.

Science/Social Studies
Provide a camera so that children can examine its parts. Display books about cameras.

Dramatic Play
Children play in "yellow land." Add as many yellow objects as possible, such as yellow sheets, a yellow duck, and a yellow toothbrush.

More Group Time Activities

1. Read *Look Again* by Tana Hoban.
2. Use opposite cards or play an opposite guessing game: Say a word like "sit." Children do the opposite motion.
3. Take a class picture outside with a camera.
4. All children pick one envelope out of the basket to see whose picture they receive.

Day 3: Developing Pictures

Group Time Activities

1. Show rolls of film and film that was exposed to light.
2. Go through process of developing film, using mock solutions, such as developer, stop bath, and fix. Use three colors of food coloring for the three solutions and use a poster of an enlarger.
3. Discuss sending film off to be processed.
4. Discuss care of pictures, such as storing pictures in albums, touching only the edges to avoid fingerprints, and not bending photos. Model these guidelines as you share a personal photo album. Encourage children to look through this album at an exploration center.

Learning Centers

Blocks
Add a variety of boxes.

Listening/Music/Reading
Add musical instruments. Provide photography magazines, books, and picture albums for display.

Art
Films: Children create a film using comic strips. Children read through funny pages and then cut out favorite comics. Cut the comic pictures apart and glue on long strips of paper like a film.

Woodworking/Sand/Water
Sand: Provide dry, fine sand and empty food boxes with small holes punched in them.

Printing
Provide typewriters. Print these words on the chalkboard—solutions, developer, stop bath, fix, film, and negative.

Math/Language Arts
Sesame Street Puzzles (C)

Look Alikes: Houses and Dolls (C)

Sorting: Children sort pictures by size and color.

Science/Social Studies
Provide Viewmaster sets (C).

Dramatic Play
Add a clothesline. Provide magazine pictures for children to dip in food-colored water solutions labeled "developer," "stop bath," and "fix." Children use clothespins to hang the pictures on the clothesline to dry.

More Group Time Activities

1. Show a film of a favorite story or slides from a vacation.
2. Discuss differences in projectors, film, and filmstrip.

Day 4: Types of Pictures

Group Time Activities

1. Show photographs from magazines and books. Discuss the pictures on the bulletin board.
2. Discuss silhouettes and review shadows.
3. Discuss types of photographers, such as portrait, wedding, and commercial.
4. Review parts of the camera.
5. Special Project: As children work in learning centers, make a silhouette picture of each child, one at a time. Shine a flashlight or film projector toward each child and have him or her turn sideways to reveal a profile. Tape black paper to the wall behind child. Use chalk to outline the child's silhouette. Each child cuts out his or her silhouette. Hang silhouettes on a wall in the room or in the hall.

Learning Centers

Blocks

Provide flashlights for children to use while block building.

Art

Photo Albums: Provide construction paper, glue, and a stapler, so each child can make a photo album from pictures cut out of photography magazines.

Woodworking/Sand/Water

Water: Provide plastic bottles with holes punched in them.

Printing

Provide typewriters. Print these words on the chalkboard—landscape, portrait, silhouette, pictures, and wedding.

Math/Language Arts

Silhouette Board: Glue pictures of objects on a poster. Make silhouettes of the objects using black construction paper. Children match silhouettes to pictures.

Laurel and Hardy and Go Fishing Card Games (C)

Science/Social Studies

Provide Viewmasters (C).

More Group Time Activities

1. Record: *Hap Palmer: Creative Movement and Rhythmic Exploration.*
2. Language Experience Notebook: Children draw pictures of something they learned this week about photography.

Day 5: Field Trip

Group Time Activities

Discuss field trip to photography lab and studio. Talk about proper behavior.

Learning Centers

Blocks

Provide flashlights to make silhouettes of blocks.

Art

Album of Faces: Children cut out faces of people from photography magazines. Have children glue the faces on construction paper and staple to make a portrait album.

Woodworking/Sand/Water

Children continue using water and plastic bottles with holes punched in them.

Printing

Provide typewriters. Print these words on the chalkboard—landscape, portrait, silhouette, and pictures.

Math/Language Arts

Puzzles (C)   Silhouette Board

Laurel and Hardy, and Go Fishing Card Games (C)

Light Bright (C)

Science/Social Studies

Provide Viewmasters (C).

Dramatic Play

Children play in "green land." Provide as many green objects as possible.

More Group Time Activities

1. Write a thank-you letter with the class to those you visited at the photography lab or studio.
2. Draw pictures or murals of the trip.

January—
Additional Activities

▶ Play a season clue game. Children give clues about a season they are thinking of by saying "I'm thinking of a season when it is..." Have children guess the season. Encourage children to give clues. Have child who gives correct answer explain how he or she arrived at the answer.

▶ Use Ezra Jack Keats' book *The Snowy Day* to create print designs using cut up sections of fruits and vegetables, such as carrots, celery, apples. Dip in tempera paint. Talk about pattern and repetition.

▶ Write a class story titled "Our Snowy Day" modeled after *The Snowy Day* by Ezra Jack Keats. Discuss character, setting, beginning, middle, and end. Use fruit and vegetable sections and tempera paint to create prints.

▶ Read *What Will the Weather Be Like Today?* by Paul Rogers.

▶ Read *White Snow, Blue Feather* by Julie Downing.

▶ Read *Our Snow Man* by M.B. Goffstein.

▶ Read *What Causes It?* by Jane Belk Moncure.

▶ Play the game "I Spy." A child begins with "I spy with my big (color) eyes something that is (describe)." Other classmates try to guess what the child is describing.

▶ Create a winter scene using white tempera paint and cut up sponge sections. Make white sponge prints for snow on blue construction paper. Discuss what else could be in the winter scene, such as children sliding, a skating rink, snowpeople, and so on.

▶ Appoint a "Weather Person of the Day." Each day the weather person makes a forecast. Have class make predictions about weather. Make a bar graph showing how many children think it will be sunny, snowy, cloudy, foggy, and so on. At the end of the day, compare the forecast to the actual weather and see how many children made accurate predictions.

▶ Invite any parents who are health-care professionals, especially optometrists, dentists, nurses, and doctors, to come to class and share some of their experiences.

▶ Have "A Day at the Doctor." Divide the class in half. One half are patients and the other half are different health-care professionals. Children dramatize visiting at least one health-care professional. Explain the different choices and have appropriate medical instruments at each station. Switch so that each child experiences being the patient and health-care professional. Discuss different feelings associated with visiting the doctor. Summarize by emphasizing the importance of prevention in health care and what children can do to keep themselves in good health.

▶ Write a class story about visiting the doctor. Each child adds one line to the story and illustrates his or her page.

- Play a senses guessing game. Have children work in pairs with a divider between them. One child describes a "mystery object" and the other child tries to guess what it is. A variation might include having one child blindfolded. Using the sense of touch, the blindfolded child tries to identify the mystery object by asking questions of his or her partner.

- Check to see if your local police department has a canine unit. If so, arrange for a policeperson to bring one of these dogs in and explain how this trained dog uses its senses.

- Invite a guest speaker from your local sight or hearing organization to come and share some of his or her experiences. Ask the guest speaker to bring in any adaptive equipment and explain how these instruments are used.

- Discuss how different music creates a mood or tone. Provide a cassette tape of a variety of music, such as slow or fast tempo, loud or soft volume, peaceful or exciting melody, and so on. Show the children how to "draw what they hear" using different colors and different kinds of lines. Encourage children to experiment.

- Provide a recording of different sounds, such as water running, people walking down the hall, toilet flushing, rain, dogs barking, and so on. Have children see how many sounds they can correctly identify.

- Set up a taste-testing station with the assistance of a parent. Blindfold children and have them taste various foods, such as lemon, pickle, strawberry, and so on. Have children name what they tasted. Write each child's one word response on a card. Give the children the cards that are numbered to coincide with the food items. As a class, discuss the results, such as how many children guessed lemon for #1 and so on.

- Read *I Have a Sister-My Sister is Deaf* by Deborah Ray.

- Read *Think About Smelling* by Henry Pluckrose.

- Compare a camera to the eye. Use correct terminology when comparing the parts of the eye to the parts of a camera.

- Assign children a specific day during the photography unit to bring in a photo album from home. Have the albums available at an exploration center.

- Read *Shadows and Reflections* by Tana Hoban.

- Songs: "Snowman, Snowman" (Tune: "Twinkle, Twinkle Little Star"). *More Piggyback Songs*. Everett, WA: Warren Publishing House, 1984.

  "Snowflakes Falling Down" (Tune: "Row, Row, Row Your Boat"). *More Piggyback Songs*. Everett, WA: Warren Publishing House, 1984.

  "Brush Away." *Hap Palmer Favorites—Songs for Learning Through Music and Movement*. Sherman Oaks, CA: Alfred Publishing Co., 1981

  "Listen and Do." *Hap Palmer Favorites—Songs for Learning Through Music and Movement*. Sherman Oaks, CA: Alfred Publishing Co., 1981

  "One Fine Face." *The Sesame Street Song Book-64 Favorite Songs*. New York, NY: Macmillan Publishing Co., 1992.

February
Week 1

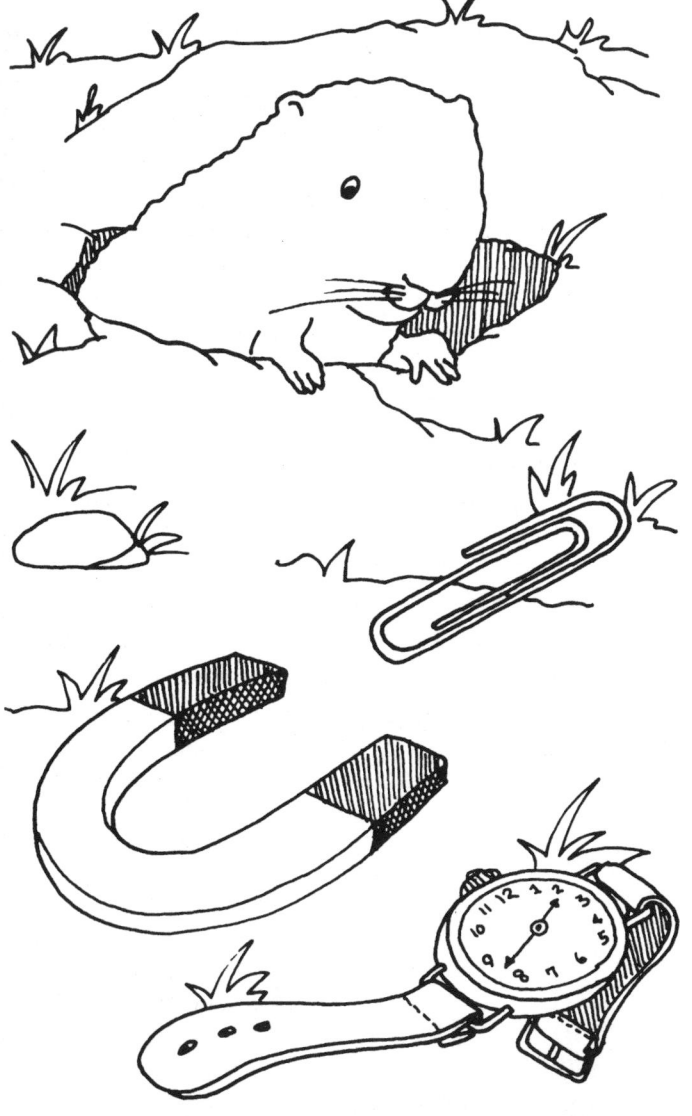

Groundhog Day/Magnets/ Time

Day 1: Groundhog Day

Group Time Activities
1. Show pictures of a groundhog. Discuss what a groundhog eats (alfalfa, clover), how it lives, and where it lives (burrow).
2. Talk about shadows. Use a projector or flashlight to show shadows. Explain the groundhog tradition.
3. Song: "Mr. Groundhog" (Tune: "Frere Jacques").
4. Film: *Tale of the Groundhog's Shadow*.

Learning Centers
Blocks
Provide a tunnel for children to use playing with the blocks.

Listening/Music/Reading
Provide the cassette and book *Groundhog's Day at the Doctor* by Judy Delton.

Art
Groundhogs: Each child draws a burrow, a groundhog, and a shadow on construction paper. Tell children to spread glue over the ground area, sprinkle sand over the paper, and shake off the extra.
Pop-up Groundhog: Children draw small groundhogs on construction paper, cut them out, and glue the groundhogs on popsicle sticks. Provide white styrofoam cups with the bottoms cut out. Children turn cups upside down and move their puppets in and out of the burrow (cup).

Woodworking/Sand/Water
Wet Sand: Provide sand toys, cardboard or plastic tunnels (paper towel rolls), and small plastic bowls.

Printing
Provide a tray of sand for children to write these words using their fingers—hibernate, spring, winter, burrow, groundhog, and shadow.

Math/Language Arts
Animal Puzzles (C)   Light Bright (C)
My Shadow: Glue pictures of animals on a poster. Make black construction-paper shadows to cover animals. Children match shadows with pictures.

Science/Social Studies
Language Experience Notebook: Groundhog's Day.
Hang a sheet on the wall. Children make shadows using a film projector, flashlight, or overhead projector.

Dramatic Play
Children use puppets from the puppet show for their own puppet shows.

Outside Play Idea
Shadow Fun: Children try stepping on their own shadows and each other's shadows. Tell children to try outrunning shadows or making shadows tall and short.

More Group Time Activities
1. Song: "See My Shadow" (Tune: "Frere Jacques").
2. Read *Will Spring Be Early? or Will Spring Be Late?* by Crockett Johnson.
3. Share the book *Shadows Here, There, and Everywhere* by Ron and Nancy Goor. Demonstrate how to create some different shadow puppets. Provide materials to create shadow puppets. Leave the book and materials at an exploration center.
4. Poem: "Ground Hog Day" by Lilian Moore from *The Random House Book of Poetry for Children*.

Day 2: Magnets

Group Time Activities

1. Show a magnet and demonstrate what it will do.
2. Demonstrate what magnets will attract and will not attract.
3. Discover where the force of a magnet is strongest.
4. Demonstrate how the force of magnets can pass through materials that are not magnetic.
5. Read *Mickey's Magnet* by Franklyn Branley.

Learning Centers

Blocks

Instead of block play, provide balance boards and rollers for children to use.

Listening/Music/Reading

Provide recording and book *Mickey's Magnet* by Franklyn Branley.

Art

Easel Paint: red and black. (Leave out all week.)

String Painting: Provide string and trays of paint with a small amount of glue or liquid starch added. Children dip strings in paint and move them over paper to make designs.

Roll It On: Children paint on construction paper with roll-on deodorant bottles that have been cleaned and filled with thickened tempera paint.

Woodworking/Sand/Water

Water: Provide various magnetic objects and a variety of magnets. Allow children to discover if magnets work in water.

Printing

Children print in tray of clay using a nail. Print these words on the chalkboard—magnet, iron, poles, steel, and magnetism.

Math/Language Arts

Magnetic Letters and Shapes with Magnetic Board (C)

Magnasticks (C)　　　　　Magnetic Train (C)

Science/Social Studies

Provide a variety of objects and several magnets. Children divide objects into two groups—magnetic and nonmagnetic materials.

Dramatic Play

Provide housekeeping furniture, dishes, dress-up clothes, and magnets.

More Group Time Activities

1. Ask children to complete the statement "If I Were a Magnet, I'd..." Write children's ideas on a large poster.
2. Read *Look at Magnets* by Rena K. Kirkpatrick.

Day 3: How to Make Magnets

Group Time Activities

1. Discuss the meaning of the words *temporary* and *permanent*.
2. Demonstrate how to make temporary magnets from soft iron.
3. Read *Stepping Into Science: Magnets* by Illa Podendorf.
4. Make conclusions with the class about the kinds of materials that can be made into magnets.

Learning Centers

Blocks

Provide balance boards and rollers.

Listening/Music/Reading

Provide the recording and book *Mickey's Magnet* by Franklyn Branley. Add safety pins and magnets for children to use when the story is over.

Art

Chalk Painting: Children dip colored chalk in milk or water and draw pictures on construction paper.

Woodworking/Sand/Water

Sand: Hide metal bottle caps in sand. Children find caps using magnets.

Printing

Children print in a tray of clay with a nail. Print these words on the chalkboard—magnet, steel, iron, temporary, and permanent.

Math/Language Arts

Magnetic Letters and Shapes and Magnet Board (C)

Magnasticks (C)　　　　　Magnetic Train (C)

Science/Social Studies

Provide nails and permanent magnets. Encourage children to experiment with magnets.

Dramatic Play

Provide housekeeping furniture, dishes, dress-up clothes, and magnets.

More Group Time Activities

1. Language Experience Notebook: Magnets
2. Discuss the concept of first, second, and third in line. Children pretend the magnet you are holding is pulling them out of the line because of something in their pockets. "The magnet is attracting the second person in line. Oh, what should we do?"
3. Review *Mm*. Children can make *M's* with magnets.
4. Game: "Magnetism." Ask one child to be the magnet. That child winds around among the children and touches one child. The child the "magnet" touched is now magnetized. The two children hold hands and wind among the children until the second child touches a third child. Continue until all children are attached to the "magnet."

Day 4: Clocks and Watches

Group Time Activities

1. Use a manipulative clock to set times to the hour and discuss the concept of an hour.
2. Song: "Hickory, Dickory, Dock."
3. Children listen to a watch ticking.
4. Show pictures of a variety of clocks and famous clocks.

Learning Centers

Blocks

Provide pictures or real clocks for children to examine as they build with blocks.

Listening/Music/Reading

Record the song "Hickory, Dickory, Dock" on a cassette tape.

Art

Clocks: Provide paper plates, construction paper, and brads for children to make clocks.

Woodworking/Sand/Water

Provide screws, bolts, nuts, screwdrivers, and pieces of wood.

Printing

Arrange these words on a large circle to look like the numerals on a clock—clock, minute, time, second, and hour. Children spin the hand on the word clock to find which words to copy.

Math/Language Arts

Flannel Board Clock (C)   Clocks and Numerals (C)

Sorting: Children arrange Legos (C) from smallest to largest.

Science/Social Studies

Provide books and pictures of clocks and watches. Provide old watches and clocks so that children can examine the insides.

Dramatic Play

Provide housekeeping furniture, dishes, watches, clocks, dress-up clothes, timer, egg timer, and calendars.

More Group Time Activities

1. Film: *What Time Is It?*
2. Continue discussing the meaning of *first*, *second*, and *third*. Use a timer in the discussion. Pretend with children to be waiting to see something special. When the timer rings, the first person in line has a turn, then the second person, and so on.
3. Read *Clocks and More Clocks* by Pat Hutchins.
4. Song: "Paper Clock."

Day 5: Days and Months

Group Time Activities

1. Use calendar to discuss days of the week.
2. Discuss months of the year. Note birthdays and holidays in each month.

3. Film: *Calendar Bird.*
4. Review the letter *Yy*.

Learning Centers

Blocks

Add pictures of famous clocks.

Listening/Music/Reading

Add the chant "Wee Willie Winkie" from *Chants for Children* to the cassette tape.

Art

Painting: Provide water, paints, and construction paper for children to paint creatively.

Woodworking/Sand/Water

Sand: Provide a variety of plastic bottles with caps.

Printing

Arrange these words on a large circle to look like the numerals on a clock—months, weeks, days, and years. Children spin the clock hand to find words to copy.

Math/Language Arts

Flannel Board Calendar (C)   Clocks and Numerals (C)

Numerals and Pegs and Peg Boards (C)

Flannel Board Clock (C)

Science/Social Studies

Provide books and pictures of clocks, old watches, and egg timers.

Dramatic Play

Provide housekeeping furniture, dishes, watches, clocks, dress-up clothes, timer, egg timer, and calendars.

More Group Time Activities

1. Film: *Heather and the Haunted Hayloft.*
2. Play Rhyming Bingo (C) with the class.
3. Read *When Is Tomorrow?* by Nancy Watson.
4. Song: "Tick-Tock."

February
Week 2

Preparation:

▶ Plan a field trip to the local post office for Day 5. Ask each child to bring money to buy a stamp.

Post Office

Day 1: Mail Delivery

Group Time Activities

1. Discuss the history of mail delivery using the pony express and stage coach.
2. Discuss today's mail delivery methods and compare them to the early delivery methods.
3. Read *I Want to Be a Postman* by Carla Green.
4. Song: "The Mailman."

Learning Centers

Blocks

Provide pictures of a post office for children to look at while they are building with blocks. Encourage free construction all week.

Listening/Music/Reading

Provide cassette and book *A Letter to Amy* by Ezra Jack Keats.

Art

Mail Carrier Pouches: Children use construction paper, string, and a stapler to make mail pouches.

Woodworking/Sand/Water

Sand: Provide sand toys.

Printing

Print these words on envelopes—stagecoach, mail carrier, pony express, and delivery. Provide a list of children's names. Have children write letters or draw pictures for their classmates. Have these letters delivered in person or at the dramatic-play post office.

Math/Language Arts

Consonant Bingo (C)   Postal Truck Puzzle (C)

Deliver the Letter: Glue paper houses on a posterboard. Write a numeral on each house. Address envelopes to the houses by writing a number on them. Have children deliver the letters.

Science/Social Studies

Provide display of stamps, magnifying glasses, money, and books about stamps.

Dramatic Play

Set up a post office. Children use mail pouches made during art. Provide cardboard box with dividers. Write a child's name in each section of the box. As children write letters or draw pictures for their classmates, they can mail the letters at the post office. Children working at this center can sort and deliver mail. Provide ink pad, paper stamps, a date stamper, and a set of scales.

More Group Time Activities

1. Film: *Postal Workers*.
2. Review the letter *Ll*.
3. Read *The Jolly Postman or Other People's Letters* by Janet Ahlberg.
4. Chant: "Every Morning at Eight O' Clock" from *Chants for Children*.

Day 2: Our Post Office

Group Time Activities

1. Discuss the post office's outside appearance, such as flags, the words *U.S. Post Office*, mail boxes, and so on.
2. Discuss what people do at a post office, such as buy stamps, mail letters and packages, and so on.
3. Discuss machines in the post office.
4. Song: "The People in Your Neighborhood."

Learning Centers

Listening/Music/Reading

Record the songs "The People in Your Neighborhood" and "The Mailman" on a cassette tape.

Art

*Crayon Shavings (special project): Conduct this activity with a small group of children while others are working in learning centers. Using scissors, children scrape pink, red, and white crayon shavings on waxed paper. Place another piece of waxed paper on top of shavings. Cover with newspaper, and iron over paper until shavings melt. Help children cut their pictures into heart shapes. Tape hearts to window.

Woodworking/Sand/Water

Sand: Provide sand toys.

Printing

Print these words on envelopes and put them in a mailbag—U.S. Post Office, mail, cancelled stamp, postal worker, and weighing. Children remove one envelope at a time to copy.

Math/Language Arts

Design Cubes (C)   USA Puzzle (C)

Deliver the Letter (p. 85)

Science/Social Studies

Display stamps, magnifying glasses, and books about stamp collecting.

Dramatic Play

Have children to continue play using the post office.

More Group Time Activities

1. Film: *Our Post Office*.
2. Game: "Over-Under." Line up entire class. Children pass a letter over their heads and through their legs. Time the game. Try to beat the fastest time when playing again.
3. Game: "Itisket, Itasket." Children stand in a circle. "It" skips around the outside of circle while class sings the song. "It" drops letter behind a child's back. That child must pick up the letter and try to catch "It." "It" tries to get back to that child's place in line without getting caught. The child with the letter becomes the new "It."

Day 3: Letters and Addresses

Group Time Activities

1. Using an oversized paper envelope, discuss the parts of an address, return address, stamps, and zip code.
2. Discuss how the number and value of stamps is based on the weight of the letter. Show examples.
3. Discuss cancelled stamps, importance of zip codes, and addresses.
4. Read *A Letter to Amy* by Ezra Jack Keats.
5. Song: "The People in Your Neighborhood."

Learning Centers

Listening/Music/Reading

Children continue to listen to the recordings of songs about the post office.

Art

Mail a Valentine: Children make valentines to mail at the real post office on Day 5's field trip. Help children address envelopes. Each child picks out a classmate to receive his or her valentine. Be sure each child will receive a letter.

Woodworking/Sand/Water

Sand: Provide a variety of small plastic bags, such as Ziplock or sandwich bags.

Printing

Print one word on each envelope—letter, envelope, address, and zip code. Put envelopes in a mailbag for children to remove one at a time to copy. Children continue writing and mailing letters to friends.

Math/Language Arts

Design Cubes (C)   USA Puzzle (C)

Deliver the Letter (p. 85)

Science/Social Studies

Provide a set of scales, packages, and letters.

Dramatic Play

Encourage children to continue play using the post office.

More Group Time Activities

1. Model writing a postcard. Use the books *The Jolly Postman or Other People's Letters* by Janet Ahlberg and *Stringbean's Trip to the Shining Sea* by Vera B. Williams. Have postcards available in the post office.
2. Game: "I'm Lost." One child pretends to be lost. Another child pretends to be a police officer. The lost child tells his or her address to the police officer.
3. Read *The Merry Mailman* by Marcia Martin.
4. Game: "Itisket, Itasket."

Day 4: Abraham Lincoln's Birthday

Group Time Activities

1. Discuss Abraham Lincoln as our 16th president. Explain his accomplishments and tell his life story. Show children Lincoln's pictures on a penny, a five-dollar bill, and at the Lincoln Memorial.
2. Poem: "Lincoln's Birthday" from *Growing with Music*.
3. Sing "Happy Birthday" to Lincoln.

Learning Centers

Blocks

Provide pictures of Lincoln's log cabin.

Listening/Music/Reading

Provide books about President Lincoln.

Art

Penny Rubbings: Each child places paper over a penny and rubs a crayon over paper to make a print. Children make rubbings of the fronts and backs of the pennies. Cut out the coin rubbings and glue the two sides together.

Log Cabin Pictures: Children glue popsicle sticks on construction paper. Or, children turn cardboard lightbulb covers inside out, color the covers brown, and add a paper roof.

Woodworking/Sand/Water

Sand: Add small sticks.

Printing

Provide stamp kit and ink pads. Print these words on paper—Abraham Lincoln, Abe, February 12, and President.

Math/Language Arts

Lincoln and Valentine Puzzles (C)

Birthday Cakes (W)   Lincoln Logs (C)

Jars and Pennies: Write numerals on baby food jars. Children put correct number of pennies in each jar.

Science/Social Studies

Children examine old pennies, shiny pennies, and dirty pennies with magnifying glasses.

Dramatic Play

With brown paper, cover a large refrigerator box that has been cut open. Make Lincoln's log cabin by drawing logs on the brown paper. Add cardboard bricks, a candle, a wooden candle holder, small logs or long blocks, and several books.

More Group Time Activities

1. Film: *Lincoln*.
2. Game: "Penny, Penny, Who Has the Penny?" Two "Its" are needed. The other children sit in a circle. One "It" passes a penny to another child in the circle secretively. The second "It" tries to guess which child received the penny.

Day 5: Field Trip

Group Time Activities

1. Discuss appropriate behavior on the field trip. Instruct children to take their letters along with them to mail at the post office.
2. Review favorite songs learned this week about the post office.

Learning Centers

Blocks

Display pictures of the post office.

Listening/Music/Reading

Provide the book and cassette *A Letter to Amy* by Ezra Jack Keats.

Art

Mail Carrier Hats: Cut off a paper bag about four inches from the bottom. Add tape for each child to tape a blue visor to the front of the bag.

Woodworking/Sand/Water

Sand: Provide plastic bags.

Printing

Print these words on envelopes—letter, envelope, address, and zip code. Place envelopes in a mailbag. Children remove one at a time to copy.

Math/Language Arts

Design Cubes (C)   USA Puzzle (C)

Deliver the Letter (p. 85)

Science/Social Studies

Provide an assortment of stamps. Children find stamps that match.

Dramatic Play

Set up a post office.

More Group Time Activities

1. Language Experience Notebook: Post Office.
2. Write a thank-you letter with the children for the post office workers. Have each child sign the letter.

February
Week 3

Preparation:

▶ Ask several parents to come to the classroom for the Valentine's Day party to help children read their valentines.

▶ Invite some older elementary children to come and read with kindergarten children on Day 4.

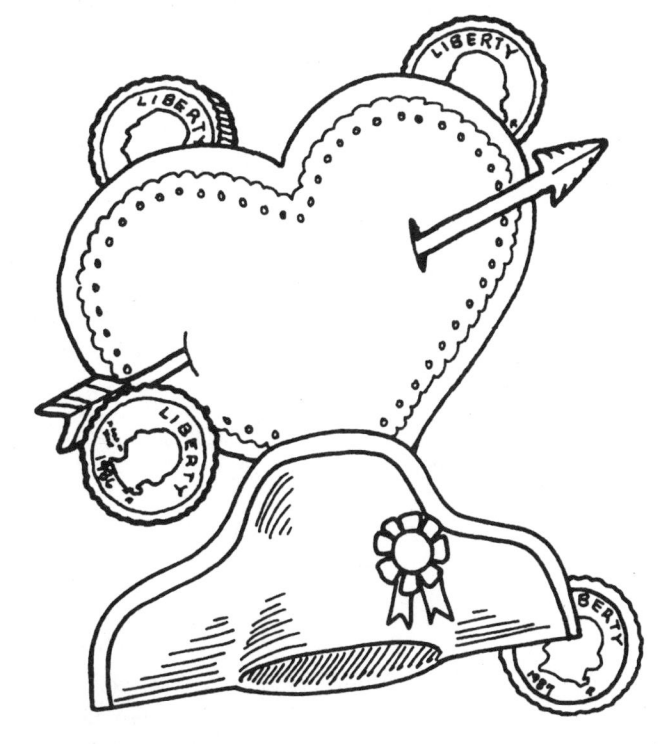

Valentine's Day/ Money/ George Washington

Day 1: Valentine's Day

Group Time Activities

1. Discuss Valentine's Day celebrations.
2. Read *The Valentine from Outer Space* by Linda Pike Hiller. Write the children's names backward on the board (as in the story) and see if the children can read the writing.
3. Song: "Valentine Song."
4. Film: *A Goofy Look at Valentine's Day.*

Learning Centers

Blocks

Instead of block play, use this area for the Valentine Beanbag Game. Paint a large box red. Cut out heart-shaped holes in the box for children to throw beanbags in.

Listening/Music/Reading

Record Valentine's Day songs on a cassette tape.

Art

Easel Paint: red and white. (Leave out all week.)

Valentine Holders: Each child cuts one paper plate in half and staples a half paper plate to a whole paper plate. Children then tie yarn bows at the top and color and decorate the holders.

Valentine Trees: Children cut out hearts to hang on a branch you've brought into the classroom. Spray paint the branch white.

Woodworking/Sand/Water

Add red food coloring in water trough and provide heart-shaped sponges. Or, fill the cleaned water trough with red fingerpaint.

Printing

Provide red clay in cookie sheet. Children use nails to write in the clay "I love you, Valentine."

Math/Language Arts

Red Ink Pad and Shape Stamps (C)

Valentine Puzzle (C)   Sharing Puzzle (C)

Textured Wallpaper Hearts: Cut out matching pairs of hearts from wallpaper samples. Children match hearts by texture.

Science/Social Studies

Display valentines and boxes of candy. Provide scales so that children can weigh and balance the boxes.

Dramatic Play

Children continue to mail valentines at the post office that was set up during the post office unit in Week 2 (p. 85).

More Group Time Activities

1. Game: "Musical Valentines." Tape paper hearts in a circle on the floor. Each child stands on a heart. Take one heart away. Play a record. Children walk around circle of hearts. When the music stops, the children must stand on a heart.
2. Game: "St. Valentine Says" (a version of "Simon Says").
3. Read *Bee My Valentine* by Miriam Cohen and *A Valentine Fantasy* by Carolyn Haywood.

Day 2: Valentine's Day Party

Group Time Activities

1. Discuss customs of Valentine's Day.
2. Fingerplay: "Five Valentines" from *Mitt Magic*.
3. Song: "Valentine's Song."
4. Discuss letter *Vv* and list words that begin with *Vv* on the chalkboard.
5. Write a story entitled "The Velvet Valentine" using *V* words.
6. Game: "Valentine, Valentine, Who's Got the Valentine?" Played like "Penny, Penny, Who's Got the Penny?" using a candy heart instead of a penny.

Learning Centers

Listening/Music/Reading

Record the Valentine's Day songs "Valentine Song" and "My Valentine" (Tune: "The Muffin Man").

Provide books *Arthur's Valentine* by Marc Brown, *Valentine Fantasy* by Carolyn Haywood, and *Little Love Story* by Fernando Krahn.

Art

Crown of Hearts: Children cut out construction-paper hearts and staple hearts to a paper headband.

Woodworking/Sand/Water

Water: Provide red water and heart-shaped sponges.

Printing

Provide a tray of red clay for children to print these words using a nail—Valentine's Day, love, and sweetheart.

Math/Language Arts

Heart Puzzle: Cut out and laminate a large paper heart. Cut it up to make a puzzle.

Addition Box: Use Valentine's Day candy.

Heart Cards: Cut playing cards so that the numeral is separated from the hearts. Children match the numeral to the correct heart card.

Science/Social Studies

Valentine Taste Center: Provide several candy hearts to taste. Pin a heart on each child that says, "I 8 a valentine."

Shades of Red: Cut up a red paint chart from a paint store. Each child places paint samples in order from darkest to lightest.

Dramatic Play

Children continue to mail valentines at the post office.

Snack Idea

Valentine's Day Party

More Group Time Activities

1. Game: "St. Valentine Says" (Simon Says).
2. Game: "Musical Valentines."
3. Ask parents who came to school to help the children open and read their valentines.

Day 3: Money

Group Time Activities

1. Discuss the history of money and how money is made.
2. Discuss and explain the process of writing checks.
3. Fingerplay: "One for the Money" from *Chants for Children*.

Learning Centers

Blocks

Provide pictures of banks, toy cars and trucks, and traffic signs.

Listening/Music/Reading

Record these songs on a cassette tape:

"A Penny Is One Cent"
(Tune: "Farmer in the Dell")
A penny is one cent.
A penny is one cent.
Oh yes, I know that.
A penny is one cent.
Second verse: A nickel is five cents.
Third verse: A dime is ten cents.

"Save Your Nickels"
(Tune: "Are You Sleeping")
Save your nickels.
Save your pennies.
In a bank.
In a bank.
Save all your money.
Save all your money.
In a bank.
In a bank.

Art

Banks: Children make piggy banks from oatmeal boxes, Band-Aid boxes, or soda pop cans. Use construction paper to decorate sides of the bank. Children can glue play coins or coin rubbings on the top and sides of the banks.

Woodworking/Sand/Water

*Woodworking: Provide bolts, boards, screws, nails, hammers, wrenches, and screwdrivers.

Printing

Provide crayons and paper. Print these words on the chalkboard—money, bank, checks, coins, and paper.

Math/Language Arts

Beginning Sounds: Write On Wipe Off Cards (C)

Addition Box: Use coins.

Jars and Pennies (p. 87)

Memory Game: Use coins.

Science/Social Studies

Provide money, money value charts, and books about money.

Dramatic Play

Set up a bank. Provide cash registers, play money, telephone, paper, pencils, and play checks.

More Group Time Activities

1. Read *Alexander, Who Used to Be Rich Last Sunday* by Judith Viorst.
2. *Cleaning Pennies (special project): Soak dirty pennies in solution of 4 T salt and 1/2 vinegar. Discuss with children the changes they observe.
3. Game: "Penny, Penny, Who Has the Penny?"
4. Review the letters *Nn* and *Qq*.
5. Fingerplay: "Five Little Pennies" from *Mitt Magic*.

Day 4: Money Values and the Bank

Group Time Activities

1. Discuss and show simple money values. Use real money.
2. Film: *Making Change for a Dollar.*
3. Discuss machines that take money, such as pay telephones and vending machines selling stamps or soft drinks.
4. Chant: "Miss Mary Mack, Mack, Mack" from *Chants for Children.*

Learning Centers

Blocks

Provide pictures of banks, toy cars and trucks, and traffic signs.

Listening/Music/Reading

Provide a cassette and read-along book of a favorite fairy tale.

Art

Making Money: Children make play money out of green construction-paper rectangles. Children make paper wallets by folding construction paper and stapling ends. Have the children write their names on the wallets.

Woodworking/Sand/Water

Water: Provide various pieces of wood. Encourage children to experiment to see if the different kinds of wood float or sink.

Printing

Provide crayons and paper. Print these words on the chalkboard—money, penny, coins, nickel, dollar, dime, cents, and quarter.

Math/Language Arts

Sorting: Sort pennies, nickels, dimes, quarters in bowls.

Sewing Cards (C)   Consonant Bingo (C)

Penny Puzzles   Jars and Pennies (p. 87)

Science/Social Studies

Provide display of money value charts, pictures of money used long ago, and books about money.

Dramatic Play

Encourage children to dramatize working in a bank.

More Group Time Activities

1. Have older elementary children read with individual children.
2. Review *Mm*.
3. Read *Annie's Spending Spree* by Nancy Watson and *Gogo's Pay Day* by Anne Rockwell.

Day 5: Washington's Birthday

Group Time Activities

1. Film: *George Washington's Birthday.*
2. Show pictures of Washington.
3. Discuss Washington's observed and official birthday (February 22, 1732).
4. Point out Washington's face on a dollar bill.

Learning Centers

Blocks

Provide pictures of the Washington Monument.

Listening/Music/Reading

Provide the Hap Palmer record *Patriotic and Morning Time Songs* and a variety of musical instruments.

Art

Cherry Trees: Children use a hole puncher to make red cherries. Provide toothpicks so that children can glue cherries to green construction-paper trees.

George Washington Hats: Children make three-sided George Washington hats from black construction paper.

Woodworking/Sand/Water

*Woodworking: Provide wood scraps, glue, hammers, and nails.

Printing

Provide typewriters. Print these words on the chalkboard— George Washington, president, cherry tree, and Martha.

Math/Language Arts

George Washington Puzzle (C)

Cherri-O Game (C)

Bingo (C): Use paper cherries as markers.

Puzzle of United States (C)

Science/Social Studies

Display stamps and currency with Washington's face on them, such as a quarter or a dollar bill. Display books and pictures about Washington.

Dramatic Play

Provide black coats and patriotic hats for dress-up. Provide a large box (buggy), stick horse, and housekeeping furniture.

More Group Time Activities

1. Give each child a cherry to eat. Write comments on butcher paper as children describe how the cherries taste.
2. Have the letters in George Washington's name printed on the board. See how many words can be made from his name.
3. Read *Washington's Birthday* by Clyde Bulla.
4. Poem: "Washington's Birthday" from *Growing with Music.*

February
Week 4

Preparation:

▶ Prepare a feelings chart. Each day as children arrive, have them draw a face showing how they feel beside their names.

Feelings

Day 1: Happy

Group Time Activities

1. Use first and last name cards.
2. Film: *Dealing With Feelings*.
3. Use pictures to discuss what makes everybody happy.
4. Discuss how yellow is associated with feeling happy.
5. Song: "Feelings."

Learning Centers

Blocks

Encourage free construction in the block center all week.

Listening/Music/Reading

Provide a favorite record or cassette.

Art

Easel Paint: yellow and pink.

Happy Creatures: Each child cuts out a yellow circle, draws a happy face, and attaches legs and arms with one paper fastener.

Woodworking/Sand/Water

Sand: Provide sifters, funnels, and plastic bowls.

Printing

Provide markers and paper. Print these words on the chalkboard—happy, fun, feelings, smile, glad, and excited.

Math/Language Arts

Circus Puzzles (C)   The Button Game (W)

Lemonade Stand Game (C)

Science/Social Studies

Children cut out magazine pictures of happy faces and glue them on a huge group mural.

Dramatic Play

Provide housekeeping furniture, dress-up clothes, toy telephone, dishes, empty food boxes, and dolls. Leave these materials out all week.

More Group Time Activities

Begin interviews with the children. Ask individual children about things that make them happy. Record each child's answer on cassette tapes. Listen to this tape on Day 5.

Day 2: Mad

Group Time Activities

1. Use first and last name cards.
2. Film: *Tell 'Em How You Feel*.
3. Discuss pictures and things that make us mad.
4. Discuss the difference between feeling mad at others and being mad at ourselves.
5. Discuss how to get over being mad. Talk about appropriate responses.
6. Discuss how red is associated with feeling mad.
7. Review letter *Ff*.

Learning Centers

Listening/Music/Reading

Provide the Hap Palmer record *Ideas, Thoughts, and Feelings*.

Art

Easel Paint: red.

Fingerpaint: Children fingerpaint on waxed paper using pudding colored with red food coloring.

Woodworking/Sand/Water

*Woodworking: Children pound out emotions. Provide a large tree stump or slice of a tree, nails, and hammers.

Printing

Provide markers and paper. Print these words on the chalkboard—mad, frustrated, angry, disgusted, furious, and upset.

Math/Language Arts

Let's Make Faces (C)   Match a Pair (C)

ABC Bingo (C)   Apple Tree Game (C)

Science/Social Studies

Children write about and draw pictures of what makes them mad. Give children magazines to cut out pictures of mad faces. Glue pictures on class mural.

More Group Time Activities

1. Continue interviewing children about their feelings. Record their comments.
2. Read *My Mean Old Mother Will Be Sorry* by Martha Alexander.
3. Song: "The Grouch Song."

Day 3: Scared

Group Time Activities

1. Use first and last name cards.
2. Film: *The Something*.
3. Discuss and list things that scare us.
4. Read *Where the Wild Things Are* by Maurice Sendak.
5. Review letter *Ff*.

Learning Centers

Listening/Music/Reading

Provide the cassette and book *Where the Wild Things Are* by Maurice Sendak.

Art

Easel Paint: yellow and black.

Bag Monsters: Provide small paper bags, newspaper for stuffing, construction paper, lace, yarn, and buttons. Children create monster puppets for a puppet show at group time.

Woodworking/Sand/Water

*Woodworking: Children build wooden monsters from wood scraps. Provide odd shapes of wood, glue, boards, nails, hammers, yarn, and buttons.

Printing

Provide markers and paper. Print these words on the chalkboard—scared, afraid, shocked, haunted, fear, and horrified.

Math/Language Arts

Let's Make Faces (C)   Crazy Animal Puzzles (C)

Snap and Play (C)   Light Bright (C)

Science/Social Studies

Children cut out magazine pictures of scared faces to glue on a class mural.

More Group Time Activities

1. Children use puppets they made in art for a puppet show.
2. Discuss what children can do when they are scared. Dramatize situations and discuss solutions.
3. Read *My Mama Says There Aren't Any Zombies, Ghosts, Vampires, Creatures, Demons, Monsters, Friends, Goblins, or Things* by Judith Viorst.
4. Review the letter *Aa*.

Day 4: Sad and Lonely

Group Time Activities

1. Use first and last name cards.
2. Use pictures to discuss things that make us sad.
3. Let children tell what makes them sad.
4. Song: "If You're Sad and You Know It" (Tune: "If You're Happy and You Know It").
5. Read *Alexander and the Terrible, Horrible, No Good, Very Bad Day* by Judith Viorst.
6. Film: *Blackberries in the Dark*.

Learning Centers

Listening/Music/Reading
Provide the record *Hap Palmer Sings Classic Nursery Rhymes*.

Art
Quilt: Give each child a square of cotton material. Each child draws his or her own picture using crayons on the material square. As children continue to work in the learning centers, iron the colored squares to set the designs. Save squares and sew them together as a quilt or wall hanging.

Woodworking/Sand/Water
*Woodworking: Children continue making wooden creatures.

Printing
Provide markers and paper. Print these words on the chalkboard—sad, unhappy, lonely, and sorry.

Math/Language Arts
Let's Make Faces (C)   Beetle Puzzle (C)

Snap and Play (C)

Patterns: Children make necklaces using Fruit Loops cereal and yarn.

Science/Social Studies
Children draw pictures of what makes them sad. Children look for pictures in magazines of things that make them sad. Have children cut out sad pictures and glue them on a class mural.

More Group Time Activities

1. Discuss what we can do when we are lonely.
2. Compare lonely feelings to times when we want to be alone. Discuss cubbies and other places where children can be alone in the classroom.
3. Read *Ira Sleeps Over* by Bernard Waber.
4. Put many objects that begin with *Ff* in a box. Each child takes out one object, identifies it, and tells what letter the word begins with.

Day 5: I Like Me

Group Time Activities

1. Song: "I Like Me."
2. Bring a mirror to group time. Children tell what they like about themselves as they look in the mirror.
3. Take a picture of the group.

Learning Centers

Quilt (Special Project): As the children work in learning centers today, sew the children's fabric squares together on a sewing machine. The children will enjoy watching the sewing machine work and seeing the squares become a quilt.

Listening/Music/Reading
Provide cassette tapes of children's interviews. Encourage all the children to listen to them.

Art
Painting: Children paint pictures and portraits of themselves using watercolor paints. Provide mirrors.

Woodworking/Sand/Water
*Woodworking: Provide hammers, nails, wood scraps, boards, and wood shavings for children to finish their wooden creatures.

Printing
Provide markers and paper. Print these words on the chalkboard—me, I like me, you, I like you, and myself.

Math/Language Arts
Fisher Price School Days Desk (C)

Snap and Play (C)   Number Bingo (C)

Plastic Links (C)

Science/Social Studies
Language Experience Notebook: Children draw pictures of what they like about themselves.

Provide a big box with a large hole cut in the side for a TV. Let children pretend to be on TV.

More Group Time Activities

1. Listen to the cassette tape of interviews with children.
2. Share some poems from *I Like You, If You Like Me: Poems of Friendship* by Myra Cohn Livingston.

February—
Additional Activities

- Provide non-fiction books about magnets for children to explore independently throughout this unit. Allow children to check these books out and bring home.

- Read *Magnets* by Irving and Ruth Adler.

- Begin to incorporate the use of a timer during learning-center time to expose children to some sense of time. Set the timer for various amounts of time, such as 5 minutes, 10 minutes, and so on. Tell the children how long the timer is set for so the children begin to grasp a sense of how long 5 or 10 minutes is.

- Point out when the clock is "on the hour." Explain the "hour hand." Make clocks from paper plates. Use brads and construction paper for the hour hand. Periodically have children display an "on the hour" time, such as 8 o'clock, 12 o'clock, and so on.

- Incorporate a basic calendar routine into your Group Time Activities. Include the day, date, month, and perhaps the concepts of yesterday, today, and tomorrow.

- Have children work in teams. Each team has a set of cards with the days of the week and months written on each. Set the timer and have each team put the days of the week and months in order. After the timer has rung, as a class, rearrange the cards in the correct order. A variation might include a whole group activity where each child is a specific day or month. The class works together to arrange themselves in the correct order by days or months.

- Assign roles in the class post office, such as postmaster, stamp checker, address checker, and so on. Have each child take a turn playing one of the roles during this unit.

- Make individual mailboxes from 1/2 gallon milk containers. Have the children decorate and write their names on their mailboxes. Place the mailboxes in the class post office that was set up in Week 2 (p. 85).

- Have the children write postcards to Abraham Lincoln or George Washington asking questions or telling one thing the children admire about the two former presidents.

- Poem: "Lincoln" by Lilian Moore from *The Random House Book of Poetry for Children*.

- Poem: "Washington" by Nancy Byrd Turner from *The Random House Book of Poetry for Children*.

- Make "heart people." Provide heart patterns of various sizes and pink, red, and white construction paper. Use a large heart for the body and smaller hearts for the head, arms, and legs. Explain how "arms" and "legs" attach to body with thin rectangular strips of construction paper folded accordian style. Have a sample at this station. Encourage children to make their own creations, as well.

- Share a Valentine's song and dance: "Masked Valentines" from *Holiday Singing & Dancing Games* by Esther L. Nelson (pp. 11-13).

- Read *A Valentine For You* by Wendy Watson.

- Read *Secret Valentine* by Catherine Stock.

- Read *The Best Valentine in the World* by Marjorie Weinman Sharmat.

- Read *Berenstain Bears' Trouble With Money* by Stan Berenstain.

- Read *The Monster Money Book* by Loreen Leedy.

- Read *Dollars and Cents for Harriet* by Betsy Maestro.

- Make a simple gameboard with a path leading from start to finish. In each box on the path, make a face depicting happy, sad, mad, or scared. Each child rolls the dice and moves marker to appropriate box. Child can then share a particular time when he or she experienced the same feelings as shown in the box.

- Tell and tape record a scary class story. Brainstorm scary words and ideas about what makes a story scary. Before recording, discuss the main character, outline a simple plot, and have conclusion decided upon. Leave this recording out at the listening station.

- Make "happy" coupons. Give each child a specific number of coupons to give away. Encourage the children to give out coupons to classmates after someone has done something to make them happy. The child giving the coupon should tell the other child what he or she did to make him or her feel happy. Follow up on some of these exchanges at next group time.

- Read *If I Ran the Family* by Lee and Sue Kaiser Johnson.

- Read *Sometimes I Feel Like a Mouse* by Jeanne Modesitt.

- Read *I Was So Mad* by Mercer Mayer.

- Read *Caring Is What Counts* by Ward Johnson.

- Songs: "Seven Days in a Week" (Tune: "For He's a Jolly Good Fellow"). *More Piggyback Songs*. Everett, WA: Warren Publishing House, 1984.

   "Count the Day" (Tune: Twinkle, Twinkle Little Star"). *More Piggyback Songs*. Everett, WA: Warren Publishing House, 1984.

   "George Washington" (Tune: "Yankee Doodle"). *More Piggyback Songs*. Everett, WA: Warren Publishing House, 1984.

   "Washington the Great." *The Holiday Song Book*. New York, NY: Lothrop, Lee & Shepard Company, 1977.

   "Everybody Has Feelings." *Hap Palmer Favorites—Songs for Learning Through Music and Movement*. Sherman Oaks, CA: Alfred Publishing Co., 1981

March
Week 1

Preparation:

▶ Plan a field trip for Day 4 to a rock museum, archaeological museum, gravel company, or even to a driveway full of rocks.

Rocks, Minerals, and Fossils

Group Time Activities

1. Display some rocks and discuss what they are made of. Give each child a cookie to eat. Discuss how a rock is like a cookie. It's made of many different ingredients that are mixed together. Discuss how the earth and moon are made of rocks.
2. Discuss sizes, shapes, colors, and textures of rocks. Write the following describing words—smooth, shiny, flat, and brown—on paper and post in the room for children to refer to and incorporate in their language experiences this week.
3. Demonstrate how to use a scale and magnifying glass.
4. Discuss different meanings of the word *rock*, such as stones, rock music, rock back and forth, and discuss uses of rocks.
5. Review the letter *Rr*.

Learning Centers

Blocks

Instead of block play, provide three roller boards for children to find ways of rocking back and forth.

Listening/Music/Reading

Record the song "I Don't Want to Live On the Moon."

Art

Easel Paint: brown, red, and yellow. (Leave out all week.)

Pet Rocks: Children glue felt on the bottom of large rocks and paint rocks with watercolors. Provide Q-Tips to use for painting instead of paintbrushes.

Woodworking/Sand/Water

Sand: Provide pocketscopes (C) or magnifying glasses, funnels, tunnels, a sand wheel, a sand bucket, and small shovels.

Printing

Provide a tray of sand. Print these words on the chalkboard—rocks, scale, arrowhead, sand, and mineral.

Math/Language Arts

Estimating Game: Provide a quart jar full of rocks. Each child puts his or her name on a piece of paper with an estimate of the number of rocks in the jar. At group time, check the estimates with the class to see who guessed the closest. Do this activity each day this week. Change the number each day.

Science/Social Studies

Display rocks. Provide scales, buckets, and magnifying glasses.

Dramatic Play

Provide a large box, such as a freezer box. Children can color or paint the sides of the box to resemble the Flintstones' rock house. Provide a stuffed dinosaur and other boxes of different sizes. Leave out all week.

More Group Time Activities

1. Check the Estimating Game.
2. Film: *What's Under the Earth*.
3. Discuss words with rock in them (rocket, rocker, rock candy, rock-a-bye).
4. Game: "Drop the Rock." Play like "Drop the Handkerchief." Children stand in a circle. "It" skips around the outside of circle and drops a small rock behind another child's back. That child picks up the rock and chases "It" around the circle. "It" tries to get back to that child's place without getting caught. That child is the new "It."

Day 2: Minerals

Group Time Activities

1. Review the "cookie" concept that rocks are a combination of substances. Rocks are made of many ingredients called *minerals*.
2. Discuss what a mineral is. Use the book *Rocks and Minerals: A New True Book* by Illa Podendorf as a guide.
3. Show pictures of minerals and show examples.
4. Crystal Experiment: Combine 6 T water, 1 T ammonia, 6 T laundry bluing, and 6 tsp salt. Pour over 6 pieces of charcoal. Put in warm place and watch crystals grow during the next few days. Discuss how minerals are made of crystals. Keep out of children's reach.

Learning Centers

Blocks

Display pictures of rock museums, caves, mountains, and other pictures of places where rocks are found.

Listening/Music/Reading

Make a recording of "Rock-a-Bye Baby."

Art

Sand Designs: Children draw designs on construction paper. Children put glue on the lines of the designs, shake sand on top of the glue, let sit for a few seconds, then shake excess sand off.

Woodworking/Sand/Water

Water: Provide a bucket of rocks.

Printing

Provide a tray of sand. Print these words on the chalkboard—rock, salt, fossil, coal mine, and mineral.

Math/Language Arts

Sesame Street Puzzles (C)   Rubber Band Boards (C)

Estimating Game (p. 96)

Fisher Price School Days Desk (C): Make new cards to be used with the Fisher Price Deck of Words (C) that pertain to the rock unit. Children match the magnetic letters to the letters in the new cards.

Science/Social Studies

Provide display of rocks, minerals, magnifying glasses, scale, and books about rocks. Provide sandstone rocks. Let children rub them together to make sand.

Rough/Smooth Game: Children sort rocks (rough and smooth). This game could be modified to sort rocks based on any property, such as color, size, shape, and so on.

More Group Time Activities

1. Song: "I Don't Want to Live on the Moon."
2. Write a class story about Robbie Ringo using *Rr* words.
3. Game: "Drop the Rock."
4. Check the Estimating Game (p. 96).

Day 3: Fossils

Group Time Activities

1. Show real fossils and pictures of fossils.
2. Use playdough to show how a fossil is made.
3. Explain what a paleontologist is.
4. Rock Candy: Combine 1 c water, 2 c sugar, 1 c Karo syrup, 1/4 tsp vanilla flavoring, and 1/4 tsp food coloring. Boil on a hot plate until it spins a thread. Pour into a buttered pan. After candy cools and hardens, cut into pieces using a scissors.

Learning Centers

Blocks

Add pictures of places where fossils have been found.

Listening/Music/Reading

Provide a recording of the song "Rockin' Hula" from *Hap Palmer: Feelin' Free.* This song requires movement, so you will not want to use headsets.

Art

Fossils: Provide clay for children to make fossils using seashells.

Woodworking/Sand/Water

Wet Sand: Children make fossil prints with shells, rocks, or other items.

Printing

Provide a tray of sand. Print these words on the chalkboard—rocks, prints, minerals, stone, and fossil.

Math/Language Arts

Dinosaur Puzzles (C)

Feed the Dinosaur: Put small plastic dinosaurs in upside-down cherry tomato baskets. Write a numeral on each basket. Provide small green paper leaves. Children feed the dinosaurs the correct number of leaves.

Sorting: Children arrange rocks in order from smallest to largest.

Science/Social Studies

Provide display of rocks, fossils, and minerals. Provide a large cookie sheet with a thin layer of clay in it. Provide cleaned turkey or chicken bones. Children arrange the bones on the clay like dinosaur bones.

More Group Time Activities

1. Check results from the Estimating Game (p. 96).
2. Use tray of objects for visual recall. Remove an object. Ask children to recall the missing object.
3. Children imitate an object that has movable parts. Other children guess what each child is imitating.
4. Discuss the importance of rocks. Long ago, rocks were used to skin animals, build fires, and make tools. Today, rocks are used to build roads and buildings. Rocks provide pencil lead, salt, lime, aluminum, borax, and jewelry.

Day 4: Field Trip

Group Time Activities

1. Introduce and discuss museums. Discuss appropriate behavior in museums.
2. Read *Lost in the Museum* by Miriam Cohen.

Learning Centers

Blocks
Provide three roller boards for children to explore ways of rocking back and forth.

Listening/Music/Reading
Record the songs "Big Beautiful Planet" and "I Don't Want to Live on the Moon."

Art
Gems: Children draw pictures of mineral mines on black construction paper. Provide sequins for children to glue on the pictures to represent valuable minerals.

Woodworking/Sand/Water
*Woodworking: Provide small hammers, a small amount of sand, and small rocks for children to break rocks into smaller pieces.

Printing
Provide a tray of sand. Print these words on the chalkboard—rocks, scale, arrowhead, sand, and mineral.

Math/Language Arts
Estimating Game (p. 96)   Dinosaur Puzzles (C)

Feed the Dinosaur (p. 97)

Science/Social Studies
Provide a display of rocks and books about rocks.

More Group Time Activities

1. Write a class thank-you letter to the museum personnel who allowed you to visit.
2. Language Experience Notebook: Rocks.
3. Check the results from the Estimating Game (p. 96).

Day 5: Numbers (Just for a change!)

Group Time Activities

1. Read *Count and See* by Tana Hoban.
2. Chant: "Five Little Monkeys Jumping on the Bed" from *Chants for Children*.
3. As a class, make a list of reasons why numbers are important.
4. Put a masking-tape hopscotch game on the floor. Have each child take a turn.

Learning Centers

Blocks
Provide roller boards.

Listening/Music/Reading
Add any songs with the word *rock* in them to the cassette.

Art
Create Your Own: Provide bottle caps, confetti, construction paper, and material scraps for children to use for free and creative art.

Woodworking/Sand/Water
Sand: Provide rocks and several sand buckets that have been labeled with a numeral. Children put the correct number of rocks in each bucket.

Printing
Provide a tray of sand. Print these words and numerals on the chalkboard—one, 1, two, 2, three, 3, four, 4, and five, 5.

Math/Language Arts
Hopscotch

Addition Box: Use rocks.

The Nail Board (W)   Number Bingo (C)

Science/Social Studies
Allow experimentation with rocks using a pan of water, a pan of sand, and a balance scale.

More Group Time Activities

1. Make large cardboard dice. Each child rolls the dice and counts the dots. The child then counts out that number of rocks.
2. Read *One Little Kitten* by Tana Hoban.
3. Chant: "One, Two, Buckle My Shoe" from *Chants for Children*.
4. Song: "Song of Five."
5. Check the results from the Estimating Game (p. 96).

March
Week 2

Preparation:

▶ Plan to dye Easter eggs on Day 1 Either boil the eggs in the classroom or ask each child to bring 4-6 hard-boiled eggs from home.

▶ Invite a Jewish family or members of the Jewish community to share their Passover practices. Plan for Day 3.

▶ Plan to have a Spring party on Day 5.

Spring Holidays

Day 1: Easter Customs

Group Time Activities

1. Discuss Easter customs around the world.
2. Review the process of how an egg gets from a farm, to the grocery store, to a home.
3. Put a hard-boiled egg in a jar of clean, unsalted water. Add 1/2 c salt to another jar of water. Put an egg in the salty water. Discuss what happens.
4. Review the meaning of the word *dozen*.
5. Talk about the process of dyeing eggs.
6. Read *The Easter Bunny That Overslept* by Otto and Priscilla Friedrick.

Learning Centers

Blocks

Provide stuffed farm animals for children to use while building with blocks. Leave out all week.

Listening/Music/Reading

Provide the cassette and book *Seven Diving Ducks* by Margaret Friskey.

Art

Easel Paint: yellow, white, and pink. (Leave out all week.)

Easter Eggs (special project): While the class works in the learning centers, dye Easter eggs with six children at a time at the art center. Save the dyed eggs in the cafeteria refrigerator for the egg hunt on Day 5.

Woodworking/Sand/Water

Wet Sand: Provide plastic eggs of several different sizes.

Printing

Provide stamp kits. Children make pictures of chicks and ducks using fingerprints. Print these words on the chalkboard—Easter eggs, chicks, ducks, and dozen.

Math/Language Arts

Chicken and Egg Sequence Puzzle (C)

Bacon and Eggs (WII)   Easter Baskets (W)

Egg Carton Eggs: Children make a dozen paper eggs out of construction paper for their own egg cartons.

Science/Social Studies

Provide a hard-boiled egg, one jar of clean water, two spoons, and one jar of water with 1/2 c salt added to it. Children continue with the experiment that you introduced at group time.

Dramatic Play

Provide housekeeping furniture, dress-up clothes, plastic Easter eggs, Easter egg baskets, and a stuffed Easter rabbit. Leave out all week.

More Group Time Activities

1. Game: "Easter Egg March." (Played like "Musical Chairs.")
2. Read *Daddy Long Ears* by Robert Kraus.
3. Talk with children about how to tell if an egg has been boiled or not. Let children experiment with a raw egg and a hard-boiled egg to discover which one has been cooked. (The boiled egg will spin.)

Day 2: Meaning of Easter

Group Time Activities

1. Fingerplay: "Easter Rabbits" from *Mitt Magic*.
2. Let children tell what Easter means to them.
3. Using the book *Lilies, Rabbits, and Painted Eggs: The Story of the Easter Symbols* by Edna Barth, discuss and explain some of the symbols of Easter.

Learning Centers

Listening/Music/Reading
Provide a favorite Easter record.

Art
Easter Pictures: Children make grass out of green construction paper and glue it on a larger piece of construction paper. Children can make paper eggs, paper flowers, and cottonball bunnies to add to the picture.

Woodworking/Sand/Water
Sand: Provide paper or plastic carrots and paper garden signs. On each sign, draw a carrot and write a numeral. Have children plant the correct number of carrots in each row.

Printing
Provide stamp pads. Ask children to make pictures of chicks, ducks, and rabbits using fingerprints. Print these words on the chalkboard—rabbits, eggs, spring, yellow, pink, and celebrate.

Math/Language Arts
Easter Baskets (W)

Sandpaper Letters and Blindfolds (C)

Pegs and Peg Number Board (C)

Let's Make Faces (C)

Color and Shape Bingo (C)

Science/Social Studies
Humpty Dumpty Egg: Provide a picture of Humpty Dumpty that has been cut into puzzle pieces. Children put Humpty back together again. Display pictures of and books about animals that hatch from eggs.

More Group Time Activities

1. Hide paper carrots or eggs in the room. Give each child a paper with a numeral on it. Children find that number of carrots or eggs.
2. Game: "Pin the Tail On the Rabbit." Use white paper circles, and play the game like "Pin the Tail On the Donkey."
3. Have an Easter parade. Children can dress up and give each child a musical instrument to play. Children march around the classroom to Easter music.
4. Read *Jennie's Hat* by Ezra Jack Keats.
5. Review the letter *Jj*.

Day 3: Passover

Group Time Activities

1. Invite the guest speaker(s) to share their Passover experiences. Encourage the guest speaker to explain the history of Passover and the symbolism of matzoh.
2. Read *My First Passover* by Tomie dePaola.
3. Discuss and explain the Seder meal and the Haggadah.
4. Ask how many children in the class are the youngest in the family. Explain the Passover custom of the youngest child asking the four questions about the meaning of the holiday.
5. Song: "Preparing for Seder."

Learning Centers

Listening/Music/Reading
Provide the recording and book *I Love Passover* by Marilyn Hirsh.

Woodworking/Sand/Water
Wet Sand: Provide plastic eggs of several different sizes.

Printing
Provide stamp pads. Print these words on the chalkboard—Passover, matzoh, Seder, Haggadah, and egg.

Math/Language Arts
Spring Puzzles (C)   Color and Shape Bingo (C)

Pegs and Peg Number Board (C)

Science/Social Studies
Discuss the foods of the Seder meal. Talk about the symbolism of the egg. Provide a large sheet of paper for a mural of "Egg Land." Children draw an egg village by drawing everything egg shaped, such as egg houses, egg cars, and egg-shaped people.

Dramatic Play
Children play in "green land." Provide as may green objects as possible.

More Group Time Activities

1. Passover Song and Dance: "Dayenu" *Holiday Singing & Dancing Games* by Esther L. Nelson (pp. 24-27).
2. Review the letter *Pp*.

Day 4: Rabbits

Group Time Activities

1. Discuss rabbits with the children—food, environment, and so on. Show children pictures of different varieties of rabbits. If possible, have a guest speaker visit the classroom to talk about how to care for rabbits.
2. Song: "Here Comes Peter Cottontail." Let one child be Peter and hop down the bunny trail.
3. Read *The Tale of Peter Rabbit* or *The Tale of Benjamin Bunny* by Beatrix Potter.

Learning Centers

Listening/Music/Reading

Record songs about rabbits, such as "Here Comes Peter Cottontail," on a cassette tape.

Provide the recording and book *The Runaway Bunny* by Margaret Wise Brown.

Art

Cottontail Rabbits: Encourage children to cut out rabbit shapes from wallpaper samples. Use cottonballs to make tails. Glue the wallpaper rabbits on construction paper.

Woodworking/Sand/Water

Wet Sand: Provide plastic eggs of different sizes. Encourage children to use two fingers to hop in the sand like rabbits.

Printing

Print these words on little pieces of paper—rabbit, bunny, cottontail, hop, ears, and so on. Place the words inside plastic eggs and arrange the eggs in a basket. Have several children pick out words for the class to copy.

Math/Language Arts

Easter Rabbit Puzzle (C)   Color and Shape Bingo (C)

Number Lotto (C)   Number Bingo (C)

Science/Social Studies

Discuss how rabbits hop. Rabbits use their front legs for balance and their back legs to hop. Show the children pictures of rabbit footprints. Encourage children to look for rabbit footprints in their own yards.

More Group Time Activities

1. Read *Bunnies, Bunnies, Bunnies* from Silver Press.
2. Review the letter *Ee*.
3. Teach the children the dance the "bunny hop." Provide music for the children to "bunny hop."

Day 5: Spring Party

Group Time Activities

1. Game: "Egg Roll." Provide large, plastic eggs. Children try to roll their eggs on the floor using only their noses.
2. Passover Song and Dance: "Dayenu" *Holiday Singing & Dancing Games* by Esther L. Nelson (pp. 24-27).
3. Game: "Egg in a Spoon." Each child tries to walk around the classroom while carrying an egg on a spoon without dropping it. This activity could be set up in a relay format.
4. Read *The Bunny Who Found Easter* by Charlotte Zolotow.

Learning Centers

Listening/Music/Reading

Record the Easter songs "Easter Basket," "Itisket, Itasket" and Passover songs "Preparing for Seder," and "Dayenu" on a cassette tape.

Art

Bunny Ears: Children draw, cut out, and staple bunny ears on a headband to be used during next group time while doing the "Bunny Hop."

Woodworking/Sand/Water

Provide dried kidney beans instead of sand. Provide large plastic Easter eggs and Easter baskets.

Printing

Provide stamp pads. Children make pictures of chicks, ducks, and rabbits using fingerprints. Print these words on the chalkboard—rabbit, Peter, and cottontail.

Math/Language Arts

Easter Puzzles (C)   Color and Shape Bingo (C)

Nutrition Game (C)   Easter Baskets (W)

Science/Social Studies

In separate bowls, display an eggshell, a boiled egg that has been cut into pieces, a raw egg that has been cracked open, and a scrambled egg. Provide magnifying glasses.

Outside Play Idea

Egg Hunt

Snack Idea

Spring Party

More Group Time Activities

1. Read *It's the Easter Beagle Charlie Brown*, by Charles Schulz.
2. Game: "Peter Rabbit." Children hold hands in a circle. One child is Peter on the inside of the circle. One child is Mr. McGregor on the outside of the circle. "Mr. McGregor" tries to get into the circle to get "Peter." Children must hold hands tightly and not let "Mr. McGregor" in.
3. Fingerplay: "Easter Eggs" from *Mitt Magic*.
4. Teach children how to do the "Bunny Hop."

March
Week 3

St. Patrick's Day/Good Manners

Day 1: St. Patrick's Day

Group Time Activities

1. Introduce the country of Ireland, and locate it on the globe or map.
2. Discuss St. Patrick, St. Patrick's Day in the United States and Ireland, and its customs.
3. Show pictures of shamrocks. Go outside with the class and pick clover, if possible.
4. Review *Pp*.

Learning Centers

Blocks

Allow free play all week. Display pictures of shamrocks.

Listening/Music/Reading

Record the song "Rig-a-Jig-Jig" on a cassette tape.

Art

Easel Paint: green and yellow. (Leave out all week.)

Shamrock Prints: Children make shamrock prints using thumbprints. Provide green ink, stamp pads, and construction paper.

Woodworking/Sand/Water

Water: Allow children to mix colors. Provide white egg cartons, three jars of colored water (primary colors), and medicine droppers. Children use medicine droppers to mix colors in the egg cartons. Have children see how many different colors they can make.

Printing

Provide typewriters. Print these words on the chalkboard— St. Patrick's Day, shamrock, March 17, clovers, and Ireland.

Math/Language Arts

Sesame Street Puzzles (C)	Let's Make Faces (C)
Strawberries (WII)	Animal Habitat (W)

Science/Social Studies

Language Experience Notebook: Children draw pictures of Ireland's flag.

Shamrocks: Provide green construction paper and patterns of shamrocks for children to trace.

Dramatic Play

Set up a shoemaker shop. Provide a bench, small table and chairs, hammers, rulers, paper, pencils, and many, many shoes.

More Group Time Activities

1. Film: *Rumpelstiltskin*.
2. Film: *The Elves and the Shoemaker*.
3. Read *Little Bear Marches in St. Patrick's Day Parade* by Janice Brustlein.

Day 2: Leprechauns

Group Time Activities

1. Discuss and show pictures of leprechauns.
2. Songs: "I'm a Little Leprechaun" (Tune: "I'm a Little Teapot") and "Leprechaun's March" (Tune: "Twinkle, Twinkle Little Star").
3. Make green Jell-O with the class. Pour into shamrock-shaped pans to gel. Have class go with you to the cafeteria to put the Jell-O in the refrigerator. Eat it at snack time.

Learning Centers

Listening/Music/Reading

Provide a favorite recording.

Art

Shamrock Masks: Provide large shamrock patterns, green construction paper, and yarn. Each child traces and cuts out two shamrocks. Then the child cuts an eye hole in each shamrock. Use yarn to tie mask on the face.

Woodworking/Sand/Water

Water: Children continue mixing colors.

Printing

Provide typewriters. Print these words on the chalkboard—St. Patrick, jelly, leprechaun, and green.

Math/Language Arts

Clocks and Numbers (C)   Numbers, Pegs, and Peg Board (C)

Around The World Lotto (C)   First-Sound Sorting Box (W)

Science/Social Studies

Provide clover, grass, and leaves. Children examine these items using pocketscopes or magnifying glasses.

Dramatic Play

Shoemaker shop.

More Group Time Activities

1. Game: "Rhyming Bingo."
2. Make a list of *Pp* words.
3. Read *The Hungry Leprechaun* by Mary Calhoun.
4. Fingerplay: "Shamrocks" from *Mitt Magic*.

Day 3: School Manners

Group Time Activities

1. Discuss good school manners and make a list of children's ideas on butcher paper.
2. Read *That's Mine!* by Elizabeth Winthrop.
3. Review the letter *Mm*.

Learning Centers

Listening/Music/Reading

Provide the Hap Palmer record *Learning Basic Skills Through Music—Health and Safety*.

Art

Language Experience Notebook: Children draw pictures about school manners.

Woodworking/Sand/Water

Water: Provide straws and kitchen utensils.

Printing

Provide typewriters. Print these words on the chalkboard—"Excuse me," "I'm sorry," "Thank you," "No thank you," and "Please."

Math/Language Arts

Light Bright (C)   Legos (C)

Bacon and Eggs (WII)

Sorting: Provide a bucket of objects. Children sort objects according to shape.

Science/Social Studies

Provide several types of scales and a basket of objects.

Dramatic Play

Set up a shoe store. Provide many pairs of shoes and purses. Also, provide a toy cash register, play money, shoeboxes, paper bags, and chairs.

More Group Time Activities

1. Game: "Rhyming Bingo."
2. Film: *Little Red Riding Hood*.
3. Song: "Courtesy Song."
4. Review the letter *Kk*.

Day 4: Verbal Manners

Group Time Activities

1. Children suggest good verbal manners. Write the words on the chalkboard.
2. Read *Manners Can Be Fun* by Munro Leaf.
3. Song: "Courtesy Song."

Learning Centers

Listening/Music/Reading

Provide the Hap Palmer record *Learning Basic Skills Through Music—Health and Safety.*

Art

Children make people puppets out of construction paper and popsicle sticks or straws. Encourage children to present a puppet show about good manners in group time.

Woodworking/Sand/Water

Water: Add plastic bottles with caps.

Printing

Provide letter stamps and ink pads. Print these words on the chalkboard—"Please," "Thank you," "Excuse me," and "I'm sorry."

Math/Language Arts

Lincoln Logs (C)   Tinker Toys (C)

Large/Small Sort: Provide a bucket of objects. Children sort objects according to size.

Smooth/Rough Sort: Provide a shoebox of rocks. Children sort the rocks according to smoothness or roughness.

Science/Social Studies

Provide several types of scales and a bucket of objects.

Dramatic Play

Shoe Store

More Group Time Activities

1. Children give a puppet show using puppets from art.
2. Flannel Story: *Hansel and Gretel.*
3. Song: "Courtesy Song."
4. Review the letter *Kk*.

Day 5: Table Manners

Group Time Activities

1. Song: "The Mulberry Bush."
2. Ask children to role-play good table manners using puppets, a table, utensils, and napkins.

Learning Centers

Listening/Music/Reading

Provide a favorite record.

Art

Paper-Towel Art: Each child folds a paper towel as many times as desired and dips the corners in bowls of food coloring. The child then unfolds the paper towel and places it on newspaper to dry. Hang paper towels on a clothesline in the room for display.

Woodworking/Sand/Water

Water: Provide a bucket of objects for children to discover which ones float and which ones sink.

Printing

Provide letter stamps and ink pads. Print these words on the chalkboard—fork, napkin, knife, spoon, and "thank you."

Math/Language Arts

Legos (C)   Rough/Smooth Sort

Snap and Play (C)   Sesame Street Puzzles (C)

Science/Social Studies

Provide pictures of different ways to set a table. Provide a few plastic dishes. Encourage children to practice setting the table.

Dramatic Play

Provide table, chairs, utensils, dishes, and napkins.

More Group Time Activities

1. Read *A, B, See* by Tana Hoban.
2. Review left and right.
3. Sing favorite songs learned this year.

March
Week 4

Preparation:

▶ Paint or draw a large tree to put on the wall. Children will add popcorn "buds" to the tree on Day 1.

Spring

Group Time Activities

1. Discuss and show pictures of signs of spring, such as warmer temperatures, rain, trees budding, wind, and so on.
2. "What causes spring?" Use the globe to explain.
3. Song: "Kite Song."
4. Pop some popcorn with the class, and compare the popcorn to the budding of tree leaves and blossoms.
5. Song: "Popcorn" (Tune: "Frere Jacques").

Learning Centers

Blocks
Provide spring pictures for children to observe while building with blocks.

Listening/Music/Reading
Record the song "Popcorn" on a cassette tape. Provide books about spring for children to look at or read.

Art
Easel Paint: green, yellow, and pink. (Leave out all week.)

Popcorn Trees: Children cut brown tree trunks out of construction paper and glue on a sheet of blue construction paper. Children glue popcorn on the paper trees to represent buds.

Woodworking/Sand/Water
Sand: Provide plastic flowers and a water can.

Printing
Provide small chalkboards and chalk. Print these words on the chalkboard—buds, spring, green, rain, and wind.

Math/Language Arts
Tree Puzzle (C)	Sequence Season Puzzle (C)
Tulip Puzzle (C)	Four Seasons Puzzle (C)

Science/Social Studies
Children cut spring pictures out of magazines and make a class mural entitled "Signs of Spring."

Dramatic Play
Provide spring cleaning items, such as a broom, dust pan, rags, and a bucket of soapy water. Leave out all week.

More Group Time Activities

1. Children dramatize what to do in windy, stormy, and rainy spring weather.
2. Explain the saying "March comes in like a lion, out like a lamb."
3. Read *Leo the Late Bloomer* by Robert Kraus.
4. Read *Jennie's Hat* by Ezra Jack Keats.

Day 2: Spring Plants

Group Time Activities

1. Use the globe to review the cause of spring.
2. Song: "Big Beautiful Planet."
3. Use charts to discuss plant parts. Discuss why there's new growth in spring.
4. Plant seeds in two containers. Place one in light and water it. Place one in the dark without water. Tell children to observe over a period of time.
5. Discuss germination and place some seeds on wet paper towels. Have children watch for growth during the day.
6. Song: "Rain Falls."

Learning Centers

Blocks

Provide pictures of spring.

Listening/Music/Reading

Add the spring songs "Kite Song" and "Rain Falls" to the cassette tape.

Art

Egg-Carton Flowers: Give each child an egg-carton cup. Have children slit the egg-carton sides and fold out. Tell children to insert pipe cleaners in the center of the egg cartons for stems. Children make several different egg-carton flowers.

Daffodil Art: Children glue yellow muffin or cupcake papers on construction paper and draw stems with crayons.

Woodworking/Sand/Water

Sand: Provide flowerpots with numerals written on them. Children place the correct number of plastic flowers in each pot.

Printing

Provide chalkboards and chalk. Print these words on the chalkboard—plant, root, green, blossoms, stem, fruit, germinate, and leaf.

Math/Language Arts

Spring Puzzles (C)   Apple Tree Game (C)

Flowers and Vases (W)

Science/Social Studies

Display these roots in water—carrots, beets, radishes, turnips, pineapples. Germinate seeds, some in the light and some in the dark. Provide a jar containing red colored water with celery stalks in it.

More Group Time Activities

1. Film: *Why Plants Grow Where They Do.*
2. Song: "Springtime" (Tune: "Skip to My Lou").
3. Review the letter *Oo.*

Day 3: Spring Animals

Group Time Activities

1. Show pictures of baby animals or use the book *The Animals of Buttercup Farm* by Judy Dunn.
2. Discuss baby birds and nests.
3. Review names of baby animals. Use Fisher Price Farm See and Say (C), such as goose-gosling, cow-calf, sheep-lamb, cat-kitten, dog-puppy, horse-colt.
4. Song: "Five Little Ducks."

Learning Centers

Blocks

Provide wooden figures of farm animals and Fisher Price Farm (C).

Listening/Music/Reading

Provide the cassette and book *Seven Diving Ducks* by Margaret Friskey.

Art

Paper-Bag Puppets: Children make lion or lamb puppets using small paper bags, construction paper, yarn, newspaper for stuffing, and sticks.

Jennie's Hat: Children use wallpaper scraps to make a spring hat on construction paper like the one in *Jennie's Hat* by Ezra Jack Keats.

Woodworking/Sand/Water

Sand: Provide small plastic farm animals.

Printing

Provide small chalkboards and chalk. Print these words on the chalkboard—babies, nest, spring, and young.

Math/Language Arts

Peg Boards and Farmer, Pig, Sheep, and Horse Pegs (C)

Farm Lotto (C)   Pig and Blue Jay Puzzles (C)

Legos (C)   Animal Puppets and Puppet Stage

Science/Social Studies

Provide pictures of animals and baby animals. Children match pictures of baby animals to mother animals.

More Group Time Activities

1. Game: "Guess Who I Am." Each child imitates an animal. The other children guess which animal is being imitated.
2. Read *Make Way for Ducklings* by Robert McCloskey.
3. Song: "Jumping Frog."

Day 4: Spring Activities and Clothing

Group Time Activities

1. Use a fan to demonstrate how wind cannot be seen—only its effects.
2. Discuss the saying "March comes in like a lion and out like a lamb."
3. Discuss spring activities, such as flying kites, playing baseball, and housecleaning.
4. Read *Springtime in Noisy Village* by Astrid Lindgren.
5. Song: "Kite Song."

Learning Centers

Blocks

Provide pictures of spring.

Listening/Music/Reading

Add the song "Springtime" to the cassette tape of spring songs.

Art

Kites: Provide construction paper, cloth strips, and yarn for children to make kites.

Woodworking/Sand/Water

Sand: Provide large seeds and small garden signs indicating how many seeds to plant in each row.

Printing

Provide small chalkboards and chalk. Print these words on the chalkboard—baseball, wind, garden, flowers, and kite.

Math/Language Arts

The Letter Boxes (W)   Number Bingo (C)

Cans and Straw Counting: Provide cans with numerals written on them. Children put the correct number of straws in each can.

Addition Box: Use large seeds.

Science/Social Studies

Language Experience Notebook: Children draw spring pictures and write words they have learned about spring.

More Group Time Activities

1. Write a story about spring with the children.
2. Read *The Wind Blew* by Pat Hutchins.
3. Review the letter *Uu*.

Day 5: Living and Nonliving Things

Group Time Activities

1. "What does the word *living* mean?" Discuss characteristics of living things and have children identify several living things. Show pictures.
2. "What does the word *nonliving* mean?" Discuss characteristics of nonliving things and have children name some nonliving things.
3. Film: *Living Things and Non-Living Things*.
4. Sort selected items into 2 groups—living and nonliving.
5. Read *It Looked Like Spilt Milk* by Charles Shaw.

Learning Centers

Blocks

Provide kites for children to observe as they play.

Listening/Music/Reading

Provide the recording of spring songs or another favorite record or cassette tape.

Art

Clouds: Children tear cloud shapes and glue them on blue paper, the same way as in *It Looked Like Spilt Milk* by Charles Shaw.

Woodworking/Sand/Water

Sand: Children continue to plant seeds.

Printing

Provide small chalkboards and chalk. Print these words on the chalkboard—living, people, nonliving, rocks, clouds, plants, and food.

Math/Language Arts

Various Puzzles of Living and Nonliving Things (C)

Addition Box: Use large seeds.

Phonics Boards (W)

Science/Social Studies

Provide two charts labeled "living" and "nonliving" things. Provide pictures of living and nonliving things. Children put pictures on correct chart.

More Group Time Activities

1. Read *Gilberto and the Wind* by Marie Hall Ets.
2. Games: "Mirrors." Put children in pairs. One child pretends to be a mirror and must copy movements of the other child.
3. Fingerplay: "Kites" from *Mitt Magic*.

March—
Additional Activities

▶ Share the book *The Magic School Bus: Inside the Earth* by Joanna Cole. This language may be difficult for young children. It may be more appropriate to retell the story in your own words. *Rock Collecting* by Roma Gans is another good reference book to use in this discussion. Give a simple explanation of the relationship between volcanoes and earthquakes. Discuss how volcanoes are made of rock.

▶ Have several non-fiction books about earthquakes, volcanoes, and rocks available for children to explore independently during this unit.

▶ Show the children where Japan, Hawaii, and Alaska are on a map or globe. Discuss the volcanic activity and earthquakes in these areas. Show pictures.

▶ Begin a class rock collection. Label each rock with 3 descriptive words and an explanation of where the rock could be found.

▶ Create treasure maps with simple directions to find "fossils" hidden in the room. Have children work in teams.

▶ Read *Visiting the Art Museum* by Laurene Krasny Brown and Marc Brown.

▶ Read *It Could Still Be a Rock* by Allan Fowler.

▶ Read *Rock Collecting* by Roma Gans.

▶ Read *Mr. Meredith and the Truly Remarkable Stone* by Grace Chetwin.

▶ Read *Mr. McGoogan Moves the Mighty Rock* by Dick Gackenbach.

▶ Read *Easter Parade* by Mary Chalmers.

▶ Read *The Easter Egg Farm* by Mary Jane Auch.

▶ Read *Danny and the Easter Egg* by Edith Kunhardt.

▶ Read *Happy Easter Day* by Wendy Watson.

▶ Write a "Good Luck, Bad Luck" book. Discuss the four-leaf clover and its significance. Follow up with a discussion about "luck." Have children "write" a page for this book, drawing an instance of good luck on one side and bad luck on the other.

▶ Role-play different situations involving verbal manners and table manners. Have children demonstrate appropriate as well as inappropriate manners. Follow up with a class discussion about manners.

▶ Have a class manners poster. Each child may sign the poster when they have used polite manners during the day. At group time, call on some of these children and have them share when and how they used polite manners.

▶ Create a spring mural. Discuss different signs of spring, such as budding trees, blooming flowers, baby animals, and so on. Talk about spring activities. Have each child add to this class mural.

▶ Take a spring walk. Encourage and point out the many signs of spring. Have children share the signs they see. When the class returns, write a story about this walk. Discuss fiction and non-fiction stories and have children vote on which kind of story they want to write.

▶ Make a tape recording of spring sounds. Play the tape for the class and have children identify as many sounds as possible. Have children make spring sounds and encourage classmates to try to identify them.

▶ As a class, "adopt" something living on the school grounds, such as a tree, a bush, a flower, and so on. Visit this living object at least twice during this unit. Record the children's observations. Discuss two things to observe prior to the visit, such as growth (measure height), buds, flowers, leaves, and so on.

▶ Have children bring in a kite from home and spend time outside flying kites. You may wish to have parental assistance for this activity.

▶ Read *Spring Snowman* by Jill Barnes.

▶ Read *End of Winter* by Sharon Chmielarz.

▶ Read *When the Root Children Wake Up* by Helen Dean Fish.

▶ Songs: "We Are All Earthlings." *The Sesame Street Songbook: 64 Favorite Songs*. New York, NY: Macmillan Publishing Co., 1992.

"Picture A World." *The Sesame Street Song Book*. New York, NY: Simon & Schuster, 1971.

"Ladybugs' Picnic." *The Sesame Street Songbook: 64 Favorite Songs*. New York, NY: Macmillan Publishing Co., 1992.

"Frogs In the Glen." *The Sesame Street Songbook: 64 Favorite Songs*. New York, NY: Macmillan Publishing Co., 1992.

"Easter Time Is Here Again." *Hap Palmer Favorites—Songs for Learning Through Music and Movement*. Sherman Oaks, CA: Alfred Publishing Co., 1981.

"St. Patrick Was a Gentleman." *The Holiday Song Book*. New York, NY: Lothrop, Lee & Shepard Company, 1977.

"Michael Finnegan." *The Holiday Song Book*. New York, NY: Lothrop, Lee & Shepard Company, 1977.

April
Week 1

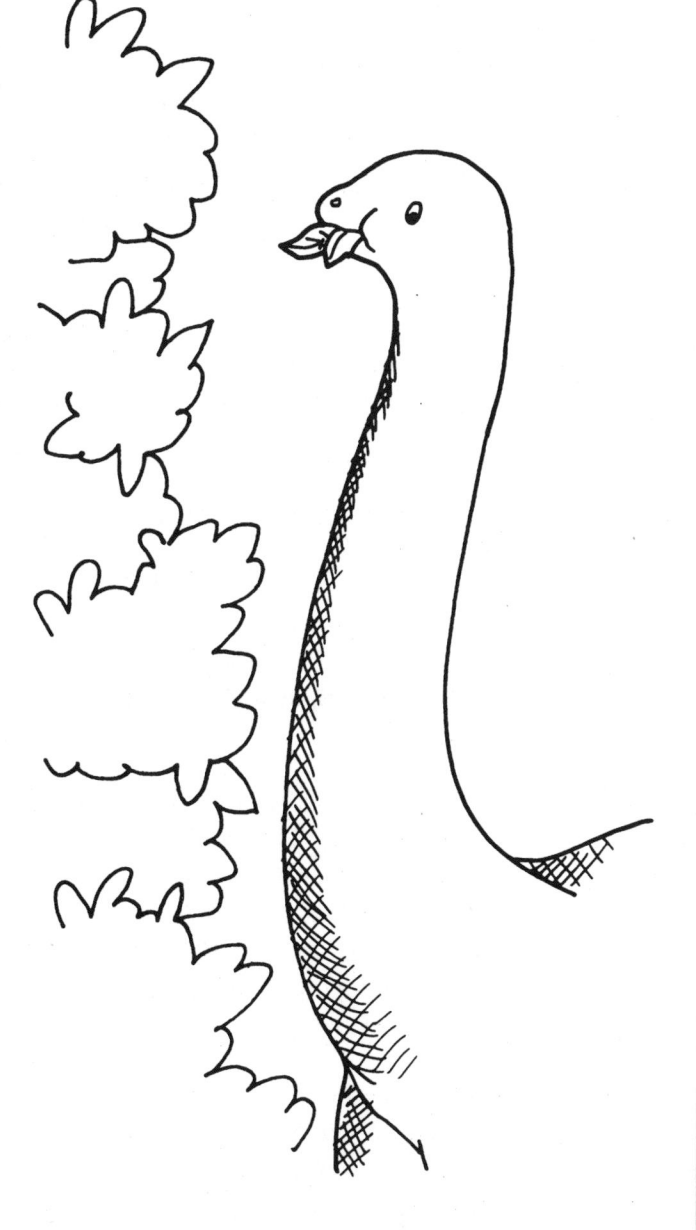

April Fool's Day/ Dinosaurs

Group Time Activities

1. Begin the day with a note hunt around the room. Plan this activity so that one note leads to another and the last note says "Hope you enjoyed the hunt. April Fools!"
2. Discuss the origin of April Fool's Day.
3. Read *Arthur's April Fool* by Marc Tolon Brown.
4. Make egg salad with the class. Children help peel one dozen hard-boiled eggs and mash them with a fork. Add pickle relish, mayonnaise, and salt to taste. Serve the egg salad at snack time. Pretend the boiled eggs are dinosaur eggs as an April Fool's joke!

Learning Centers

Blocks

Provide large plastic dinosaurs for children to use with the blocks.

Listening/Music/Reading

Provide a record and read-along book about the Flintstones.

Art

Easel Paint: brown and green. (Leave out all week.)

On Your Own: Provide a variety of art materials for children to use creatively.

Woodworking/Sand/Water

Sand: Hide clean turkey bones. Children pretend to be paleontologists and dig for fossils. Provide khaki shirts, hats, paintbrushes, and sticks to hunt for bones. Leave out all week.

Printing

Children print in a tray of clay with a stick. Print these words on the chalkboard—triceratops, apatosaurus, ankylosaurus, and stegosaurus.

Math/Language Arts

Dinosaur Puzzle (C)   Crazy Animal Puzzle (C)

Dinosaur Card Game (C)

Skeleton Sequence: Children arrange pictures of dinosaur skeletons from smallest to largest.

Addition Box: Use small plastic dinosaurs.

Science/Social Studies

Display pictures and books about dinosaurs. Provide charts of dinosaur skeletons.

Dramatic Play

Cover the walls with brown paper or provide a large box. Children draw rock shapes on the wall or box to make the Flintstones' house. Provide a stuffed dinosaur, housekeeping furniture, and dishes. Leave out all week.

More Group Time Activities

1. As a class, write a story on a large piece of paper titled "If I Had a Dinosaur for a Pet."
2. Fingerplay: "Dinosaurs" from *Mitt Magic*.

Day 2: Introduction to Dinosaurs

Group Time Activities

1. Ask this riddle: "What was huge, laid eggs, had tough skin, and lived over 100 million years ago?"
2. Children tell their ideas about dinosaurs. Discuss the meaning of the word *extinct*.
3. Tell what the word *dinosaur* meant in Greek (terrible lizard).
4. Discuss facts about dinosaurs and show pictures.
5. Song: "The Elephant." (Change the word *elephant* in the song to *dinosaur*.)
6. Read *Danny and the Dinosaur* by Sydney Hoff.

Learning Centers

Blocks

Provide posters of dinosaurs and dinosaur skeletons.

Listening/Music/Reading

Provide the song "The Animal Song" on a cassette tape. Have children substitute the word *dinosaur* for *alligator*. Encourage the children to move like dinosaurs.

Art

Mold a Dinosaur: Combine 2 c flour, 1 c salt, and just enough water to make playdough consistency. Children can use the playdough to mold dinosaurs. Let dinosaurs dry.

Printing

Provide a tray of clay. Print these words on the chalkboard—dinosaur, reptile, egg, shell, large, and terrible lizard.

Math/Language Arts

Dinosaur Puzzles (C)

Skeleton Sequence: Children arrange pictures of dinosaur skeletons from smallest to largest.

Addition Box: Use small plastic dinosaurs.

Bacon and Eggs (WII)

Science/Social Studies

Provide pictures, words, books about dinosaurs, and models of dinosaurs.

More Group Time Activities

1. Song: "The Elephant." Children move like dinosaurs.
2. Song: "The Animal Song."
3. Read *The Tyrannosaurus Game* by Steven Kroll.

Day 3: Plant-Eating Dinosaurs

Group Time Activities

1. Review paleontologist. Give each child a dinosaur hunting license. Hide plastic or paper plant-eating dinosaurs in the room. Each child finds one dinosaur and brings it back to the group.
2. Discuss the earth's habitat during the reign of the plant-eating dinosaurs—triceratops, apatosaurus, ankylosaurus, stegosaurus, and so on.
3. Discuss the characteristics of the stegosaurus, such as plates, eggs, and brain.
4. Use plastic dinosaurs to show other plant-eating dinosaurs.
5. Dinosaur Chant: "Here comes a dinosaur, walking down the sidewalk. I think he is someone who doesn't want to talk." Invite children to reword the chant.

Learning Centers

Blocks

Provide pictures of the plant-eating dinosaurs.

Listening/Music/Reading

Provide a record about the Flintstones.

Art

Dinosaur Dioramas: Provide shoeboxes, construction paper, plants, and small rocks for children to create dinosaur dioramas.

Printing

Provide a tray of clay. Print these words on the chalkboard—triceratops, apatosaurus, ankylosaurus, and stegosaurus.

Math/Language Arts

Dinosaur Puzzles (C)   Crazy Animal Puzzle (C)

Dinosaur Card Game (C)

Skeleton Sequence: Children arrange pictures of dinosaur skeletons from smallest to largest.

Addition Box: Use small plastic dinosaurs.

Science/Social Studies

Display pictures and books about dinosaurs. Display fossils, rocks, and magnifying glasses.

More Group Time Activities

1. Game: "Mother May I." Children stand on a line. Tell different children to take two triceratops steps or three stegosaurus steps. If they say "Mother May I," they can move forward. If they forget, they must stay still. Continue until all children have moved to the finish line.
2. Read *In the Time of the Dinosaurs* by William Wise or *The Wonderful Egg* by Dahlov Ipcar.

Day 4: Flesh-Eating Dinosaurs

Group Time Activities

1. Practice the "Dinosaur Chant."
2. Introduce tyrannosaurus and allosaurus.
3. Show pictures of dinosaur skeletons and a human skeleton. Compare the differences in size.
4. Discuss contributions dinosaurs have made (oil).
5. Review *Dd*.

Learning Centers

Blocks

Provide pictures of flesh-eating dinosaurs.

Listening/Music/Reading

Provide music that stimulates imaginative animal movements. Have children fly like a pteranodon or make a noise like a triceratops.

Art

Dinosaur Eggs: Provide small blown-up balloons for dinosaur egg bases. Children dip newspaper strips into liquid starch and lay the strips on the balloon until it is completely covered. Allow to dry.

Printing

Provide a tray of clay. Print these words on the chalkboard—flesh eater, tyrannosaurus, egg, skeleton, ton, and oil.

Math/Language Arts

Legos (C)   Dinosaur Puzzles (C)

Mosaics (C)

Science/Social Studies

Provide a display of rocks and fossils.

More Group Time Activities

1. Language Experience Notebook: Dinosaurs.
2. Read *If the Dinosaurs Came Back* by Bernard Most, *Mitchell Is Moving* by Marjorie Sharmat, or *Quiet on Account of Dinosaur* by Catherine Wooley.

Day 5: Flying Dinosaurs

Group Time Activities

1. List the ancestors of dinosaurs, such as turtle, snake, alligator, lizard, and so on.
2. Discuss and show pictures of theories about what happened to the dinosaurs. Discuss the word *extinct*.
3. Read selected sections of *Flying Reptiles In the Age of Dinosaurs* by John Kaufmann.

Learning Centers

Blocks

Provide pictures of flying dinosaurs.

Listening/Music/Reading

Provide music to stimulate children to move about like dinosaurs.

Art

Dinosaur Eggs: Children paint their dinosaur eggs.

Printing

Provide a tray of clay. Print these words on the chalkboard—dinosaur, reptile, and flying.

Math/Language Arts

Etch-A-Sketch (C)   Dinosaur Puzzles (C)

Crazy Puzzles (C)

Plastic Eggs: Print a capital letter on one half of plastic eggs and a lower-case letter on the other half. Children match the halves.

Science/Social Studies

Display charts and books about dinosaurs and fossils.

More Group Time Activities

1. Discuss opposites, such as old-new; past-present; yesterday-today. Children can list examples.
2. Read *The True Book of Dinosaurs* by M.L. Clark.
3. Ask children to make up a recipe for apatosaurus steak, dinosaur soup, or dinosaur egg salad. Write recipes on large sheets of poster paper.

April
Week 2

Preparation:

▶ Plan a field trip for Day 5 to a farm.

▶ Provide an incubator and eggs for children to observe. If possible, plan ahead so that eggs will hatch this week!

Farm Animals

Group Time Activities

1. Use the Fisher Price See and Say (C) to guess animal sounds.
2. Discuss facts about chickens using pictures, feathers, and eggs.
3. Crack an egg and let children look at the inside.
4. Boil an egg. Have children peel and taste the egg.
5. Discuss hatching and put eggs in an incubator.
6. Read *Green Eggs and Ham* by Dr. Seuss or *What Is a Chicken?* by Gene Darby.

Learning Centers

Blocks

Provide plastic farm animals and Fisher Price Farm (C) for children to use all week with the blocks. Display pictures of a farm and farm animals.

Listening/Music/Reading

Provide the books *Green Eggs and Ham* by Dr. Seuss, *Don't Count Your Chicks* by Ingri and Edgar Aularie, and *What Is a Chicken?* by Gene Darby.

Art

Easel Paint: brown, red, green. (Leave out all week.)

Eggshell Art: Dye eggshells with water and food coloring. Children glue the dried, colored eggshells in shapes and designs on construction paper.

Chicks: Mix cottonballs in dry yellow tempera to color them. Shake the excess tempera off the cottonballs. Children glue yellow cottonballs on construction paper in the shape of chicks or ducks. Then draw the legs, feet, and beaks on the chicks.

Woodworking/Sand/Water

Sand: Provide small plastic farm animals and toy tractors. Leave out all week.

Printing

Provide alphabet stencils. Print these words on the chalkboard—rooster, hen, chicken, comb, and chicks.

Math/Language Arts

Find a Pair: Puppy (C)

What's Cooking Game (C)   The Feely Board (W)

Bacon and Eggs (WII)   Chicken Puzzle Sequence (C)

Science/Social Studies

Allow children to observe the eggs in the incubator. Children cut animal-product pictures from magazines.

Dramatic Play

Set up a farm. Provide farm dress-up clothes, stuffed animals, a bucket, a small stool, and a large cardboard cow. Stuff a rubber glove and attach it to the cardboard cow to be the cow's udder. Leave out all week.

More Group Time Activities

1. Film: *Old MacDonald Had a Farm*.
2. Encourage children to put on a puppet show with farm animal puppets (C).
3. Read *The Little Red Hen* by Jean Horton Berg.
4. Review the letter *Xx*.

Day 2: Cattle and Goats

Group Time Activities

1. Discuss cows. Make and use a flow chart to explain the process of milk going from the farm to the market. Show objects or foods that come from cows.
2. Discuss goats and what they provide—cashmere, mohair, goatskins, milk, cheese, and so on.
3. Make pudding with the class.
4. Read *Flip* by Wesley Dennis.
5. Song: "Farmer in the Dell."

Learning Centers

Listening/Music/Reading
Provide the cassette and book *Chester's Barn* by Lindee Climo.

Art
Button Art: Children glue a button on construction paper for an animal's eye and draw a farm animal around the button.

Printing
Provide alphabet stencils. Print these words on the chalkboard—farm, goat, cow, kid, calf, and cattle.

Math/Language Arts
Nutrition Board Game (C) Nutrition Cards (C)

Flannel Set of Farm Animals (C)

Count the Milk Bottles (See October, Week 1)

Farm Animal Puzzles (C) Farm Lotto (C)

Ice Cream Cones (W)

Science/Social Studies
Children continue to observe the eggs in the incubator.

Mother/Baby Match: Provide a poster with pictures of mother animals on one side and baby animals on the other side. Tie strings to the pictures on one side of the board. Tell children to connect the strings to the correct baby animal pictures.

More Group Time Activities

1. Distribute capital letters and lower-case letters to children. Children then find their letter partners. For example, the child with capital *A* must find the child with lower-case *a*.
2. Song: "Farmer in the Dell." Children dramatize the song.
3. Read *Animal Families* by Ann Weil.

Day 3: Sheep and Pigs

Group Time Activities

1. Nursery Rhyme: "Little Boy Blue" from *Chants for Children*.
2. Discuss facts about sheep and show products we get from them.
3. Song: "Baa, Baa Black Sheep."
4. Nursery Rhyme: "Little Bo Peep" from *Chants for Children*.
5. Discuss facts about hogs and show products we get from them.
6. Read *Three Little Pigs* by Barbara Brenner. Have children act out the story.

Learning Centers

Listening/Music/Reading
Provide the recording and book *Three Little Pigs*. Also, continue with the recording and book *Chester's Barn*.

Art
Sheep: Children draw the outline of a sheep on construction paper. Provide sheep wool or cottonballs for children to glue on the drawings.

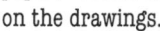

Printing
Provide alphabet stencils. Print these words on the chalkboard—sheep, lamb, sow, pig, and hog.

Math/Language Arts
Pig Puzzle (C) Bacon and Eggs (WII)

Goose Puzzle (C) Sequence Chicken Puzzle (C)

Peg Boards with Animal Pegs (C)

Animal Habitat: Children sort pictures of animals according to where they live—air, land, or water.

Science/Social Studies
Provide magazines for children to cut out pictures of products we get from sheep and pigs. Children glue these pictures on a mural. Children continue observing the eggs or baby chicks in the incubator.

More Group Time Activities

1. Song: "Mary Had a Little Lamb."
2. Discuss methods of preserving food (freezing, canning, preservatives). Show products and pictures.
3. Introduce subtraction using familiar objects. Make up word problems with children.
4. Read *The Truffle Pig* by Claire Huchet Bishop.
5. Fingerplay: "Piggies" from *Mitt Magic*.

Day 4: Horses and Donkeys

Group Time Activities

1. Discuss the uses of horses in the past and how they are helpful today.
2. Discuss facts about horses and donkeys. Show pictures.
3. Read *Flip* by Wesley Dennis or *Donkey, Donkey* by Roger Duvoisin.
4. Show horseshoes, saddle, spurs, chaps, hat, and bridle.

Learning Centers

Listening/Music/Reading

Provide the record and book *Old MacDonald Had a Farm*. Also, provide these and other books about farm animals—*Donkey, Donkey* by Duvoisin and *Horses* by Posell.

Art

Farm Dioramas: Provide shoeboxes, construction paper, and an assortment of art materials.

Printing

Provide alphabet stencils. Print these words on the board—horse, colt, hoof, mare, tail, foal, and donkey.

Math/Language Arts

Horse Puzzle (C)   Winnie the Pooh Game (C)

Three Billy Goats Gruff Puzzle (C)

First-Sound Sorting Boxes (W)

Beginning Sounds: Provide small plastic animals and cherry tomato baskets turned upside down. Label each basket with a letter. Children put the plastic animals in the correct animal pen according to the beginning letter.

Science/Social Studies

Observe the activity in the incubator. Provide paper and crayons for children to draw pictures and write stories about their observations.

More Group Time Activities

1. Film: *Old MacDonald Had a Farm*.
2. Game: "Farmer in the Dell." Have children dramatize the song.
3. Read *The Big Book of Horses* by Edward Chase.

Day 5: Ducks and Fish

Group Time Activities

1. Read *Two Lonely Ducks* by Roger Duvoisin.
2. Use a down jacket, stuffed duck, and a duck decoy in a discussion about ducks.
3. Teach children how to do the duck walk.
4. Song: "Five Little Ducks."
5. Show pictures and talk about why fish are important to us.
6. Take an imaginary trip with children to a duck or fish pond.
7. Prepare for the field trip to the farm.

Learning Centers

Listening/Music/Reading

Provide the cassette and book *Seven Diving Ducks* by Margaret Friskey.

Art

Feather Art: Provide an assortment of feathers and styrofoam meat trays of paint. Children paint on large sheets of paper using the feathers.

Printing

Provide alphabet stencils. Print these words on the chalkboard—flock, webbed feet, drake, bill, duck, fish, duckling, and catfish.

Math/Language Arts

Go Fishing (C)   Farm Lotto (C)

See and Say (Fisher Price) (C)   Flannel Farm Animals (C)

Science/Social Studies

Children draw pictures of eggs and baby chicks. Provide a display of products that come from ducks and fish.

Dramatic Play

Children play in "green land." Provide as may green objects as possible.

More Group Time Activities

1. Language Experience Notebook: The Farm.
2. Read *Make Way for Ducklings* by Robert McCloskey.
3. Write a thank-you letter with the class to the farm personnel.
4. Fingerplay: "Five Yellow Ducklings" from *Mitt Magic* and "Five Little Fishes" from *Mitt Magic*.

April
Week 3

Preparation:

▶ Prepare "Astronaut Training School" graduation certificates to be presented to each child at the end of the week.

Space

Day 1: Introduction to Space/Astronauts

Group Time Activities

1. Discuss outer space.
2. Discuss astronauts' health, qualifications, preparations, functions, duties, and spacesuits.
3. Have children pretend they are in astronaut training school all week. Each morning, conduct physical exercises with the class as part of group time.
4. Discuss astronauts' experience in space, such as blastoff, countdown, weightlessness, and so on. Show pictures.
5. Song: "I Don't Want To Live On the Moon."

Learning Centers

Special Project: Provide a black light, black construction paper, and fluorescent paint. Children paint pictures of space. Painting with fluorescent paint will work best in a dark corner or closet, but this is also a fun activity in a lighted room.

Blocks

Provide pictures of space and spaceships, and toy spaceships for children to use all week.

Listening/Music/Reading

Record the songs "One Light, One Sun" and "I Don't Want to Live On the Moon" on a cassette tape. Leave out all week. Provide books about space.

Art

Space Helmets: Provide white paper bags. Children cut out holes for the face.

Astronauts: Tell children to draw an astronaut on construction paper, cut the astronaut out, and glue the figure on a meat tray. Then children can cut the tray into the shape of a spaceship.

Woodworking/Sand/Water

*Woodworking: Provide wood boards, wood scraps, nails, hammers, and glue.

Printing

Provide Silly Putty (C) and newspapers. Print these words on the chalkboard—astronaut, spacesuit, and space.

Math/Language Arts

Space and Astronaut Puzzles (C)

Snap and Bolt (C)   Snap and Play (C)

Science/Social Studies

Provide space charts, pictures of space, rocks, and scales.

Dramatic Play

Set up a space station. Make a spaceship out of a large appliance box. Provide white jackets (T-shirts), a control station (be creative), and helmets (boxes covered with foil). Leave out all week.

More Group Time Activities

1. Song: "One Light, One Sun."
2. Read *Space Alphabet* by Irene Zacks.
3. Poem: "The Universe" by Mary Britton Miller from *The Random House Book of Poetry for Children*.

Day 2: Spaceship and Launching Pad

Group Time Activities

1. Use pictures to discuss the spaceship and launching pads. Use a balloon to illustrate and talk about blastoff.
2. Discuss weightlessness and parachutes.
3. Lay chairs flat with the backs on the floor. Children sit in the chairs while taking a "trip" through space. Include in the dramatization the blastoff and walking on the moon.
4. Encourage the children to do astronaut exercises.

Learning Centers

Listening/Music/Reading

Add the song "Sally Go Round the Sunshine" to the cassette of songs.

Art

Spaceships: Provide cardboard cylinders, cones, spools, and juice cans, so children can tape together and cover with construction paper to make spaceships and rockets.

Woodworking/Sand/Water

*Woodworking: Provide wood scraps, boards, nails, hammers, and glue.

Printing

Provide Silly Putty (C) and newspapers. Print these words on the chalkboard—spaceship, rocket, blastoff, decontaminator, lunar module, and command module.

Math/Language Arts

Space and Astronaut Puzzles (C)   Legos (C)

Octons (C)   Light Bright (C)

Science/Social Studies

Provide pictures and charts of outer space.

Flannelboard Set: Planets (C)

More Group Time Activities

1. Children make up a story that begins: "While I was in outer space..." Write the children's words on a large sheet of paper cut into the shape of a spaceship.
2. Poem: "I'm Glad the Sky Is Painted Blue," anonymous, from *The Random House Book of Poetry for Children*.
3. Poem: "This Little Pig Built a Spaceship" by Frederick Winsor from *The Random House Book of Poetry for Children*.

Day 3: Stars and Sun

Group Time Activities

1. Song: "Twinkle, Twinkle, Little Star."
2. Discuss stars.
3. Discuss facts about the sun (source of energy). Use pictures.
4. Discuss galaxy, astronomer, and constellation.
5. Show telescope.
6. Film: *Stars and More Stars*.
7. Have the children do astronaut exercises.

Learning Centers

Listening/Music/Reading

Record the song "Twinkle, Twinkle, Little Star." As children listen to the recording, have them draw and cut out paper stars. Hang stars with string from the ceiling in the dramatic-play center.

Art

Constellations: Give each child a paper with a constellation outlined on it. Provide stick-on stars for children to add to the constellations.

Woodworking/Sand/Water

Wet Sand: Provide objects that could be used to shape the moon's surface.

Printing

Provide Silly Putty (C) and newspaper. Print these words on the chalkboard—stars, sky, shooting stars, and comets.

Math/Language Arts

Space Puzzles

Space Match: Children match space pictures to space words.

The World about Us Lotto (C)

Triominoes (C)

Rubber Bands and Rubber Band Boards (C)

Science/Social Studies

Provide a telescope and books about telescopes, stars, and space. Display star constellation posters.

Flannel Set: Planets (C).

More Group Time Activities

1. Language Experience Notebook: Space.
2. Read *I Want to Be an Astronaut* by Carla Greene.

Day 4: Planets

Group Time Activities

1. Show pictures and discuss the nine planets.
2. Swing a ball on a rope to illustrate orbiting.
3. Discuss a planetarium.
4. Illustrate the relationship between the earth and sun with a ball and flashlight or lamp. Ask one child (earth) to rotate while walking in an orbit around the lamp (sun).
5. Read *Is There Life in Outer Space?* by Franklyn M. Branley.
6. Astronaut exercises.

Learning Centers

Listening/Music/Reading

Children listen to the cassette of songs. Also, provide the book and recording *I Want to Be An Astronaut* by Byron Barton.

Art

Galaxies: Children cut out a yellow construction-paper sun and glue it in the center of a piece of black construction paper. Children put nine planets in orbit around the sun. Children can spread glue and sprinkle glitter on the pictures.

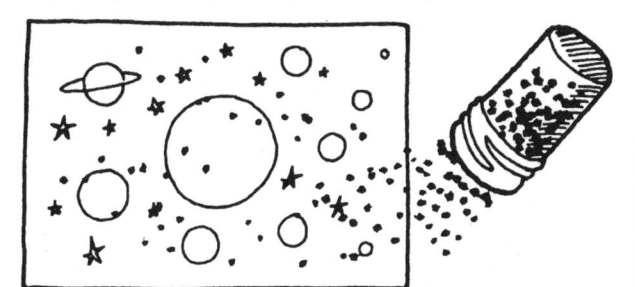

Woodworking/Sand/Water

Wet Sand: Provide objects that could be used to shape the moon's surface. Display pictures of the moon.

Printing

Provide Silly Putty (C) and newspapers. Print these words on the chalkboard—sun, earth, planet, and orbit.

Math/Language Arts

Space Puzzle (C)   Marbles and Marble Magic (C)

Dominoes (C)   Sewing Cards (C)

Addition Box: Use marbles.

Science/Social Studies

Provide a telescope and books about telescopes, stars, and space. Display charts and pictures of the moon and outer space.

Provide Flannel Set: Planets (C).

More Group Time Activities

1. Make class murals of space. Provide large sheets of black bulletin-board paper. Divide class into groups of 4 or 5.
2. Song: "One Light, One Sun."
3. Poem: "The Marrog" by R.C. Scriven from *The Random House Book of Poetry for Children.*

Day 5: Moon

Group Time Activities

1. Nursery Rhyme: "Hey Diddle, Diddle." Discuss the saying "The Man in the Moon." Use pictures to discuss the moon. Demonstrate with mirror and light.
2. Discuss and look at pictures of craters.
3. Song: "Sally Go Round the Sunshine."
4. Write and narrate a puppet show called "Space Flight." Use pictures to illustrate as the puppets discuss what is seen.
5. Read *Moon Man* by Tomi Ungerer.

Learning Centers

Listening/Music/Reading

Make a recording of the story *Moon Man* by Tomi Ungerer.

Art

Space Monsters: Provide paper plates and construction paper for children to make space monsters.

Woodworking/Sand/Water

Wet Sand: Provide objects to use on the moon's surface. Provide toy trucks.

Printing

Provide Silly Putty (C) and newspapers. Print these words on the chalkboard— moon, craters, and meteorites.

Math/Language Arts

Space and Astronaut Puzzles (C)

Pegs and Peg Boards (C)   Initial Sound Bingo (C)

Light Bright (C)   Marble Magic (C)

Science/Social Studies

Display a telescope, star charts, and pictures about space.

More Group Time Activities

1. Game: "Space Flight." Children stand in a circle. Two children at a time can be astronauts. Count down with the class and the two children blast off. The two children run around the outside of the circle until re-entry. Then the astronauts break into the inner circle for splash down into the ocean.
2. Mix up a gallon of Tang. Provide Ziplock bags and straws for children to use to drink the Tang. Discuss use of Tang in space.
3. Children pretend to walk in space while listening to music. Use Hap Palmer record *Movin'.*
4. Present "Astronaut Training School" certificates.

April
Week 4

Preparation:

▶ Plan a field trip for Day 5 to a pet shop.

▶ Provide a gerbil or hamster in a cage for the class to keep as a pet.

▶ Provide an aquarium for the class to observe and enjoy.

▶ Prepare a bulletin board titled "Our Pets." Children will add pictures to the bulletin board throughout the week.

Classroom Pets

Day 1: Pets

Group Time Activities

1. Use first and last name cards.
2. Read *Pet Show* by Ezra Jack Keats.
3. Each child talks about his or her pet. Ask children to bring pictures of pets to school on Day 2. Display pictures on bulletin board entitled "Our Pets."
4. Make a chart showing proper pet care.
5. Make a class bar graph of pets children would like to have in class.
6. Song: "Mary Had a Little Lamb."

Learning Centers

Blocks

Provide plastic animals and pictures about pets and pet shops for children to observe as they build.

Listening/Music/Reading

Provide the cassette and book *Whistle for Willie* by Ezra Jack Keats.

Art

Easel Paint: blue, green, and yellow. (Leave out all week.)

Paper-Bag Puppets: Children make puppets to look like pets they have. Provide small paper bags, newspaper, yarn, and construction paper.

Woodworking/Sand/Water

Children mold clay pets. Recipe: 1 c flour, 1/2 c salt, 2 tsp cream of tartar, 1 c water, 1 tsp oil, and food coloring. Combine and cook in skillet until desired clay consistency is formed. Knead.

Printing

Provide typewriters. Print these words on the chalkboard—dog, cat, puppy, hamster, and pet.

Math/Language Arts

Puppy Match (C)   Fish Puzzles (C)

Zoo Lotto (C)

Science/Social Studies

Display a gerbil or a hamster, a hamster cage, supplies, hamster and gerbil books, and magnifying glasses.

Dramatic Play

Set up a pet shop. Provide stuffed animals, toy cash register, play money, big boxes, and shoeboxes. Leave out all week.

More Group Time Activities

1. Provide a box of objects. Each child tells what letter an object begins with and places the object in the appropriate pile.
2. Game: "ABC Bingo."
3. Film: *Are You My Mother?*
4. Chant: "I Know a Little Puppy" from *Chants for Children*.

Day 2: Fish and Other Aquarium Pets

Group Time Activities

1. Discuss characteristics of fish. Use charts and pictures of goldfish, guppies, snails, and tetras.
2. Songs: "Over In the Meadow" and "Jumping Frog."

Learning Centers

Blocks

Provide pictures of and books about aquariums. Add balance beams.

Listening/Music/Reading

Provide a recording of the songs "Song of the Fishes" and "Fishing Blues" from *Sharon, Lois & Bram: Stay Tuned.* Provide watercolor paints and white paper for children to paint pictures while listening.

Art

Make a Fish: Children cut out two fish shapes, color, decorate, stuff with paper, and staple together. Hang in room.

Woodworking/Sand/Water

Water: Provide wind-up water animals.

Printing

Provide a tray with a thin layer of blue clay in it. Children write in the clay using a stick. Print these words on the chalkboard—goldfish, snail, guppy, tetra, turtle, and neon.

Math/Language Arts

Zoo Lotto (C)   ABC Frog and Lily Pad Match (C)

Fish Puzzle (C)   Mosaics (C)

Animal Sequence Cards (C)

Science/Social Studies

Display an aquarium. Provide books about aquariums, magnifying glasses, and books about fish as pets.

More Group Time Activities

1. Song: "Fishing Blues" from *Sharon, Lois & Bram: Stay Tuned.*
2. Fingerplay: "Turtles" from *Mitt Magic.*
3. Use the songs "Song of the Fishes" and "Fishing Trip" and have children explore ways of moving like fish.
4. Share chldren's pictures of pets they brought from home.

Day 3: Aquarium

Group Time Activities

1. Song: "The Animal Fair."
2. As a class, sit by the aquarium and discuss the contents. Explain what is needed—plants, sand or gravel, thermometer, heater, pump, and filter. Clean the filter with children.

Learning Centers

Blocks

Provide books and pictures about aquariums.

Listening/Music/Reading

Provide recording of "Song of the Fishes." Children can draw pictures of fish while listening.

Art

Crayon Resist: Draw an aquarium and fish with crayons. Paint over the drawing with very thin blue water paint.

Woodworking/Sand/Water

Water: Provide wind-up water toys and plastic fish.

Printing

Put a thin layer of blue clay on cookie sheet for children to write in with a nail. Print these words on the chalkboard—aquarium, fish, oxygen, and water.

Math/Language Arts

Go Fishing Cards (C)   Fish Puzzle (C)

Crazy Animal Puzzles (C)   Mosaics (C)

Light Bright (C)

Science/Social Studies

Children observe the aquarium. Also, have the hamster available for observation. Display books on aquariums, fish, and other classroom pets.

More Group Time Activities

1. Divide class into groups of four. Each group draws a mural of an aquarium. Display in hall. Help each group write a story about their mural.
2. Review mystery letter *Gg*. Write on the board *Gg* words, such as *guppy* or *goldfish*.

Day 4: Hamsters and Gerbils

Group Time Activities

1. Use book *Golden Hamsters* by Herbert Spencer Zim to discuss care of pet hamsters.
2. Read *Benjamin Bounces Back* by Alan Baker.
3. Provide the cassette and book *Fat Cat*.

Learning Centers

Blocks

Provide pictures of mice, hamsters, and gerbils.

Listening/Music/Reading

Provide the cassette and book *Annie's Prize Pet*.

Art

Milk-Carton Hamsters: Mix a small amount of liquid detergent with tempera paint. Children paint milk cartons. Using construction paper, have children decorate cartons to look like hamsters.

Pecan Hamsters: Children make hamsters out of pecans. Children glue on tiny black dot eyes and a short piece of yarn for the tail. Each child then glues the pecan hamster on a piece of matboard and glues a cherry tomato plastic basket turned upside down over the pecan hamster.

Woodworking/Sand/Water

Wet Sand: Provide a plastic mouse, paper-towel rolls, or plastic tunnels.

Printing

Provide a tray of sand for children to write in using their fingers. Print these words on the chalkboard—cage, gerbil, hamster, germ, teddy bear, Germany, and golden.

Math/Language Arts

Zoo Lotto (C)   ABC Frog Lily Pad Match (C)

Crazy Animal Puzzle (C)   Biscuits (WII)

Science/Social Studies

Stay close to the hamster cage to help the children learn how to hold the hamster. Provide magnifying glasses and books on hamsters.

More Group Time Activities

1. Game: "ABC Bingo" (C).
2. Read *Max* by Giovannetti, *Benjamin's Book* or *Benjamin's Dreadful Dream* by Alan Baker.

Day 5: Field Trips and Birds

Group Time Activities

1. Use Big Bird puppet (C) to discuss birds (feathers, bills, eggs).
2. Review *Bb*.
3. Discuss how some birds may carry diseases and how people must be careful.

4. Review and show pictures of various birds, such as parrots or parakeets.
5. Review *Pp*.
6. Prepare for the field trip to local pet shop. Discuss rules and manners.

Learning Centers

Blocks

Provide pictures of birds.

Listening/Music/Reading

Provide the cassette of songs from this week.

Art

Button Art: Children draw and color favorite birds on construction paper. Provide buttons for the eyes.

Woodworking/Sand/Water

Wet Sand: Provide a plastic turtle, frog, rocks, and plastic plants.

Printing

Provide typewriters. Print these words on the chalkboard—bird, parakeet, and parrot.

Math/Language Arts

Light Bright (C)   Rhyming Word Match (C)

Button Sort: Provide a box of buttons and tray for sorting.

Science/Social Studies

Continue helping children handle the new classroom pet (hamster). Provide magnifying glasses. Children observe the aquarium and fish. These are now a permanent part of your classroom.

More Group Time Activities

1. Give "Mr. B" (puppet) a birthday party. Children find objects to give him. Everything must start with the letter *Bb*.
2. Language Experience Notebook: Pets.
3. Make a *Bb* box together as a class. Walk around the class and look for objects that begin with the letter *Bb*, such as book, button, and so on.
4. Help the children write a thank-you letter to the pet shop personnel.

April–
Additional Activities

▶ Have 3 pieces of poster paper labeled with different dinosaur types, such as stegosaurus, tyrannosaurus, allosaurus, and so on. Using pictures and books, have children describe these dinosaurs as you write or draw the adjectives under the correct dinosaur type. Hang pictures of dinosaurs and adjective posters in the room.

▶ Play "Who Am I?" game. Review dinosaur descriptions. Have "It" give adjective clues and have classmates guess which dinosaur the child is describing.

▶ Create a prehistoric mural. Discuss what the world was like in "dinosaur times." Have the class create a mural of what they think the world looked like then.

▶ Read *Fossils Tell of Long Ago* by Aliki.

▶ Read *Dinosaurs Are Different* by Aliki.

▶ Read *A Dinosaur Named After Me* by Bernard Most.

▶ Read *Dinosaurs* by Gail Gibbons.

▶ Play a memory game about a visit to a farm. The first child starts by saying "I went to the farm and I saw a (blank)." The next child follows by saying "I went to the farm and I saw a (blank) and a (blank)." Continue as long as children can remember, then start a new game. Play until everyone has had at least one turn.

▶ Create a bar graph titled "My Favorite Farm Animal."

▶ Write a class story titled "A Day On the Farm." Have children decide whether they want to tell a fantasy story or a realistic story. Illustrate and dramatize if desired.

▶ Read *Rosie's Walk* by Pat Hutchins.

▶ Read *The Spring Hat* by Madelaine Gill Spring.

▶ Read *Gemma and the Baby Chick* by Antonia Barber.

▶ Read *We Keep a Pig in the Parlor* by Suzanne Bloom.

▶ Have children create "planet creatures" from various odds and ends, such as construction paper, egg cartons, pipe cleaners, sequins, and so on. Have each child name his or her creature and tell which planet it is from.

▶ Show pictures of astronauts on the moon. Children can pretend that they will be going on the next space shuttle to the moon. Have children dictate a story or draw things they would take with them to the moon.

▶ Record a class story about visiting another planet. Have each child add a sentence or two to the story. Before recording, discuss characters, setting, and events in the beginning, the middle, and the end.

- Pretend "Peter the Plutonian" has come to visit your class. Children should decide on three things they would like to give Peter to bring back with him to Pluto.

- Read *Mooncake* by Frank Asch.

- Read *Happy Birthday, Moon* by Frank Asch.

- Create a class pet. Talk about imagination. Show pictures of imaginary creatures and create an imaginary class pet. Describe and name the pet. Decide what it likes to eat and what it likes to do.

- Have children choose one pet they would like to be. Have children draw and dictate a few sentences that begin with "If I were a ..."

- Assign children specific days during the week to bring their pets from home to school.

- Vote on a class pet. Narrow choices to four or five animals. Have children discuss which animals would make good pets and why. Children should choose one of the choices and be able to explain why they chose this animal. Have a class vote or make a bar graph to see which animal gets the most votes.

- Read *Theodor and Mr. Balbini* by Petra Mathers.

- Read *Arthur's Pet Business* by Marc Tolon Brown.

- Read *My Friend Fish* by Mamie Hegwood.

- Read *I Took My Frog to the Library* by Eric A. Kimmel.

May
Week 1

Cowboys

Day 1: Cowboy Clothes and Equipment

Group Time Activities

1. Discuss the term "cowboy." Emphasize the fact that both women and men can be cowboys, but in the past these responsibilities were mostly assumed by men.
2. Ask children to name things cowboys wear, such as boots, belts, chaps, bandanas, and hats.
3. Show pictures or real examples of cowboy clothing and equipment.
4. Discuss purposes of the cowboys' clothing. (The hat can be used to shade eyes, to keep the head cool, and as a cup.)
5. Discuss and contrast the role and responsibilities of women in frontier times to the role and responsibilities of women in ranching today.
6. Read *Cowboy Sam and Freckles* by Edna Walker Chandler.

Learning Centers

Blocks

Provide plastic horses, pictures of cowboys, Lincoln Logs (C), and toy trucks for children to use with the blocks all week.

Listening/Music/Reading

Provide the cassette and book *The True Book of Cowboys* by Teri Martini.

Art

Easel Paint: brown, red, and black. (Leave out all week.)

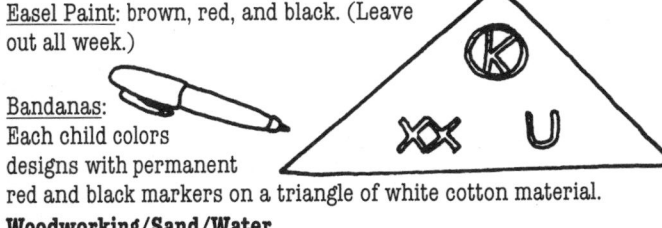

Bandanas:
Each child colors designs with permanent red and black markers on a triangle of white cotton material.

Woodworking/Sand/Water

Sand: Provide small plastic cowboys, horses, and fences. Leave out all week.

Printing

Provide paper and pencils. Print these words on small pieces of paper—boats, saddle, cowboy, chaps, bandanas, and rope. Place the words in a cowboy hat. Children take out one word at a time to copy.

Math/Language Arts

Candy Land Bingo (C)	Cowboy Jigsaw (C)
Play Tiles (C)	Horseshoe Game (C)

Memory Game: Branding Symbols.

Science/Social Studies

Provide recent magazines and books on cowboys. Display cowboy clothes and equipment.

Dramatic Play

Provide sleeping bags, blocks or sticks to build a "fire," a saddle, books, a bucket, hats, and dress-up clothes. Leave out all week.

More Group Time Activities

1. Discuss the different sounds of *Cc*.
2. Play the record *The Sons of the Pioneers: 25 Favorite Cowboy Songs*. Make a pretend fire using blocks. Children sit around the fire and sing and listen to the cowboy songs.

Day 2: Cowboy Life

Group Time Activities

1. Discuss foods cowboys ate and utensils they used. Also, discuss where cowboys lived and what they did in their spare time.
2. Read *Cowboy Sam and Shorty* by Edna Walker Chandler.
3. Cook beans or stew with the class on a hot plate, and pretend you are eating around a campfire. Sing cowboy songs while cooking.

Learning Centers

Listening/Music/Reading

Provide the record *The Sons of the Pioneers: Tumbling Tumbleweed.*

Art

Campfire Pictures: Children can make campfire scenes on construction paper by using popsicle sticks, tissue paper, construction paper, sand, and glue.

Printing

Provide paper and pencils. Print the words on paper to put inside a cowboy hat. Also, have these words printed on the chalkboard—cowboy, song, food, range, and campfire.

Math/Language Arts

Cowboy Maze: On a posterboard, draw a maze. Children move plastic cowboys on horses through the desert range to the campsite.

Marble Magic (C)   Cowboy Puzzle (C)

Science/Social Studies

Display foods that cowboys could eat easily while camping. Provide books about cowboys.

More Group Time Activities

1. Song: "Old MacDonald Moved out West" (Tune: "Old MacDonald Had a Farm"). Make up words for what Old MacDonald might have on his ranch.
2. Game: "What's Missing?" Place cowboy items in center of the rug. Have one child leave the room and hide one object. Have the child return and determine what's missing.

Day 3: Cowboy Jobs

Group Time Activities

1. Discuss jobs cowboys perform during different seasons (roundup, branding, going to market, cattle drive, ranch work).
2. Show and discuss a poster displaying various brands. Show a branding iron.
3. Song: "Home on the Range."
4. Game: "Match-O." Display large and small pictures on the chalkboard. Children find a small picture to go with each big picture. For example, saddle goes with horse.
5. Read *I Want to Be a Cowboy* by Carla Greene.

Learning Centers

Listening/Music/Reading

Provide a recording of the *William Tell Overture.*

Art

Cattle Brands: Make cattle brands from pipe cleaners. Children dip the branding irons in a tray of paint, make a print on construction paper, and draw a cow around the brand.

Printing

Provide small chalkboards. Print these words on the chalkboard—roundup, branding, cattle drive, and going to market.

Math/Language Arts

Cowboy Sound Puzzle (C)

Memory Game: Use cattle brands.

Same/Different Cowboy Game: Provide cut-off blue jeans. Write "Same" on one back pocket with permanent marker and "Different" on the other back pocket. Provide cards that have two branding symbols on them. Children place cards in the correct pocket.

Play Tiles (C)

Science/Social Studies

Display branding irons, horseshoes, bridle, and books on cowboys.

More Group Time Activities

1. Game: "Branding Guessing." Draw a brand on the board, using children's initials. Children guess who the branding symbols stand for.

2. Read *Cowboy Sam and Miss Lily* by Edna Walker Chandler.
3. Roundup: Hide paper cows around the room and have children "round 'em up."

Day 4: Cowboys in Other Lands

Group Time Activities

1. Talk about the names of cowboys in other lands, such as gauchos from Ecuador. Use the globe to show where the different cowboys live.
2. Compare the way cowboys from other countries dress to the way American cowboys dress.
3. Discuss how cowboys today are different from those in the past. Discuss again the changing role of women and their equality in this lifestyle today.
4. Review the many sounds of Cc.

Learning Centers

Listening/Music/Reading

Record the songs "Good-by Old Paint," "Old Brass Wagon," and "The Old Chisholm Trail" on a cassette tape.

Art

Pipe Cleaner Sculptures: Children design sculptures using pipe cleaners.

Printing

Provide typewriters. Print these words on the chalkboard—roundup, shoot-out, branding, and cattle.

Math/Language Arts

Play Tiles (C)   Cowboy Puzzles (C)

Etch-A-Sketch (C)   Bead Stringing(C)

Science/Social Studies

Provide books and pictures about cowboys. Children sort cowboy pictures into two groups—cowboys of the past and present.

More Group Time Activities

1. Language Experience Notebook: Cowboys.
2. Read *Cowboy Sam and Big Bill* by Edna Walker Chandler.

Day 5: Well-Known Cowboys

Group Time Activities

1. Discuss Buffalo Bill (William F. Cody), Pecos Bill, and TV cowboys (Lone Ranger). Show pictures, if possible.
2. Read *Hunters Blaze the Trail* by Edith McCall.
3. Game: "I'm Going On a Cattle Drive." A new version of "Let's Go On a Bear Hunt" from *Chants for Children*.

Learning Centers

Listening/Music/Reading

Provide recording of *William Tell Overture*. Provide headsets.

Art

Lone Ranger Masks: Provide black construction paper and yarn.

Printing

Provide typewriters. Print these words on the chalkboard—Buffalo Bill, Pecos Bill, and Lone Ranger.

Math/Language Arts

Etch-A-Sketch (C)

Cowboy Puzzle (C)

Memory Game: Use branding symbols.

Bead Stringing (C)

Science/Social Studies

Provide a display of cowboy equipment. Provide scales to weigh horseshoes.

More Group Time Activities

1. Play a recording of the *William Tell Overture* and let children pretend to be the Lone Ranger riding a horse.
2. Read *Cowboy Sam* by Edna Walker Chandler.

May
Week 2

Preparation:

▶ Prepare a bulletin board entitled "Let's Go to the Beach." Have children bring pictures of themselves at the sea to add to the bulletin board.

Sea Life

Group Time Activities

1. Present an introduction to the sea.
2. Show pictures and objects from the sea.
3. Read *Emma's Sea Journey* by Patricia Quinlan.

Learning Centers

Blocks

Instead of block play, provide a boat and a fishing pole with a magnet tied to it. Provide paper fish and sea animals with paper clips attached. Allow children to go fishing in this center all week.

Listening/Music/Reading

Provide the cassette and book *Six Foolish Fishermen* by Benjamin Elkin.

Art

Easel Paint: blue, green, and yellow. (Leave out all week.)

Sea Mural: Children draw large pictures of sea animals, color, and cut them out. Tape sea animals on the blue paper that is covering the wall in the dramatic-play center.

Woodworking/Sand/Water

Water: Provide sand, magnets, plastic sea animals, shells, bottle caps, and paper. Add blue food coloring to the water.

Printing

Provide a tray filled with sand or blue clay. Children write with a nail. Print these words on the shapes of the sea animals and on the chalkboard—sailing, sea, sunbathing, sand, swimming, surfing, scuba diving, skin diving, and skiing.

Math/Language Arts

Go Fishing Cards (C)   Sea Animal Puzzles (C)

Addition Box: Use small plastic fish.

Sea Animal Lacing Cards: Make lacing cards of sea animals from old X-rays. X-ray material is strong and durable.

Science/Social Studies

Provide a display of shells, pictures of shells, books of the sea, weighing scales, and magnifying glasses.

Dramatic Play

Cover the walls at the dramatic-play center with blue paper. Provide a large refrigerator box for children to use as a submarine. Add underwater masks, flippers, books about the sea, beach ball, rafts, beach towels, and sand buckets. Leave out all week.

More Group Time Activities

1. Discuss sea birds, such as the albatross and the penguin.
2. Read *Albert the Albatross* by Syd Hoff.
3. Show jars of settled sand and mixed-up sand and discuss.
4. Make tuna fish salad with the class. Serve children the tuna salad on crackers.

Day 2: Fish

Group Time Activities

1. Discuss facts about fish.
2. Discuss the sea horse and shark. Show shark's tooth, sharkskin, and any other available items or pictures.
3. Game: "Fishing." Place several fish on the rug with ABCs written on them and a paper clip attached to each. Using an old fishing pole or dowel stick with a magnet on the end, children take turns fishing. Children call out the letter when a catch is made.
4. Read *Six Foolish Fishermen* by Benjamin Elkin.
5. Review *Ff* and *Ss*.

Learning Centers

Listening/Music/Reading

Provide the book and cassette *Six Foolish Fishermen* by Benjamin Elkin.

Art

Paper Plate Fish: Children cut out and glue triangles to paper plates.

Sharks: Children draw and cut sharks from sandpaper.

Sandpaper Sea Pictures: Children draw with chalk on sandpaper. (Provide sandpaper because it's rough like sharkskin.)

Woodworking/Sand/Water

Water: Make the water blue. Encourage children to use magnets to find "trash" in the ocean.

Printing

Provide tray of blue clay. Print these words on the chalkboard—shark, jaws, teeth, sea horse, and fish.

Math/Language Arts

Shark Game: Jaws (C)   Light Bright (C)

Science/Social Studies

Display shells, pictures of shells, books of the sea, sharkskin, shark tooth, magnifying glasses, and scales.

Dramatic Play

Children play in "yellow land." Add as many yellow objects as possible, such as yellow sheets, a yellow duck, and a yellow toothbrush.

More Group Time Activities

1. Discuss products from the ocean, such as food (tuna, clams, oysters), minerals (gold, salt, iodine), jewelry (pearls), sponges, and so on. Also, many of our products contain seaweed: medicine, ice cream, candy, jelly, salad dressing, and makeup.
2. Read *Mabel the Whale* by Patricia King.

Day 3: Sea Mammals

Group Time Activities

1. Discuss mammals in the sea. Show pictures.
2. Read *The Blue Whale* by National Geographic.
3. Using a water trough, objects, and two buckets labeled "float" and "sink," encourage children to experiment and place objects in the correct bucket. Use the book *Floating and Sinking* by Franklyn Branley in the discussion.

Learning Centers

Listening/Music/Reading

Make a recording of the story *Wynken, Blynken and Nod* by Eugene Field.

Art

Crayon Resist: Children draw ocean pictures with crayons and paint over the picture with thin, blue watercolor paint.

Woodworking/Sand/Water

Sand: Provide bucket, shells, shovel, and sand toys.

Printing

Provide a tray of blue clay. Print these words on the chalkboard—whale, seal, mammal, and walrus.

Math/Language Arts

Light Bright (C)   Sea Animal Puzzle (C)

Count the Pearls: Cut apart an inexpensive strand of plastic pearls. Provide oyster shells that have been labeled with numerals. Children count the correct number of pearls into each shell.

Science/Social Studies

Display foods that originated in the ocean.

More Group Time Activities

1. Song: "Penguin" from *Hap Palmer: Movin'*. Have children walk like penguins to this music.
2. Read *Seal and the Slick* by Don Freeman.
3. Songs: "Charlie Over the Water," "Sailing at High Tide," and "There's a Hole in the Bottom of the Sea."

Day 4: Other Sea Creatures

Group Time Activities

1. Discuss jellyfish, coral, starfish, sand dollar, and sponge.
2. Song: "Baby Beluga." Have children move to the music.
3. Read *D.W. All Wet* by Marc Tolon Brown.

Learning Centers

Listening/Music/Reading
Provide the recording and book *Swimmy* by Leo Lionni. Provide watercolor paints and paper for children to use while listening.

Art
Shiny Starfish: Using construction paper, children draw and cut out starfish. Apply glue and glitter to the starfish.

Woodworking/Sand/Water

Sand: Provide magnets, buckets, shells, shovel, and metal objects.

Printing
Provide tray of clay. Print these words on the chalkboard—starfish, jellyfish, and sand dollar.

Math/Language Arts
Light Bright (C)
Sea Animal Lacing Cards (seal, turtle, fish)
Sea Puzzles (C)
Addition Box: Use plastic sea animals.

Science/Social Studies
Provide empty tuna cans (tape the edges of cans), crab shells, and shrimp peelings.

More Group Time Activities

1. Read *I Saw the Sea Come In* by Alvin Tresselt. Discuss the tide and waves. Show pictures. Use a rope to demonstrate the action of a wave.
2. Film: *What's Under the Ocean?*
3. Fingerplay: "Five Little Seashells" from *Mitt Magic*.

Day 5: Octopus and Shell Fish

Group Time Activities

1. Discuss lobster, crab, shrimp, octopus, scallop, oyster, and clam.
2. Show various shells and discuss shell collecting.
3. Read *Otto is Different* by Franz Brandenberg.
4. Discuss the meaning of the word *eight*. Explain that *octo* means eight, such as octabon, octopus, octave, and so on.
5. Game: "Pin the Arm on the Octopus." Play this game like "Pin the Tail on the Donkey." Tape a large picture of the body of an octopus on the wall. A blindfolded child pins the arm on the octopus. Each child has a turn. Check to see who placed the arm on the body of the octopus most accurately.

Learning Centers

Listening/Music/Reading
Record the song "Eight Beautiful Notes." Also, provide the recording and book *Herman the Helper* by Robert Kraus. Children can draw pictures while listening.

Art
Lobster Traps: Provide plastic cherry tomato baskets, yarn, and construction paper. Children lace two baskets together like a trap, cut a trap door in the top of the basket, and draw and then cut out a paper lobster to put in the trap.
Shell Sculptures: Children glue shells together.
Octopus: Children make an octopus from cardboard egg carton sections and glue on 8 arms.

Woodworking/Sand/Water
Water: Provide objects for children to test sinking and floating abilities.

Printing
Provide tray of blue clay. Print these words on the chalkboard—octopus, ocean, animal, eight, snail, arms, shell, sea, clam, and oyster.

Math/Language Arts
Pearls: Cut strands of plastic pearls into different lengths—one pearl long, two pearls long, and so on. Children put pearl lengths in order.
Match the Words: Make a set of matching words. Print half of the words on paper and the other half on clear contact paper. Match the contact-paper word with the paper word.

Science/Social Studies
Provide shells and pictures of sea life.

More Group Time Activities

1. Read *Old Hasdrubal and the Pirates* by Bertha Amoss. Each child makes an eye patch. Have a treasure hunt in the classroom.
2. Game: "Octopus." One child is the "Octopus." Other children are "swimmers" and stand behind an imaginary line or tape line on the floor. When the "Octopus" calls out "octopus," the "swimmers" dash to the other shore. The children tagged by the "Octopus" freeze in place. Game continues until one "swimmer" is left. (*The Outrageous Outdoor Games Book* by Bob Gregson.)

May
Week 3

Preparation:

▶ Invite mothers to come to school on Day 5. (Be sensitive to children's different family situations.) At second Group Time Activities, have the children's mothers tell the class what they like best about being a mother.

▶ Prepare a bulletin board entitled "Our Moms." Children will make pictures to add to it on Day 5.

Circus/
Mother's Day

Group Time Activities

1. List circus animals on the board.
2. Show circus pictures.
3. Poem: "This Little Clown" from *Mitt Magic*.
4. Read *Sammy the Seal* by Sydney Hoff.

Learning Centers

Blocks

Provide plastic circus animals to use with the blocks. Also provide Fisher Price Zoo Train (C). Display pictures of the circus. Encourage creative building all week.

Listening/Music/Reading

Provide a recording of the songs "One Elephant Went Out to Play" and "Going to the Zoo" from *Sharon, Lois & Bram's Elephant Show Record*.

Art

Easel paint: yellow, red, and blue. (Leave out all week.)

String Art: Children can make designs using three colors of paint. Mix 3 T of liquid starch or glue with 1 c of tempera paint. Children dip strings in the paint and move the strings over paper to make designs.

Woodworking/Sand/Water

Provide rocks, pipe cleaners, clay, boards, small boxes, and glue for children to make sculptures.

Printing

Provide construction paper, crayons, and staplers for children to make books about the circus. Print these words on the chalkboard—circus, elephant, tent, tiger, animals, dog, trainers, seal, and whip.

Math/Language Arts

Circus Puzzles (C)   Animal Lotto Game (C)

Color Bingo (C)

Addition Box: Use peanuts.

Science/Social Studies

Provide books, pictures, and posters about the circus.

Dramatic Play

Set up a circus. Provide stuffed animals, tires, stools, boxes, jump ropes, and dress-up clothes. Leave these materials out all week.

More Group Time Activities

1. Song: "Elephant Rhyme" from *Sharon, Lois & Bram: One Elephant, Deux Elephants*.
2. Record: *Hap Palmer: Creative Movement and Rhythmic Exploration*.
3. Fingerplay: "Circus Ponies" from *Mitt Magic*.

Day 2: Circus Acts

Group Time Activities

1. Discuss circus acts. Show pictures, such as jugglers, bareback riders, ringmasters, and trapeze artists.
2. Listen to a circus record.
3. Song: "The Animal Fair."

Learning Centers

Art

Clay Circus: Each child makes one circus character out of clay. Put all characters on display.

Woodworking/Sand/Water

Provide empty food containers and glue for children to make sculptures.

Printing

Provide alphabet stencils to make words. Print these words on the chalkboard—circus, strong man, trapeze, and ringmaster.

Math/Language Arts

Circus Puzzles: Clowns (C)
Octons (C)
Stringing Beads: Use pattern cards (C).
Apple and Trees (W)

Science/Social Studies

Language Experience Notebook: Circus.

More Group Time Activities

1. Discuss "Confusing *Cc*." Use pictures and objects to discuss the two sounds of *Cc*.
2. Think of different ways to make a *Cc* with the body and blocks.
3. Use objects in the room to make different alphabet letters.
4. Read *Paddington at the Circus* by Michael Bond or *The Cat Who Thought He Was a Tiger* by Polly Cameron.

Day 3: Clowns

Group Time Activities

1. Discuss clowns, such as dress, makeup, acts, and schools for clowns.
2. Make clown faces on children using makeup.
3. Children dress up in clown costumes and dramatize clown acts.
4. Show posters of clowns.
5. Read *Bambino the Clown* by George Schreiber.

Learning Centers

Art

Clown Masks: Children make clown masks from paper plates. Use small balloons for the nose and string or yarn to attach to head.

Woodworking/Sand/Water

Provide bark, sticks, leaves, wood scraps, wood shavings, and glue for sculptures.

Printing

Provide construction paper, crayons, and staplers for children to make books about the circus. Print these words on the chalkboard—circus, clown, faces, funny, and makeup.

Math/Language Arts

Design Boards (C)	Zoo Lotto (C)
Circus Puzzles (C)	Number Bingo (C)
Tinker Toys (C)	

Science/Social Studies

Provide large outlines of clowns drawn on paper. Children design costumes and faces for the clowns. Display on a wall.

More Group Time Activities

1. Film: *Zoo Babies*.
2. Children wear masks and parade around the room to circus music.
3. Song: "The Clown."

Day 4: Circus Foods

Group Time Activities

1. Discuss circus foods and show pictures, such as candy apples, popcorn, peanuts, cotton candy.
2. Use ABC letter cards.
3. Make candy apples.

Learning Centers

Art

Apple Prints: Provide apples that have been cut in different shapes. Provide trays of paint and construction paper. Children dip apple pieces in paint and make prints on paper.

Peanut Puppets: Children make finger puppets out of peanut shells. Using markers, children color faces on the shells and then stick the colored shells on their fingers.

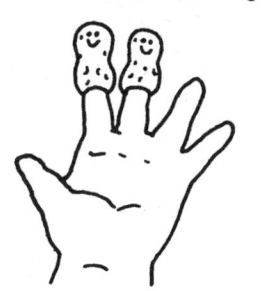

Woodworking/Sand/Water

Provide garbage bag ties, twisties, and pipe cleaners to make sculptures.

Printing

Provide a big bag of popcorn. Children print any circus word on a piece of posterboard, put dots of glue on the printed lines, and place popcorn pieces on the glue to spell the words. Print these words on the chalkboard—circus, popcorn, peanuts, and Cracker Jacks.

Math/Language Arts

Alphabet Train (W)   Triominoes (C)

Number Bingo (C)

Pegs and Peg Boards and Animal Pegs (C)

Science/Social Studies

Children divide pictures of circus foods in two groups—sweet and sour.

More Group Time Activities

1. Flannel Story: *Three Billy Goats Gruff.*
2. Have children choose their favorite songs to sing.
3. Read *The Smallest Elephant in the World* by Alvin Tresselt.
4. Snack on peanuts or popcorn.

Day 5: Mother's Day

Group Time Activities

1. Discuss the meaning of Mother's Day. Point out the correct date on the calendar.
2. Discuss things we can do for mother on "her day," such as clean room, set table, make a present, say "I Love You."
3. Name things mothers do for us. Name jobs mothers do outside the home. (Be sensitive to children's different family situations.)
4. Read *On Mother's Lap* by Ann Herbert Scott.

Learning Centers

Listening/Music/Reading

Provide a cassette and read-along book.

Art

Mother's Day Cards: Children make cards with construction paper, baking cup papers, buttons, and yarn. Provide copies of this poem for children to glue on their cards—Buttons and bows, Buttons and bows, Mother's the one, Who always knows.

Woodworking/Sand/Water

Provide magnets and metal objects for sculptures.

Printing

Provide pencils, crayons, and paper to make cards. Print these words on the chalkboard—Mother, Mom, Momma, love, Sunday, and family.

Math/Language Arts

Puzzles (C)   Apple Trees (W)

Triominoes (C)   Rhyming Bingo (C)

Science/Social Studies

Children draw their mother's faces on construction-paper cards. Write each child's mother's name on a card. Display on a bulletin board.

Dramatic Play

Provide housekeeping furniture and dress-up clothes.

More Group Time Activities

1. Invite mothers to come to school to tell the class about themselves and their jobs.
2. Read *If I Were a Mother* by Kazue Mizumura.

May
Week 4

Insects

Day 1: Honeybees

Group Time Activities

1. Show large pictures of the honeybee.
2. Read and discuss the section about honeybees in *Insects Do the Strangest Things* by Leonora Hornblow.
3. Show beeswax and candles made from beeswax.
4. Make honey butter by mixing honey with softened butter until well blended. Provide this at the art table.

Learning Centers

Blocks

Provide pictures of bees and beehives for children to observe as they build.

Listening/Music/Reading

Provide the recording and book *Bees and Honey* by Oxford Scientific Films.

Art

Easel Paint: black, yellow, and orange. (Leave out all week.)

Honey Butter Snacks: Children cut shapes out of bread, spread honey butter on the bread shapes, and eat.

Woodworking/Sand/Water

*Woodworking: Provide boards, nails, hammers, and yarn. Children hammer nails into the boards and connect the nails with yarn to make designs. Continue all week.

Printing

Provide clay for children to mold the words that are printed on the chalkboard—honey, drone, bee, worker, beehives, sting, and queen.

Math/Language Arts

Mosaics (C)	Pegs and Peg Boards (C)
Lacing Cards (C)	Insect Sequence Game (C)

Science/Social Studies

Entomology Lab: Display insect specimens and provide magnifying glasses and books about insects. Leave out all week.

Dramatic Play

Provide housekeeping furniture, dress-up clothes, dishes, empty food containers, bug boxes, fly swatters, and plastic insects. Leave out all week.

More Group Time Activities

1. Read Insects *Build Their Homes* by Gladys Conklin.
2. Fingerplays: "Five Little Bees" and "Bees" from *Mitt Magic*.
3. Song: "Over in the Meadow."

Day 2: Ants

Group Time Activities

1. Show pictures of ants.
2. Read about ants in *Insects Do the Strangest Things* by Leonora Hornblow.
3. Discuss and show an ant colony.
4. Song: "On a Picnic We Will Go" from *Sharon, Lois & Bram's Elephant Show Record.*

Learning Centers

Blocks

Provide pictures and books on ants, ant hills, and ant colonies.

Listening/Music/Reading

Provide a recording of the song "On a Picnic We Will Go."

Art

Blotto Butterfly: Provide a butterfly pattern. Children trace, cut out, and put paint drops on one side of the butterfly. Children then fold the butterfly in half to make blotto prints. Add 6 legs and antennae. Hang in room.

Butterfly: Give each child one white paper towel. The child puts dots of food coloring on the paper towel. Then the child pulls the center of the paper towel together with a garbage bag twist and adds paper antennae.

Printing

Provide small chalkboards and chalk. Print these words on the chalkboard—ant, worker, colony, butterfly, and queen.

Math/Language Arts

Puzzles (C)   Lacing Cards (C)

More Group Time Activities

1. Film: *Amazing Ants.*
2. Read *The Ants Go Marching* by Bernice Freschet.
3. Make ants on a log. Wash and cut celery into 3-inch sections. Children fill the inside of the celery with peanut butter, then put raisins (ants) on top of the peanut butter and eat.

Day 3: Grasshoppers

Group Time Activities

1. Read about grasshoppers in *Insects Do the Strangest Things* by Leonora Hornblow.
2. Play jumpy music and have children move like grasshoppers.

Learning Centers

Blocks

Provide pictures of grasshoppers.

Listening/Music/Reading

Provide a recording of the song "All the Ways of Jumping Up and Down" from *Hap Palmer: Walter the Waltzing Worm.*

Art

Grasshoppers: Children make grasshoppers out of pipe cleaners.

Printing

Provide trays of clay. Print these words on the chalkboard—locust, grasshopper, and enemy.

Math/Language Arts

Insect Puzzles (C)   Legos (C)

Lincoln Logs (C)   Insect Sequence Game (C)

More Group Time Activities

1. Play dominoes with the whole group. Use large dominoes.
2. Sing songs about insects.
3. Discuss characteristics of insects, such as three body parts, six legs, and so on.

Day 4: Friends and Enemies

Group Time Activities

1. Read "The Enemies" from *Insects Do the Strangest Things* by Leonora Hornblow.
2. Discuss the mosquito and fly life cycles. Flies and mosquitoes can also be disease carriers.
3. Film: *Insects: Friends and Enemies*.

Learning Centers

Blocks

Provide pictures of flies and mosquitoes.

Listening/Music/Reading

Provide a recording of the song "Bee Bee Bumblebee" from *Sharon, Lois & Bram: One Elephant, Deux Elephants*.

Art

Trash Collage or Sculptures: Provide trash, such as paper cups, newspapers, magazines, candy wrappers, and gum wrappers, for children to glue on construction paper.

Printing

Provide small chalkboards and chalk. Print these words on the chalkboard—mosquito, housefly, termite, honeybee, and enemy.

Math/Language Arts

Animal Lotto (C)	Lacing Cards (C)
Mosaics (C)	Dominoes (C)
Bingo (C)	Insect Sequence Game (C)

More Group Time Activities

1. Make up a story about "Freddie Fly" as a group activity.
2. Make a list of words that rhyme with fly.
3. Read *The Grouchy Ladybug* by Eric Carle.
4. Fingerplay: "Lady Bugs" from *Mitt Magic*.

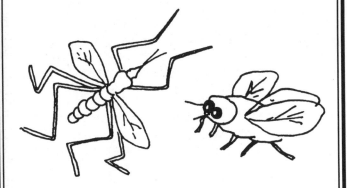

Day 5: Fireflies and Summary of Insects

Group Time Activities

1. Read *Insects Do the Strangest Things* by Leonora Hornblow. Discuss fireflies and lightning bugs.
2. Read *Fireflies in the Night* by Judy Hawes.
3. Summarize characteristics of insects.
4. Make lists of the insects that are helpful and harmful.
5. Discuss how all insects are strange and interesting.

Learning Centers

Blocks

Display pictures of insects.

Listening/Music/Reading

Provide the recording of songs about insects.

Art

Fireflies: Have children draw fireflies on black construction paper. Children can add glue and glitter on the fireflies' bodies.

Printing

Provide a tray of clay. Print these words on the chalkboard—fireflies, insects, light, friend, and beetle.

Math/Language Arts

Insect Puzzles (C)	Geozellos (C)
Bingo (C)	Dominoes (C)
Insect Sequence Game (C)	

More Group Time Activities

1. Discuss summertime and insects.
2. Language Experience Notebook: Insects.
3. Read *A Pocketful of Cricket* by Rebecca Caudill.

May–
Additional Activities

- As a class, write a fiction story titled "A Day on the Ranch." Begin this activity with a review of cowboy jobs, equipment, clothing, and so on. This would be a good way to summarize this unit.

- Have a parent dress up as a famous cowboy of the past. Have him or her visit the class and answer questions from the children. Preface this activity with a discussion of what it must have been like to have lived in early cowboy times. Write some of the children's ideas and questions on poster paper. Have your guest address some of these questions and ideas during his or her visit. Write a class thank you to this guest.

- Designate one day during this unit as cowboy dress-up day. Point out various articles of clothing on different children and have children explain possible functions of each, such as a hat was used to shade the head and so on.

- Read *Cowboy Andy* by Edna Walker Chandler.

- Read *Rosie and the Rustlers* by Roy Gerrard.

- Reference for famous women cowboys— *American Cowgirls: Yesterday and Today.*

- Read *Calamity Jane: Her Life and Her Legend.*

- Play "Who Am I?" game. As a class, select five different sea creatures. The person who is "It" gives clues about one of these creatures. The other children try to guess which creature he or she is describing.

- Draw and cut out the shapes of different sea creatures, such as turtles, whales, octopi, and so on. Brainstorm different descriptive words and write or draw these descriptions inside the shape outlines. Hang the pictures in the room.

- Create a circus mural. Have each child draw his or her favorite part of the circus on a class mural. He or she can also dictate a sentence explaining his or her picture.

- Discuss the many different circus people— clowns, lion tamer, ring master, tightrope walker, and so on. Write these names on the chalkboard. Have children choose the one they would most like to be. Make a class bar graph depicting the children's choices.

- Have children illustrate a page for a class book titled "Circus People." On each page have these words written "If I were in the circus I'd like to be the..." Have children dictate their choices from the list on the chalkboard.

- Read *Millicent the Magnificent* by Alice Bach.

- Read *C is for Clown; A Circus of "C" Words* by Stan Berenstain.

- Read *Barbar's Little Circus Star* by Laurent de Brunhoff.

- Read *Louella and the Yellow Balloon* by Molly Coxe.

- Read *Andy and the Lion* by James Henry Daugherty.

▶ Have children work in pairs to dictate or illustrate a page for a non-fiction book about insects. Read this book at the next group time. Continue to add more information to the book.

▶ Brainstorm reasons that insects are helpful to the environment. Write the type of insect, a picture of the insect, and the function it fulfills on a list titled "How Insects Help Us." Post this list in the room.

▶ Play "Insect Concentration." Cut out or draw pictures of different insects. Have two pictures for each insect. Glue each picture on a piece of construction paper and place all cards face down. Children try to make matches by turning over two cards at a time. If a match is made, the child keeps both cards. If a match is not made, the child places both cards face down in the same places.

▶ Write a class story called "The Day the Ants Came to Our Picnic."

▶ Read *The Very Quiet Cricket* by Eric Carle.

▶ Read *Deep Down Underground* by Olivier Dunrea.

▶ Read *Grasshopper on the Road* by Arnold Lobel.

▶ Film: *An Alphabet of Insects* (Coronet/ MTI Film and Video)

▶ <u>Songs</u>: "Octopus Blues." *The Sesame Street Song Book-64 Favorite Songs*. New York, NY: Macmillan Publishing Co., 1992.

"If I Were." *The Sesame Street Song Book-64 Favorite Songs*. New York, NY: Macmillan Publishing Co., 1992.

"The Clown." *Hap Palmer Favorites: Songs for Learning Through Music and Movement*. Sherman Oaks, CA: Alfred Publishing Co., 1981

"The Caterpillar." *Singing Bee!* New York, NY: Lothrop, Lee & Shepard Books, 1982.

"Picture a World." *The Sesame Street Song Book*. New York, NY: Simon & Schuster, 1971

"J Jump." *The Sesame Street Song Book*. New York, NY: Simon & Schuster, 1971

Year-End Kindergarten Program

The year-end kindergarten program should reflect what children have learned during the school year. The program should involve all children as much as possible and should require very little preparation time. The following script was written to use children's favorite songs learned during the year. The lines in the play should be divided among children as needed. Each child can be assigned a song to dramatize while the other children sing. Keep in practice for the program fun, and enjoy the time when children show their families what they learned in kindergarten!

We welcome you, both parents and friends
to our first graduation day.
As with favorite songs and happy grins,
We share with you our work and play.

Song: "Beautiful Day."

Some astronauts have gone to the moon,
Maybe we, too, can go there soon.

Song: "I Don't Want to Live On the Moon."

Once a year we may get a big fright,
From witches and ghosts that go bump
in the night.
But smiling pumpkins make a happy sight,
While happy songs can make Halloween bright.

Song: "There Was an Old Witch."

With the Native Americans, the Pilgrims
shared a meal
That first Thanksgiving day.
The Native Americans had been their friends
And helped them in every way.

Song: "Navajo Happy Song."

Thanksgiving should be a happy day,
I'll bet that's not what the turkeys say!

Song: "The Turkey."

Christmas is bright
With colored lights, both red and blue,
Bringing much joy
With toys, candy, and Santa's helpers, too.

Song: "Jingle Bells."

Valentine's Day is for sweethearts, you see,
I love her, and she loves me.

Song: "Valentine Song."

Rocks may differ in size, shape, and feel,
And their uses may vary a great deal.

Song: "Big Beautiful Planet."

Spring is a special season,
We see this time every year.
When raindrops bring blossoms
Popping out bright and clear.

Song: "Kite Song" and "Rain Falls."

Now here are some of our favorite animal songs,
The cute, the brave, and the tiny.
The stories of dinosaurs can never go wrong,
They excite kids from five to ninety.

**Songs: "Six Little Ducks,"
"Over in the Meadow," and "The Elephant."**

Some songs are sung just for fun, you see,
Hope you will enjoy these with me.

**Songs: "Peanut Butter" and
"I Know and Old Lady."**

We thank you for coming to our program today
And hope you've enjoyed each song.
It's been fun for us, too,
But now we must say to all our friends...So long.

(Words by Mrs. Henrietta Moore)

References (Books)

Baratta-Lorton, Mary. *Workjobs... for Parents*. Menlo Park, CA: Addison-Wesley, 1972.

_____. *Workjobs II, Number Activities for Early Childhood*. Menlo Park, CA: Addison-Wesley, 1978.

Childcraft, The How and Why Library. Chicago, IL: World Book-Childcraft International, Inc., 1979.

Colgin, Mary Lou. *Chants for Children*. Manlius, New York, NY: Colgin Publishing, 1982.

Glazer, Tom. *Eye Winker, Tom Tinker, Chin Chopper*. New York, NY: Doubleday, 1973.

Glazer, Tom. *Tom Glazer's Treasury of Songs for Children*. Garden City, NY: Doubleday, 1964.

Gregson, Bob. *The Outrageous Outdoor Games Book*. Carthage, IL: Fearon Teacher Aids, 1984.

Hart, Jane. *Singing Bee! A Collection of Favorite Children's Songs*. New York, NY: Lothrop, Lee & Shepard, 1982.

Hogstrom, D. *My Big Book of Finger Plays*. Racine, WI: Golden Press, 1974.

Larrick, Nancy. *Songs from Mother Goose: With Traditional Melody for Each*. New York, NY: Harper & Row, Publishers, 1989.

Livingston, Myra Cohn. *"12 October" in The Malibu and Other Poems*. New York, NY: Atheneum, 1972.

Matterson, Elizabeth. *Games for the Very Young: A Treasury of Nursery Songs and Finger Plays*. New York, NY: American Heritage Press, 1969.

Nelson, D. *170 Christmas Songs and Carols*. New York, NY: The Big 3 Music Corp., 1970.

Palmer, Hap. *Hap Palmer Favorites—Songs for Learning Through Music and Movement*. Sherman Oaks, CA: Alfred Publishing Co., 1981.

Prelutsky, Jack. *The Random House Book of Poetry for Children: A Treasury of 572 Poems for Today's Child*. New York, NY: Random House, 1983.

Quackenbusch, Robert. *The Holiday Song Book*. New York, NY: Lothrop, Lee & Shepard, 1977.

Raffi. *The 2nd Raffi Songbook*. New York, NY: Crown Publishers, Inc., 1986.

Raposo, Joe and Jeffrey Moss. *The Sesame Street Song Book*. New York, NY: Simon & Schuster, 1971.

Raposo, Joe and Jeffrey Moss (and other Sesame Street Songwriters). *The Sesame Street Song Book-64 Favorite Songs*. New York, NY: Macmillan Publishing Co., 1992.

Roberts, Lynda. *Mitt Magic*. Mt. Rainier, MD: Gryphon House, Inc., 1985.

Seeger, Ruth. *American Folk Songs for Children*. Garden City, NY: Doubleday, 1948.

Sur, William R., William R. Fisher, Mary R. Tolbert, and Adeline McCall. *This is Music for Today*. Rockleigh, NJ: Allyn & Bacon, 1971.

Warren, Jean. *More Piggyback Songs*. Everett, WA: Warren Publishing House, 1984.

Weissman, Jackie. *Sniggles, Squirrels and Chicken Pox*. Overland Park, KS: Miss Jackie Music Co., 1984.

Wilson, Harry, Walter Ehret, Alice Snyder, Edward Hermann, and Albert Renna. *Growing With Music*. Englewood Cliffs, NJ: Prentice-Hall, Inc., 1970.

Winn, Marie. *The Fireside Book of Children's Songs*. New York, NY: Simon & Schuster, 1966.

References (Cassettes and Records)

A Charlie Brown Christmas (Random House)

A Letter to Amy (Weston Woods)

Counting Games and Rhythms for the Little Ones (Folkways)

Dr. Seuss's ABC (Random House)

Green Eggs and Ham (Random House)

Greg and Steve: Kidding Around with Greg and Steve (Youngheart Records)

Greg and Steve: We All Live Together, Vol. 1 (Youngheart Records)

Greg and Steve: We All Live Together, Vol. 4 (Youngheart Records)

Halloween Night (Bantam)

Hap Palmer: Creative Movement and Rhythmic Exploration (Activity Records)

Hap Palmer: Feelin' Free (Activity Records)

Hap Palmer: Getting to Know Myself (Activity Records)

Hap Palmer: Hap Palmer Sings Classic Nursery Rhymes (Activity Records)

Hap Palmer: Learning Basic Skills Through Music— Health and Safety (Activity Records)

Hap Palmer: Learning Basic Skills Through Music— Volumes 1, 2 (Activity Records)

Hap Palmer: Learning Basic Skills Through Music— Vocabulary (Activity Records)

Hap Palmer: Math Readiness, Vocabulary and Concepts (Activity Records)

Hap Palmer: Movin' (Activity Records)

Hap Palmer: Patriotic and Morning Time Songs (Activity Records)

Hap Palmer: Walter the Waltzing Worm (Activity Records)

The Hokey Pokey (Melody House)

Indian Two Feet and His Horse (Childrens Press)

The Little Red Hen (Random House)

The Littlest Angel (Childrens Press)

The Shape of Me and Other Stuff (Random House)

Sharon, Lois & Bram's Elephant Show Record (Elephant Records)

Sharon, Lois & Bram: One Elephant, Deux Elephants (Elephant Records)

Sharon, Lois & Bram: Stay Tuned (Elephant Records)

The Sons of the Pioneers: 25 Favorite Cowboy Songs (Radio Corporation of America)

The Sons of the Pioneers: Tumbling Tumbleweed (Radio Corporation of America)

Six Foolish Fishermen (Caedmon)

Stone Soup (Random House)

Three Blind Mice (Curriculum Materials)

Three Little Pigs (Listening Library, Inc.)

Twas the Night before Christmas (RCA Records)

Wee Sing America: Songs of Patriots and Pioneers (Price, Stern, Sloan)

Whistle for Willie (Weston Woods)

White Snow, Bright Snow (Weston Woods)

References (Films)

A Goofy Look at Valentine's Day (Coronet/MTI Film and Video)

A Spooky Tale for Halloween (Troll Associates)

Amazing Ants (Coronet/MTI Film and Video)

America the Beautiful (Brunswick Productions)

An Alphabet of Insects (Coronet/MTI Film and Video)

An Alphabet of Weather (Coronet/MTI Film and Video)

Are You My Mother? (Listening Library, Inc.)

Autumn (Coronet/MTI Film and Video)

Bambi Learns about: Seeing, Hearing, Touch, Taste and Smell (Disney Educational Productions)

Big Mouth Goes to the Dentist (Coronet/MTI Film and Video)

Birds, Fish and Other Pets (National Geographic Society)

Blackberries in the Dark (Disney Educational Productions)

Blueberries for Sal (Listening Library, Inc.)

Breakfast Gives You Bounce (Disney Educational Productions)

Calendar Bird (Troll Associates)

Christmas Time in Europe (Coronet/MTI Film and Video)

The Cow Who Fell in the Canal (Weston Woods)

Dealing With Feelings (Coronet/MTI Film and Video)

Dinner: A Time for Sharing (Disney Educational Productions)

Donald's Fire Drill (Coronet/MTI Film and Video)

The Elves and the Shoemaker (Coronet/MTI Film and Video)

Fast-Food Facts (Disney Educational Productions)

Feliz Navidad (Coronet/MTI Film and Video)

Firefighters (Coronet/MTI Film and Video)

The First Christmas Tree (Coronet/MTI Film and Video)

George Washington's Birthday (Troll Associates)

Goofy's Field Trips: Ships, Planes, Trains (Disney Educational Productions)

Hansel and Gretel (Random House)

Heather and the Haunted Hayloft (Troll Associates)

Here Comes Columbus Day (Troll Associates)

Holidays Your Neighbors Celebrate (Coronet/MTI Film and Video)

Hook and Ladder, The Fire Department Story (Troll Associates)

The Hopi Indian (Coronet/MTI Film and Video)

How Animals Get Ready for Winter (Coronet/MTI Film and Video)

How the Animals Discovered Christmas (Coronet/MTI Film and Video)

I'm No Fool With Safety at School (Coronet/MTI Film and Video)

Insects: Friends and Enemies (National Geographic Society)

The Life Cycle of the Honeybee (Listening Library, Inc.)

Lincoln (SVE Educational Films)

The Little Engine That Could (Coronet/MTI Film and Video)

The Little Red Hen (Coronet/MTI Film and Video)

Little Red Riding Hood (Coronet/MTI Film and Video)

The Littlest Angel (Listening Library)

Living Things and Non-Living Things (Coronet/MTI Film and Video)

Lunch: Trying New Foods (Disney Educational Productions)

Making Change for a Dollar (Coronet/MTI Film and Video)

Old MacDonald Had a Farm (Scott Educational Division)

The Plains & Woodland Indians (National Geographic Society)

Our Post Office (Encyclopedia Britannica Education Corp.)

Our Senses Working Together (Disney Educational Productions)

Postal Workers (Coronet/MTI Film and Video)

The Red Balloon (Macmillan Films)

Rescue Rangers Fire Safety Adventures (Coronet/MTI Film and Video)

Rumpelstiltskin (Troll Associates)

School Manners (Troll Associates)

School Workers (Coronet/MTI Film and Video)

Smart Snacks (Disney Educational Productions)

Sniffles, Sneezes and Contagious Diseases (Coronet/MTI Film and Video)

The Something (Listening Library, Inc.)

The Star-Spangled Banner (Bowmar)

Stars and More Stars (Troll Associates)

Tale of the Groundhog's Shadow (Coronet/MTI Film and Video)

Teeth Are for Chewing (Coronet/MTI Film and Video)

Tell 'Em How You Feel (Coronet/MTI Film and Video)

The Three Little Pigs (Listening Library, Inc.)

Twas the Night before Christmas (Coronet/MTI Film and Video)

The Valentine Mystery (Troll Associates)

What's Under the Earth (Troll Associates)

What's Under the Ocean (Troll Associates)

What Time Is It? (Coronet/MTI Film and Video)

Why Plants Grow Where They Do (Coronet/MTI Film and Video)

Why We Need Doctors: No Measles, No Mumps for Me (Coronet/ MTI Film and Video)

Woodland Indians of Early America (Coronet/MTI Film and Video)

Your Teeth (Encyclopedia Britannica Education Corp.)

Zoo Babies (Coronet/MTI Film and Video)

References (Songs)

"A, B, C, D, E, F, G..." *Chants for Children.* Manlius, NY: Colgin Publishing, 1982.

"America." *The Holiday Song Book.* New York, NY: Lothrop, Lee & Shepard, 1977.

"American Flag" (Tune: "Frere Jacques"). *More Piggyback Songs.* Everett, WA: Warren Publishing House, 1984.

"The Animal Fair." *Tom Glazer's Treasury of Songs for Children.* Garden City, NY: Doubleday, 1964.

"The Animal Song." *The Fireside Book of Children's Songs.* New York, NY: Simon & Schuster, 1966.

"Animals Are My Friends." *Sniggles, Squirrels and Chicken Pox.* Overland Park, KS: Miss Jackie Music Co., 1984.

"A-Tisket, A-Tasket." *Growing with Music.* Englewood Cliffs, NJ: Prentice-Hall, Inc., 1970.

"Baa, Baa, Black Sheep." *Growing with Music.* Englewood Cliffs, NJ: Prentice-Hall, Inc., 1970.

"Baby Beluga." *The 2nd Raffi Songbook.* New York, NY: Crown Publishers, Inc., 1986.

"Beautiful Day." *Hap Palmer Favorites*. Sherman Oaks, CA: Alfred Publishing Co., 1981

"Bein' Green." *The Sesame Street Songbook: 64 Favorite Songs*. New York, NY: Macmillan Publishing Co., 1992.

"Big Beautiful Planet." *The 2nd Raffi Songbook*. New York, NY: Crown Publishers, Inc., 1986.

"The Bus Song." *Eye Winker, Tom Tinker, Chin Chopper*. New York, NY: Doubleday, 1973.

"Charlie Over the Water." *Eye Winker, Tom Tinker, Chin Chopper*. New York, NY: Doubleday, 1973.

"Circles Everywhere." *Hap Palmer Favorites*. Sherman Oaks, CA: Alfred Publishing Co., 1981

"The Clown." *Hap Palmer Favorites*. Sherman Oaks, CA: Alfred Publishing Co., 1981

"Courtesy Song." *Growing with Music*. Englewood Cliffs, NJ: Prentice-Hall, Inc., 1970.

"Dayenu." *The Holiday Song Book*. New York, NY: Lothrop, Lee & Shepard, 1977.

"Easter Basket." *The Holiday Song Book*. New York, NY: Lothrop, Lee & Shepard, 1977.

"Eight Beautiful Notes." *The Sesame Street Song Book- 64 Favorite Songs*. New York, NY: Macmillan Publishing Co., 1992.

"The Elephant." *Hap Palmer Favorites*. Sherman Oaks, CA: Alfred Publishing Co., 1981

"Feelings." *Hap Palmer Favorites*. Sherman Oaks, CA: Alfred Publishing Co., 1981

"Fire Down Below." *American Folk Songs for Children*. Garden City, NY: Doubleday, 1948.

"Firefighters" (Tune: "Pop Goes the Weasel"). *More Piggyback Songs*. Everett, WA: Warren Publishing House, 1984.

"Fishing Trip." *Hap Palmer Favorites*. Sherman Oaks, CA: Alfred Publishing Co., 1981

"Five Little Ducks." *The 2nd Raffi Songbook*. New York, NY: Crown Publishers, Inc., 1986.

"Five Little Monkeys Jumping on the Bed." *Chants for Children*. Manlius, NY: Colgin Publishing, 1982.

"Furry Squirrel." *Sniggles, Squirrels and Chicken Pox*. Overland Park, KS: Miss Jackie Music Co., 1984.

"Go Tell Aunt Rhody." *Chants for Children*. Manlius, NY: Colgin Publishing, 1982.

"Good-by Old Paint." *Growing with Music*. Englewood Cliffs, NJ: Prentice-Hall, Inc., 1970.

"Grandma's Spectacles." *Eye Winker, Tom Tinker, Chin Chopper*. New York, NY: Doubleday, 1973.

"The Grouch Song." *The Sesame Street Song Book: 64 Favorite Songs*. New York, NY: Macmillan Publishing Co., 1992.

"Hanukkah Song." *The Holiday Song Book*. New York, NY: Lothrop, Lee & Shepard, 1977.

"Happy Birthday to America" (Tune: "Oh Christmas Tree"). *More Piggyback Songs*. Everett, WA: Warren Publishing House, 1984.

"Have You Seen the Ghost of John?" *Chants for Children*. Manlius, NY: Colgin Publishing, 1982.

"He Knew the Earth Was Round-O." *The Holiday Song Book*. New York, NY: Lothrop, Lee & Shepard, 1977.

"Hickory, Dickory, Dock." *Growing with Music*. Englewood Cliffs, NJ: Prentice-Hall, Inc., 1970.

"Home On the Range." *Tom Glazer's Treasury of Songs for Children*. Garden City, NY: Doubleday, 1964.

"I Am a Fireman" (Tune: "I'm a Little Teapot"). *More Piggyback Songs*. Everett, WA: Warren Publishing House, 1984.

"I'm a Little Leprechaun" (Tune: "I'm a Little Teapot"). *More Piggyback Songs*. Everett, WA: Warren Publishing House, 1984.

"I Don't Want to Live On the Moon." *The Sesame Street Song Book*. New York, NY: Simon & Schuster, 1971.

"I Heard My Dog Bark." *The Sesame Street Song Book: 64 Favorite Songs*. New York, NY: Macmillan Publishing Co., 1992.

"I Know an Old Lady." *Eye Winker, Tom Tinker, Chin Chopper*. New York, NY: Doubleday, 1973.

"I Like Me." *Hap Palmer Favorites*. Sherman Oaks, CA: Alfred Publishing Co., 1981

"If You're Scared (Sad) and You Know It"(Tune: "If You're Happy"). *Growing with Music*. Englewood Cliffs, NJ: Prentice-Hall, Inc., 1970.

"It's All Wrong." *The Holiday Song Book*. New York, NY: Lothrop, Lee & Shepard, 1977.

"It Is Snowing" (Tune: "Frere Jacques"). *More Piggyback Songs*. Everett, WA: Warren Publishing House, 1984.

"Itisket, Itasket." *The Holiday Song Book*. New York, NY: Lothrop, Lee & Shepard, 1977.

"Jack-o'-Lantern." *Eye Winker, Tom Tinker, Chin Chopper*. New York, NY: Doubleday, 1973.

"Jumping Frog." *Hap Palmer Favorites*. Sherman Oaks, CA: Alfred Publishing Co., 1981

"Kite Song." *Hap Palmer Favorites*. Sherman Oaks, CA: Alfred Publishing Co., 1981

"Leprechaun's March" (Tune: "Twinkle, Twinkle Little Star"). *More Piggyback Songs*. Everett, WA: Warren Publishing House, 1984.

"Looby Loo." *Singing Bee!* New York, NY: Lothrop, Lee & Shepard, 1982.

"The Mailman." *Growing with Music*. Englewood Cliffs, NJ: Prentice-Hall, Inc., 1970.

"Marching Song" (Tune: "Frere Jacques"). *More Piggyback Songs*. Everett, WA: Warren Publishing House, 1984.

"Mary Had a Little Lamb." *Growing with Music*. Englewood Cliffs, NJ: Prentice-Hall, Inc., 1970.

"The Milkman." *Growing with Music*. Englewood Cliffs, NJ: Prentice-Hall, Inc., 1970.

"Mr. Groundhog." *More Piggyback Songs*. Everett, WA: Warren Publishing House, 1984.

"Motorcycle Racer." *Hap Palmer Favorites*. Sherman Oaks, CA: Alfred Publishing Co., 1981.

"The Mulberry Bush." *Singing Bee!* New York, NY: Lothrop, Lee & Shepard, 1982.

"My Dreydl." *The Holiday Song Book*. New York, NY: Lothrop, Lee & Shepard, 1977.

"My Spanish Guitar." *The Holiday Song Book*. New York, NY: Lothrop, Lee & Shepard, 1977.

"My Valentine." *More Piggyback Songs*. Everett, WA: Warren Publishing House, 1984.

"Navajo Happy Song." *The Holiday Song Book*. New York, NY: Lothrop, Lee & Shepard, 1977.

"Numbers Tell a Lot about You." *Hap Palmer Favorites*. Sherman Oaks, CA: Alfred Publishing Co., 1981.

"Oh Christmas Tree." *The Holiday Song Book*. New York, NY: Lothrop, Lee & Shepard, 1977.

"Old Brass Wagon." *Growing with Music*. Englewood Cliffs, NJ: Prentice-Hall, Inc., 1970.

"The Old Chisholm Trail." *Growing with Music*. Englewood Cliffs, NJ: Prentice-Hall, Inc., 1970.

"On Each Hand I Have Five Fingers." *More Piggyback Songs*. Everett, WA: Warren Publishing House, 1984.

"One Light, One Sun." *The 2nd Raffi Songbook*. New York, NY: Crown Publishers, Inc., 1986.

"Over the River and Thro' the Woods." *The Holiday Song Book*. New York, NY: Lothrop, Lee & Shepard, 1977.

"Paper Clock." *Hap Palmer Favorites*. Sherman Oaks, CA: Alfred Publishing Co., 1981.

"Peanut, Peanut Butter and Jelly." *Chants for Children*. Manlius, NY: Colgin Publishing, 1982.

"The People in Your Neighborhood." *The Sesame Street Song Book: 64 Favorite Songs*. New York, NY: Macmillan Publishing Co., 1992.

"Peppermint Stick." *Growing with Music*. Englewood Cliffs, NJ: Prentice-Hall, Inc., 1970.

"Popcorn" (Tune: "Frere Jacques"). *More Piggyback Songs*. Everett, WA: Warren Publishing House, 1984.

"Preparing for Seder." *The Holiday Song Book*. New York, NY: Lothrop, Lee & Shepard, 1977.

"Put Your Finger in the Air." *Eye Winker, Tom Tinker, Chin Chopper*. New York, NY: Doubleday, 1973.

"Rain Falls." *The Sesame Street Song Book*. New York, NY: Simon & Schuster, 1971.

"Riding in an Airplane." *The 2nd Raffi Songbook*. New York, NY: Crown Publishers, Inc., 1986.

"Rig-a-Jig-Jig." *The Holiday Song Book*. New York, NY: Lothrop, Lee & Shepard, 1977.

"Sailing at High Tide." *Eye Winker, Tom Tinker, Chin Chopper*. New York, NY: Doubleday, 1973.

"Sally Go Round the Sunshine." *American Folk Songs for Children*. Garden City, NY: Doubleday, 1948.

"Save Your Nickels" (Tune: "Are You Sleeping?"). *Growing with Music*. Englewood Cliffs, NJ: Prentice-Hall, Inc., 1970.

"See My Shadow" (Tune: "Frere Jacques"). *More Piggyback Songs*. Everett, WA: Warren Publishing House, 1984.

"She'll Be Comin' Round the Mountain." *American Folk Songs for Children*. Garden City, NY: Doubleday, 1948.

"Sing After Me." *The Sesame Street Song Book-64 Favorite Songs*. New York, NY: Macmillan Publishing Co., 1992.

"Song of the Fishes." *The Fireside Book of Children's Songs*. New York, NY: Simon & Schuster, 1966.

"Special." *The Sesame Street Song Book*. New York, NY: Simon & Schuster, 1971.

"Springtime" (Tune: "Skip To My Lou"). *More Piggyback Songs*. Everett, WA: Warren Publishing House, 1984.

"Stop! Look! and Listen!" *Growing with Music*. Englewood Cliffs, NJ: Prentice-Hall, Inc., 1970.

"Ten Little Indians." *Eye Winker, Tom Tinker, Chin Chopper*. New York, NY: Doubleday, 1973.

"Ten Little Snowmen" (Tune: "Ten Little Indians"). *Eye Winker, Tom Tinker, Chin Chopper*. New York, NY: Doubleday, 1973.

"Thanksgiving at Grandma's." *Growing with Music*.

Englewood Cliffs, NJ: Prentice-Hall, Inc., 1970.

"There's a Hole in the Bottom of the Sea." *Eye Winker, Tom Tinker, Chin Chopper*. New York, NY: Doubleday, 1973.

"There Was an Old Witch." *Holiday Singing & Dancing Games*. New York, NY: Sterling Publishing Co., Inc., 1980.

"Things I'm Thankful for." *Hap Palmer Favorites*. Sherman Oaks, CA: Alfred Publishing Co., 1981

"This Is How We Make a Circle" (Tune: "The Mulberry Bush"). *Eye Winker, Tom Tinker, Chin Chopper*. New York, NY: Doubleday, 1973.

"This Is the Way We Brush Our Teeth" (Tune: "The Mulberry Bush"). *Eye Winker, Tom Tinker, Chin Chopper*. New York, NY: Doubleday, 1973.

"Tick-Tock." *Growing with Music*. Englewood Cliffs, NJ:

Prentice-Hall, Inc., 1970.

"Triangle, Circle and Square." *Hap Palmer Favorites*. Sherman Oaks, CA: Alfred Publishing Co., 1981

"The Turkey." *Growing with Music*. Englewood Cliffs, NJ: Prentice-Hall, Inc., 1970.

"Turkey in the Straw." *The Holiday Song Book*. New York, NY: Lothrop, Lee & Shepard, 1977.

"Valentine Song." *Growing with Music*. Englewood Cliffs, NJ: Prentice-Hall, Inc., 1970.

"Valentine's Song." *More Piggyback Songs*. Everett, WA: Warren Publishing House, 1984.

"Weather Song." *More Piggyback Songs*. Everett, WA: Warren Publishing House, 1984.

"Working on the Railroad." *Singing Bee!* New York, NY: Lothrop, Lee & Shepard, 1982.

Publisher's Addresses

Addison-Wesley Educational
Publishing Co.
School Publishing Group
2725 Sand Hill Road
Menlo Park, CA 94025

Bantam, Doubleday, Dell
666 5th Ave.
New York, NY 10103

The Big 3 Music Corporation
New York, NY 10167

Bowmar Records, Inc.
4563 Colorado Boulevard
Los Angeles, CA 90039

Brunswick
Box 1A1, Rte 1
Lawrenceville, VA 23868

Childrens Press
1224 W. Van Buren St.
Chicago, IL 60607

Colgin Publishing
Box 301
Manlius, NY 13104

Coronet/MTI Film and Video
108 Wilmot Road
Deerfield, IL 60015

Crown Publisher, Inc.
225 Park Avenue South
New York, NY 10003

Disney Educational Productions
108 Wilmot Road
Deerfield, IL 60015

Doubleday
245 Park Ave.
New York, NY 10167

Encyclopedia Brittanica
425 North Michigan Avenue
Chicago, IL 60611

Folkways Records
632 Broadway
New York, NY 10012

Hap Palmer
Educational Activities
P.O. Box 392
Freeport, NY 11520

Listening Library, Inc.
One Park Avenue
Old Greenwich, CT 06870-1727

Lothrop, Lee & Shepard Company
105 Madison Avenue
New York, NY 10016

MacMillan Educational
Distribution Center
Front and Brown Streets
Riverside, NJ 08370

Melody House
819 N.W. 92nd St.
Oklahoma City, OK 73114

National Geographic Society
17th & M Streets, NW
Washington, DC 20036

Prentice-Hall Media
150 White Plains Rd.
Tarrytown, NY 10591

Random House
201 East 50th St.
New York, NY 10022

RCA Educational Division
Front & Cooper Streets
Camden, NJ 08102

RCA Records
1133 Avenue of the Americas
New York, NY 10036

Simon & Schuster Building
Rockefeller Center
1230 Avenue of the Americas
New York, NY 10020

SVE
1345 Diversey Parkway
Chicago, IL 60614

Troll Associates
100 Corporate Drive
Mahwah, NJ 07430

Warren Publishing House
PO Box 2255
Everett, WA 98203

Weston Woods
Weston, CT 06883

Youngheart Music
Box 6017
Cypress, CA 90630